SURVIVAL AND TRIALS OF REVIVAL

PSYCHOANALYSIS AND JEWISH LIFE

The *Psychoanalysis and Jewish Life* book series has been established to promote scholarship, research, and a wide range of theoretical, textural, and clinical studies on the multiple interconnections between and mutual influence of Judaism and contemporary psychoanalysis. Its aim is broad, spanning a wide variety of subject areas: from the origins of psychoanalysis in Jewish circles in turn-of-the-century Vienna to clinical studies illuminating contemporary facets of Jewish identity and self-understanding; from explorations of psychological aspects of Jewish theology to psychoanalytic investigations of anti-Semitism; from studies of Jewish religious ritual to analyses of Hasidic mysticism and folklore; from psychoanalytic studies of pre-World War II Yiddish theater to the clinical practice of psychoanalysis in modern-day Tel-Aviv. The *Psychoanalysis and Jewish Life* book series provides a home for fresh and intellectually challenging contributions across the spectrum of this interdisciplinary area of scholarship.

SURVIVAL AND TRIALS OF REVIVAL:

PSYCHODYNAMIC STUDIES OF HOLOCAUST SURVIVORS AND THEIR FAMILIES IN ISRAEL AND THE DIASPORA

Hillel KLEIN

edited by ALEX HOLDER

Boston 2012

Library of Congress Cataloging-in-Publication Data:
A catalog record for this title is available from the Library of Congress.

ISBN 978-1-936235-89-6

Book design and cover illustration by Adell Medovoy

Published by Academic Studies Press in 2012
28 Montfern Avenue
Brighton, MA 02135, USA

press@academicstudiespress.com
www.academicstudiespress.com

Table of Contents

Preface

I had the privilege of working with Hillel Klein, psychiatrist, psychoanalyst, teacher, director of a mental hospital, friend, and even more importantly, a *Mensch*, a wonderful human being. We taught a research seminar for graduates together, for seven years, at the Institute of Contemporary Jewry at the Hebrew University. Hillel dealt with the psychological aspects of the Holocaust and I with the historical ones. The seminars had different names each year, but they were basically the same. We both developed in them, in dialogue with our students, our concepts and understanding of that harrowing series of events we call the Holocaust; the result was that I had the fortune to write a number of books since then in which I embodied some of the ideas I had learned from Hillel, whereas Hillel's book remained in manuscript form for years after his untimely death. It is wonderful to have the opportunity of seeing it now, at long last, in print, due to the unceasing efforts of Carl Nedelmann, Christoph Biermann, and Hillel's family.

The book deals not only with psychological and psychoanalytic theory as it relates to the life of Holocaust survivors but also, very openly of course—as befits a great psychoanalyst and teacher—with the author's own life, survival, and the aftermath of that survival. Hillel Klein was a survivor of the Krakow Ghetto. He had been a member of a resistance group, then he went through the horrors of the Plaszow camp on the outskirts of Krakow, and then through a series of camps, until the death marches at the end of the war that brought him to the ghetto of Theresienstadt (Terezin) in Czechia, where he was finally liberated by the Soviet Army. He then studied medicine and psychology at German universities before immigrating to Israel. When I got to know him, he divided his time between directing a mental hospital on the outskirts of Jerusalem and teaching at the Hebrew University. Very quickly we found out that we had a very similar approach to the subject of the Holocaust, though from different disciplines; Hillel's idea was that one cannot create an artificial abyss between these disciplines and that one should view the survivor's experiences as a whole, as a *Gestalt* and only then look at her/him from the different possible perspectives, which of course should be combined ultimately.

Hillel explained, and explains in the present book, that the common view that looks at all survivors as basically mentally disturbed people needing sympathy is completely warped and is the result of aggressions and guilt feelings on the part of individuals and social groups in the (mainly Jewish) host societies. The wonder that Hillel tries to explain in the book is the victory of the mental powers that enabled a vast majority of survivors to re-adapt to society and function within it in ways parallel to those of non-survivors; however, he also tries to point out where nevertheless, and despite this, the differences lie. He goes through the stages the survivor went through and basically concentrates his attention on Polish Jews who went through ghettos and camps. He does not deal in any detail with partisans, hidden Jews, and Jews from areas outside of the Polish-Soviet areas. I am quite sure he would have dealt with these had he lived longer. As it is, his contribution to our knowledge of the psychological processes in the face of the unprecedented events they had to live through, such as helplessness, fury, transference, desire for vengeance, adaptation, and numbing, is in my judgment, as a layman as far as psychology is concerned, tremendous.

He connects the survivor's reactions to her/his prewar experiences during childhood and draws some fascinating conclusions. His emphasis is on the individual. Hillel resists easy generalizations and is wary of speaking about the survivors as a group, emphasizing that the important thing is to see the survivors as individuals and the group as composed of individuals, each one of whom had a slightly different personal history and therefore different psychological reactions to his Holocaust experience. At the same time, he puts the experiences of the individual into the contexts of family, community, and the Jewish people as a whole because the traditions of the community and the atmosphere in which the person was reared has a lasting impact also on the behavior of the individual while he/she goes through gruesome traumatic experiences. The process of returning to this context or recreating it after the Holocaust is a central concern in this book.

Hillel Klein's vantage point is quite unique: a Holocaust survivor himself who went through many of the stages that the objects of his research also went—pre-Holocaust well-ordered childhood and early youth, war, ghetto, resistance, slave labor, concentration camp, and liberation—and then as a person who went through psychoanalysis, received his medical and psychiatric training, and returns to deal with what is in part his own history. A professional, an expert, writes the book as a profession. It is also written by somebody who has not only empathy but also a deep understanding of the trauma—from the inside so to speak.

One of his most interesting and controversial activities was the attempt to have survivors and/or their children meet with second-generation perpetrators. His observations on the parallels and the differences between the two groups in the process of these meetings are some of the more fascinating parts of his research. He was an innovator in this respect, too, and others have continued his work.

His death was a great loss—to his family, his students, his friends, and the scientific community. I, too, lost a friend who, I am sure, would have wanted his book to be published rather than speeches delivered on his grave.

Yehuda Bauer
Jerusalem, October 2002

INTRODUCTION[1]

by Carl Nedelmann

I

This book is the legacy of a survivor of the Holocaust. It calls the Holocaust "the dark core of the twentieth century" and an attack on individuality. As a consequence, it portrays an individual "whose personal survival contains memories of the past before the Holocaust and of the psychotic universe of the ghetto and concentration camp." The legacy consists in showing ways that lead to open spaces. The reality of the Holocaust remains present in the survivor, and even very small occasions suffice to make thoughts and feelings flow to the most horrendous experiences. Imre Kertész has found words for it: "I have seen the true face of this terrible century [. . . and] knew that this face will captivate me forever" (Kertész, 2000). Hillel Klein describes how it is nevertheless possible to return to life again.

Hillel Klein was born in Krakow on March 20, 1923, and grew up in a world of which he said that "Goethe's words were just as important there as the words of Yitzhak of Berditchev," a rabbi who lived and worked in Berditchev during Goethe's time and achieved a great deal of influence. The other great leaders of the Hasidic movement also manifested their unanimous esteem for him, which may be due to the fact that he did not found a school and was therefore no one's rival and everyone could cite his wisdom.

I am mentioning this just to give some idea of what it means for the German language and civilization to have Goethe's name mentioned in this way, in the same breath as Yitzhak of Berditchev, and put next to the East European Jewish tradition.

Klein said, "One has to go out of Auschwitz, to break free from Auschwitz. One has to go back to the intact sources . . . In the words of Rabbi Yitzhak of Berditchev, 'one of our Saints,' one has to say: 'I call You, God,

---

1 From the epilogue of the German edition—*Überleben und Versuche der Wiederbelebung. Psychoanalytische Studien mit Überlebenden der Shoah. Jahrbuch der Psychoanalyse,* Beiheft 20, Stuttgart: Frommann-Holzboog, 2003. Biermann, C., Nedelmann, C. (editors), Strehlow, B. (translator)—and from my article "No reconciliation, but self-searching in the sense of rapprochement—Hillel Klein's Holocaust research in Germany 40 years after." *Int. J. Psychoanal.*, 2005, 86:1133–42.

to a court of the *Torah*: What have you done?' That would really be in the true spirit of analysis. Not accepting what is bad and evil, not just the quiet work of mourning, as if it could not have been otherwise" (Klein, 1992 [1983], p. 1181).

Emphasizing the progressive meaning of the survivor's guilt, he asked, "Why am I standing here before you instead of my friend Mordechai Gebirtig?" Mordechai Gebirtig was shot and killed by a German soldier in 1942 when the Krakow Ghetto was cleared out. The survivor's guilt caused Klein to ask this question about his friend. By asking it, the world that had been lost rose up before his very eyes. That was when he started to find the world from before again.

The Kleins and the Gebirtigs had been neighbors. Mordechai was Klein's paternal friend. He was a carpenter and songwriter; an atheist and member of the *Bund*, the Jewish Socialist Party of Poland; deeply rooted in Kazimierz, the Jewish part of Krakow; and a great deal more. In 1938, when Klein was fifteen, Mordechai wrote a song that later became the anthem of the resistance in the underground and the ghetto and is still sung at Holocaust memorials today. Klein often quoted the opening lines:

Ss 'brent! Briderlech, ss 'brent!
Oj, undser orem shtetl nebech brent!
Un ir schtejt un kukt asoj sich
Mit farlejgte hent

Our Town is burning, brothers, burning,
Our poor little town is burning.
And you stand looking on
With folded arms

Klein wrote: "It was a voice of despair and a cry for help in the anxious, depressed, disbelieving shtetls and towns of Eastern Europe, on the one hand, and the emotional desert and apathy of the Western world on the other."

II

Klein was sixteen years old when the Germans marched into Poland. For a few months, until he had just turned seventeen, he was still able to attend the Gymnasium (the upper-level grammar school). Then he joined the resistance and went underground. In 1942, he was captured by the Germans and locked up. He survived the horrors of Plaszow, a camp on the edge of Kraków, and other camps until the death marches at the end of the war took him to Theresienstadt, where he was liberated by the Red Army at twenty-two years old, closer to death than life, the only survivor of a large family.

When he had physically recovered after a prolonged in-patient period in a hospital for displaced persons in Munich, he studied medicine in Munich, which he completed with the state examination and promotion. He then went to Sweden, where he married and where his first daughter was born. The family then emigrated to Israel, where his second daughter was born. He became a psychiatrist and psychoanalyst. He underwent part of his psychoanalytic training in London. He tended to sympathize with the Middle Group around Balint and Winnicott and later remained close to object-relations thinking. In Jerusalem he opened a private psychoanalytic practice and became the director of a psychiatric hospital as well as a professor at the Hebrew University of Jerusalem. Honorary posts followed. Lecture trips and research commitments often took him to the United States and to Germany during later years.

He sought discussion with German colleagues, at first only with Jewish ones, later also with non-Jewish ones. As far as the German Psychoanalytical Association was concerned, he found the following situation: psychoanalysis in Germany after 1945 was reconstructed with international help. In 1951, the newly formed German Psychoanalytical Association was accepted by the International Psychoanalytic Association (IPA). At the 1977 IPA Congress in Jerusalem, the Germans proposed to hold the 1981 Congress in Berlin. The invitation provoked the shadowy presence of the Holocaust and aroused mixed feelings among many of the analysts about a congress on German soil. It would be the first one since the 1932 congress in Wiesbaden. It was too closely associated with the time of the Nazis. The vote went against a congress in Germany. The rebuff affected the German Association deeply as a group. In 1985, the IPA Congress was finally held in Germany, in Hamburg, not in Berlin. Hamburg was less of a symbol. In the meantime, a special relationship developed between Israeli and German colleagues. Among the Israeli psychoanalysts who came to Germany, Hillel Klein was the most prominent during the period before the 1985 IPA Congress in Hamburg.

To understand the Holocaust, the study of history seemed to him to be imperative and led him, during the same period, to the cooperation with Yehuda Bauer, who was then the head of the International Institute for Research into the Holocaust at Yad Vashem, as described in the Preface of this book.

Further important sources of knowledge were for him the texts of poets and writers: "They have transmitted the external and inner conditions of life in the ghetto and concentration camp which we, as psychoanalysts, got to know in our work with survivors and their families."

III

Hillel Klein's contribution to the research of the Holocaust centers on a reversal of the evaluation of the guilt feelings of the survivors. For him, guilt feelings were a sign of "recovery" and "revival" since memories begin with feelings of guilt. "I believe," he said, "that the guilt for surviving is the only possibility to start a process of mourning and to promote a process of individuation." Martin Bergmann and Milton Jucovy praised Hillel Klein's "life-affirming attitude" and wrote:

> Klein called attention to the mistaken tendency to use the term "survivor's guilt" in a pathological sense and thus to give it a pejorative meaning. In many instances it may be appropriate to use the term in that sense. But in Klein's view there is also a healthy survivor's guilt as it links survivor and the offspring to the past, to those who died, to a sense of belonging to the Jewish group in a life-affirming way. (Bergmann et al., 1990, pp. 314–5)

This change of perspective enabled Hillel Klein "to approach the lives of the survivors from the point of view of a meaningful life experience rather than from that of 'psychic damage.'" He wrote that the difficulties "are reflected in the fact that the literature on the 'therapy with survivors' is so scant in comparison with works on the 'psychopathology of survivors.'"

Signs of *recovery* and *renewal* are signals of hope. Without hope, there would be no way into the open. He told his German colleagues, "We hardly consider hope as an analytic theme, as something we should re-find in ourselves and in our patients. We speak about defence mechanisms, we speak about techniques. But we do not speak about the only crucial subject, that of hope" (1992, p. 1183).

IV

Hillel Klein's contribution to psychoanalysis in Germany centered upon the idea of rapprochement. The term was introduced into psychoanalysis by Margaret Mahler, but he used it in a broader sense, as the *Oxford Dictionary* defined it. *Rapprochement* means "coming together again in friendly relations" or "renewal of friendship."

To meet Hillel Klein was one of my wishes when I travelled to Israel for the first time in June 1982. My wish was fulfilled with unexpected ease. Anne and Martin Wangh had just arrived from New York. In the evening of my first day in Jerusalem, they gave a housewarming party in their new apartment in Neve Sha'anan. Inviting me, Martin said, "You will meet Hillel Klein this evening. He speaks German well, but he will talk with you in English." This is precisely what happened, but after a few minutes, he switched to German, and the following day, in his consulting room, he involved me in a clinical discussion about guilt and guilt feelings. I soon felt like a candidate in the medical state examination. I seem to have passed the examination sufficiently well because Hillel suddenly broke off the discussion and asked abruptly whether I had already been to Yad Vashem. I replied that I intended to go there that day. He asked, "May I accompany you?" I answered in the affirmative. Later, we stood next to each other for a long time in silence in the Remembrance Hall. Eventually I stammered, "For me it means a lot." "For me as well," answered Hillel, which still reverberates in my ears.

We became friends. In October 1983, Hillel was my guest in Hamburg. The program included a lecture at the university. On the way to the lecture hall, he took hold of my arm, hesitating, and said, "Imagine we go in and nobody is there. We could have such a nice evening." Because his lecture was devoted to mourning, he may also have been thinking, *Will my listeners be mourning with me or just not care? Am I accepted?* We went in, and he was confronted by a big audience that followed him word for word. He spoke without notes.

The essence of this friendship showed itself in November 1983 at the autumn conference of the German Psychoanalytical Association. Hillel gave one of the plenary papers. It showed that Hillel was very engaged in a process of coming to terms with Germany again. He told his German colleagues, "What is important is not . . . to deny the past. What is important is the attempt at confrontation . . . and this is why I got the idea of approaching each other, in the sense of . . . rapprochement . . . And I might have started out with you: you and me. That would be . . . a movement with the . . . whole range of feelings, of the emotional world of hate, revenge, disappointed love" (1992, p. 1183).

V

In the summer of 1984, Hillel Klein developed a malignant brain tumor, which usually means less than a year of survival. We saw each other for the last time in January 1985. I went to Jerusalem for his sake. His illness had visibly left its mark. But he made plans that were full of hope. He intended to write about Lessing and his "Nathan" and suggested that we write an essay together with the title "No reconciliation but self-searching in the sense of rapprochement: Dialogue between an Israeli psychoanalyst and a German psychoanalyst forty years after."

In July 1985, I received a short letter from him, and it was apparent that it would be his last. It was written in a barely readable handwriting. In it he writes: "As the Jewish proverb says: man thinks and God laughs. What he laughs about I really do not know and cannot understand it." I have asked Jewish friends about the significance of the proverb. The answers that I received were manifold. But in one respect, they all agreed: God does not laugh, they said, he only smiles.

Hillel Klein died on December 14, 1985, at the age of sixty-two years.

I thought of his last letter when I read in the manuscript of his book that he used to pray at night on his plank bed in the concentration camp. His prayers connected him with the whole world. The thoughts about God in the letter seem to have the same function as the prayers in the concentration camp. They connected him to the whole world and thus became a sign of hope.

As a late sign of his influence in Germany, Klein's book *Survival and Trials of Revival—Psychodynamic Studies of Holocaust Survivors and their Families in Israel and the Diaspora*, originally written in English, appeared in German posthumously in 2003. It consists of a revised version of his contributions to psychoanalytic Holocaust research as well as further observations and a number of autobiographical features. The book describes the struggle for survival from September 1, 1939, to May 8, 1945, from the invasion of Poland to the day of liberation, and it describes trials of survival thereafter.

Prologue

One day in the winter of 1942, a young SS-man who was keeping a group of tired ditch diggers under guard asked one of them, "Tell me the truth. Who will be victorious in the war?" The boy he addressed was nineteen, one of a group of a dozen Jews who were wielding shovels and spades and who were exhausted from digging in the intense cold. A Latin proverb he had once learned came to his mind. Any answer could be risky, but he knew he had to give one that was impersonal. He hoped it would do. In a soft voice he said, "In war there are no victors, only victims."

The SS-man grew furious. Perhaps he sensed that the boy was quick-witted and was evading the question; perhaps any answer would have provoked him. He shoved a revolver at the boy's head and said, "If you do not tell the truth, Jew dog, I will kill you on the spot." His German was clipped, but he meant his threat. Work stopped. No member of the group moved. They waited and their eyes shifted from one to the other. They knew that it was likely that the boy would be murdered in cold blood and then be kicked aside when work resumed. The young man stepped out of the line. He had grown bolder. Perhaps he felt he had nothing to lose. "Germany will lose the war. You can't kill everyone." The two stared at one another for a split second. The boy, too, thought he would be shot. His stammered answer received no reply. The SS-man was silent. He slowly put the pistol away, and when moments later he emerged from his sudden calm silence, it was as if to perform a forgotten chore. "*Weiter machen!*" he shouted. "*Weiter machen!*" Then he marched away.

Later, the gang members attacked the boy, beating him and shouting obscenities. He had jeopardized their lives, they said. He had been arrogant and stupid in daring to have *his* truth spoken at a time when only lies might have saved them.

Why did this young SS-man from the "Gross-Deutschland Division," wearing the skull symbol of the SS on his forehead, ask this question of an anonymous "slave" who was officially no more than "vermin," predestined for imminent collective death? And why did the SS-man not react with rage and aggression as expected? And why did the group, whom the young man had actually saved from destruction, react with rage after the imminent danger had passed? These questions come back to my mind now, looking back in an inner dialogue between the psychoanalyst of today and the young man of 1942.

The style of the SS-man remains that of the omnipotent oppressor, but the incident implied basic doubts about the ultimate end of the war and perhaps even about its justice, the Nazi *Weltanschauung*. The reaction of the SS-man, intuitively hoped for by the young man singled out but totally unexpected by the group, who expected that the boy would be killed, seems to have been the beginning of a dialogue, the hint of a possibility of a human transaction between two young men of the same generation in a desperate situation across an abyss.

The group was supportive as long as the young adolescent representative of the disliked "intelligentsia" was a part of it, using their style, language, and identical patterns of submission, denial, avoidance, temporary submission to slavery and regression of the ego in the service of a future life.

Looking back, I cannot be angry now, I can understand their anguish: "How dare he be so provocatively proud and free, how dare he indulge in the luxury of being an individual when only anonymity was the accepted form of adaptation to hell, the only way to survive known to us?" He had removed himself from the humble submission and acquiescence that they had agreed was the safest and most pragmatic way to behave. Their reaction seems now to include an element of the relief experienced by a family or a cohesive group when an imminent threat to a beloved object has passed. Anxiety then changes into aggression and is displaced onto the object of their previous fears.

What prompted the adolescent to give these answers—absurd in the wasteland of concentration camp reality? He regained the right to answer as an individual when he physically removed himself from the group, thereby rejecting the false self that had been projected onto him by the Nazi aggressor up to this point, as part of the anonymous mass.

His answers represented his fidelity to a strong sense of self, his naïveté and perhaps also resignation, and an unacknowledged hope that truth was power. How did the adolescent know—or did he?—that the German SS-man also needed a break from the insanity of torture and dominance, a momentary return to sanity? If mass destruction was an automatic response at this time of death, what were the forces at work in the basic preservation of the victim's spiritual and moral sense of self? Is there a reconstructive power within human beings that enables them to preserve their bonds with others and to triumph over death? It seems that when the victim overcame the brutality and the absurdity of the camp existence by adopting a moral orientation connected with their internal sense of national identity, he gave the SS-man a chance to get in touch with his evolving humanity.

Despite the confrontation with death, the victims demonstrated that their spiritual and moral self could remain autonomous, influencing their decision making when their ego was not totally depleted. The spectrum of emotions ordinarily experienced within families and transmitted from parents to children (love, fidelity to a system of values, tenderness, anger, and disappointment) still existed in them. The continuing attachment and responsibility of human beings to others in and after a time when such ties were deliberately severed were indicative of the enduring strength of these bonds.

Through studies of individuals and recreated families of survivors gathered in Israel, Europe, and the United States over many years, I have attempted to answer the haunting questions of the Holocaust: Could the Nazis have destroyed the human feelings and sense of self of those men and women gathered together on that winter day? If they had survived the Holocaust, what kind of people are they today? Did the fact that they survived physically mean that they survived psychologically? Who among the survivors preserved a continuing sense of self, a drive toward reconstitution of emotional attachments, hope, and curiosity about life? How has such a survivor altered society's perceptions of life? To what extent do we share their difficulties and achievements? Had the young Nazi's experience as the aggressor destroyed his human feelings and sense of self? What is he like today?

The Nazi persecutor is rarely mentioned in scientific studies and certainly never psychiatrically analyzed in the myriad papers and books dealing with the Holocaust. Did he not also suffer massive psychic traumatization? His dehumanization and hopelessness, the fabric of his psychological experience, should be the subject of scientific inquiry so that we can learn more about survival and revival in the framework of the specific "transactions" between victim and aggressor.

I recognize that I am suggesting answers in my statements about the relations of survivors and their role in society, in the possibility of reshaping the world in which we live. I hear my readers ask, "Isn't it a rather late wish to conjure up this memory of life and death confrontation of so many years ago?" Some of my questions are, I admit, rather rhetorical and naive in this post-Auschwitz era, when we are filled with doubts about ourselves and our relationship to our common human history.

When I asked myself why I wanted to write about the Holocaust, I found that the answer lay in my own need, both as a survivor and psychiatrist, to render it in a more balanced perspective. I believe that some of my insights about my personal experience and observations as an involuntary participant-observer will be conducive to an understanding of the world of today in the light of the world that has vanished.

I wish to share with the readers something about the human capacity to work through massive traumatization and transform painful memories and survival guilt into responsibility. The hope is that readers may be able to recognize within themselves the means by which they not only suffer, endure, and physically survive but also their ability to recover from massive traumatization.

After treating survivors and their families for many years, I have learned the process by which survivors recover from and transform suppressed, denied, and avoided experiences and memories through confrontation and clarification. This therapeutic process has enabled them to rid themselves of experiences of shame and despair. The newly accepted psycho-historical identification with their heritage—one in which pain and confrontation with death are connected with rebirth and new beginnings—is expressed in the lives of the families of survivors as well.

For the purposes of this book, I reject the normally respected boundaries between the disciplines of psychology, sociology, and history. I disavow as well the separation between the realm of the researcher/observer and the realm of the object of the research as an individual whose personal survival incorporates memories to the pre-Holocaust past as well as the psychotic universe of the ghetto and the concentration camp. A precedent for such a disclaimer I found in the psychoanalytic setting. In psychoanalytic practice, the analyst's ego is both cognitively observing and empathically responding in an attempt to give meaning to the patient's experiences, thoughts, and emotions.

I speak in this book with many voices: the adolescent of then and the man of now, the victim/survivor of then, and the psychiatrist/

psychoanalyst and researcher today. These voices blend, and the roles interconnect as I try to derive meaning and hope from my own and others' experiences. This book is a dialogue between the adolescent experiencing the utter destruction of his humanistic *Weltanschauung*—the *Weltuntergang* of his beloved private world and the mature man living between resignation and hope in an anxiety-ridden time.

Chapter 1:
The Survivor's Search for Meaning

The Holocaust is the darkness at the heart of the twentieth century. It has gained a place among those events that have permanently shaped our perception of man, alerting our view of the present and our expectations of the future. As time passes, the need to interpret the relationship of the Holocaust to the whole fabric of human experience becomes more pressing so that we neither blind ourselves to the aggressor/victim within ourselves nor ignore the human capacity for recovery, healing, and revival. It is the strength of the latter that urges us to reproduce our own kind, restoring our vision of immortality through our children.

The totality of terror in the psychotic cosmos of the concentration camps produced a trauma of apocalyptic proportions. Most unique is the Nazis' regression to bestiality. The unfathomable "wasteland" of the ghettos and concentration camps has been described in the metaphors of writers such as Elie Wiesel (1958), Ilona Carmel (1969), and Paul Celan (1959), who have recorded those outer and inner facts of ghetto and concentration camp life that we psychoanalysts have come to know in our work with survivors and their families. The full impact of the Holocaust cannot be understood solely through studying the survivors themselves. They must also be seen in relation to their families, particularly their children.

There are many conflicting published opinions about Holocaust victims and survivors based upon differing cultural backgrounds, personal experiences, intellectual traditions, and scientific disciplines. Two widely divergent views of survivors are found in the works of Bettelheim (1943) and Des Pres (1976). Bettelheim's approach to human behavior and survival in the concentration camps has strongly shaped public thinking today about survivors in Nazi-occupied Europe. Bettelheim's crucial point as enunciated in the chapter "Self Determination" is the ideal of assertion of personal autonomy that he thought he personally preserved during his incarceration in Dachau in 1938, before the Holocaust. In Bettelheim, there seems to exist the need for illusion and comforting thought, and that even in the psychotic cosmos of the concentration camps. In Auschwitz, there was some measure of individual freedom of action and thought. In contrast to himself, Bettelheim describes other survivors collectively as a regressed, submissive group whose survival was purchased at the cost of inner autonomy, humanity, and assertion and whose later lives continued to bear the stigma of that psychosocial regression.

Des Pres, approaching the survivor from a different discipline and questioning the relevance of psychoanalytic theory, portrayed the intensely human quality of the survivor's past experiences in the most degrading and loftiest aspects. He does not, however, relate to the survivor's pre-Holocaust past, neither to his family nor to his personality. Both approaches deprive survivors of psycho-historic identities as individuals as well as a group in which specific systems of values and cherished traditions exist. The traditional defenses that are transmitted from one generation to another and that characterized and influenced their experiences of the Holocaust and their later adaptation to life as survivors are overlooked by both authors.

Nazi racial ideology and action aimed at the destruction not only of individuals and communities but of an entire civilization. Because the traumatization was both individual and collective, individual victims of this trauma could seek love and both physical and emotional support from other survivors, creating a "new family" to replace the lost one, a supportive system in the form of a small group of friends. This small group of comrades worked together in a gang and shared basic necessities such as food; they were united by common attitudes against the German tormentors, at times transforming them with a joke from almighty killers to stupid creatures. Common experiences such as praying, singing, and conveying universal and personal strivings for hope and love were important group activities, an antidote to dehumanization, supporting the self and ego ideal.

This was especially true for those individuals who shared a common language and came from the same area. During the Holocaust, people used psycho-social defenses and coping mechanisms that were embedded in their cultural tradition and family. Black humor and ironic wit were used to describe the relation between victim and aggressor. Many identified with martyrs from the past, such as those who died for the "sanctification of God" during the Inquisition and others with ideologies ranging from religious to utopian and universalist socialistic. Some survivors resorted to fantasy; others relied on social support systems of a particular kind between the victims.

Ignoring these elements impoverishes our understanding of the survivor, as does negligence of such factors as his pre-Holocaust family structure, personal life, and the situation when the traumatization occurred.

While there is no questioning the importance of establishing what were the common issues, features, defenses, and coping mechanisms employed by survivors in order to better understand their traumatization, it is equally imperative scientifically and morally to distinguish the survivors as individuals. In order to do so, we deal with each of the several factors in the survivor's experience: the psychological, social, and cultural universalities on the one hand and the unique and subjective features of each survivor on the other. Conceptualizing these experiences will allow us to draw scientific inferences from them.

It is also important to emphasize here that when we speak of the "survivor experience," we address ourselves to the continuity between the period of persecution and that which followed liberation as a psychosocial environment that could either be rejecting or supportive. Such massive traumatization and exposure to extreme situations involving collective death and dehumanization overwhelm the adaptive and recuperative capacities of the psyche. This degree of traumatization had never before been a subject of study. Many psychiatrists have since described the phases that the individual undergoes when psychic defenses are overwhelmed by a reality that is of a psychotic nature, as in ghettos and concentration camps (Davidson, 1979; Klein, 1974b).

Holocaust victims were forced to become the passive witnesses of the massive destruction of their families and communities. Common features and psychosocial patterns in their response to the persecution appear in their personal histories. The first reaction to oppression was an attempt to master whatever could be manipulated and rescued in the external environment, including an increased emotional investment in family members and a diminished level of interpersonal conflicts. Intrapsychic conflicts of childhood origin were also characteristically diminished in the face of real danger and the pressure to have to answer existential questions with life-or-death consequences for the self and the family. Aggression was diverted to the external, hostile environment. All the survivors suffered physical impairment as a result of continuous extreme hunger and sleep deprivation, in addition to infections and deficiency diseases. They also suffered extreme emotional deprivation with consequent doubts about their own body and self-image as men or women.

As long as conditions in the ghetto permitted, the survivors maintained a relatively active personal and social life. Some attended and others taught in underground schools. However, they had little opportunity for social role experimentation and for finding solutions to intrapsychic life-cycle problems, which remained unresolved until after liberation. Personal relationships continued, as well as courtship and marriage between ghetto inmates. Poems were written, relating the ghetto experiences, and scientific investigations by doctors were undertaken. One example is the studies undertaken on the effects of malnutrition on health, social relations, and community life during different phases of the Warsaw Ghetto. But in every ghetto, there was a continuous development of underground resistance, organizations with numerous revolts, most of which failed.

When the oppression became so pervasive that active resistance was not feasible, they became, in most cases, helpless and passive and, of necessity, had suppressed massive feelings toward their oppressors. This suppressed aggression caused a temporary state of paralysis of action and numbness of feeling (Lifton, 1967, 1968).

From a psychological perspective, the conflicts of ghetto life were much more complex and intense than those of the concentration camp. The survivor had the freedom to choose different pathways at the time, although the choices were limited. He could, for example, choose to leave the ghetto as an "Aryan" or remain with his family. Issues related to his attachment-separation, his slowly evolving realization of the genocide taking place, his feelings of total isolation and loneliness, and his basic need for life and tenderness intermingled and evolved into a counterpointed theme, contrasting the fugue of death and the fugue of love.

Fragments of a poem written by a poet friend, Chaskiel Anisfeld from Krakow, with whom I shared dialogues and the anguish of the Krakow Ghetto and experienced the agony of working in the stone quarries of the Plaszow concentration camp, illustrate the polarities of this life experience. The young, promising poet was seventeen years old when he died. He was killed by an SS officer whom he and the others called "The Angel of Death" and "*Lalke*" (puppet) because he seemed to have a demonic blond beauty mixed with a passion for murder. At the time of his death, I found stanzas in his pocket of what was originally a sonnet in Polish that had been written only days before he was murdered. These were taken from me immediately, and only fragments come back to me now.

Sonata of Love and Death
Was it as a punishment that God sent me love
That hovers over me like the vengeful ghost Hekata,
Condemns me to pain because I have lost
All feelings, now consumed by the passion's flame?

I carry this burden like a crown of thorns
Entwined from my sighs.
It cuts to my brow, a payment for sins that I don't know
How I ever committed or was guilty of.

My youth, pale with grief, now passing me by
Spins like a puppet on a slippery stage.
Someone put it in motion in an insane rage
And it whirls and it twirls until the finale.

Then it stops, now defeated, my youth pale with grief
And tells me to hate and I obey
Carrying the new burden unto my last day
Like a bloody stigma, like a gory sign.

But sometimes I dream of a place far away
A desert, a tundra, a deep shady forest
Where one day I'll put down my head and rest
A helpless dream of a damned one, one sentenced to death.

(Chaskiel Anisfeld, born in Krakow, 1924, killed in KZ Plaszow, 1942, at the age of seventeen)

Creativity was a form of dealing with human losses, the loss of love, the anticipation of one's own death, and most important a way of preserving a human image and an image of God in one's self. Often, as in the case of Anisfeld, the language and the metaphors of the pre-war adolescent world, with its images from Greek and Judeo-Christian mythology and humanistic traditions, were the only concepts that could be used in relation to the unspeakable.

The persecution period consisted of several phases of psychosocial responses, including trials of active mastery of the traumatic situation, cohesive pairing behavior with intense emotional ties, and finally induced passive compliance with the oppressors. These phases may be understood as trial periods, involving adaptation and development of specific coping mechanisms for the strains and dangers of the unspeakable reality of the Holocaust.

The uniform picture of Holocaust survivors was that of suffering from a static concentration camp syndrome, as it was described during the initial phase of investigation following their liberation. Simon Minkovski's 1946 paper about "affective anesthesia," that is, the superficiality of object relationships, and later Paul Friedman's work (1948) and the development of the concept of the "survivor syndrome" are a consequence of these early observations of survivors (Targowla, 1955; Niederland, 1968a, 1968b; Eitinger, 1964; Krystal, Niederland, 1968). At first, psychiatrists working with survivors were struck by the common patterns of traumatization of genocidal persecution. However, this clinical syndrome was not static, as is shown by longitudinal psychoanalytic and psychological studies. Rather, later studies highlight significant differences in the psychological profiles and life histories of survivors.

Because the goal of the studies that took place soon after liberation was to establish the consequences of the experiences of the survivors (evidenced by the concentration camp syndrome as a recognized psychopathological categorization of the survivors), the clinical and theoretical research focused on the psychopathology rather than on the question of coping, and the development of specific ego-adaptive pathways during the Holocaust and in the life of the survivor after liberation. The description of the concentration camp syndrome in the late 1950s and 1960s created a new modality of diagnosis for psychiatry and the behavioral sciences and became a model that has served as a focal concept for examining the sequel of catastrophic stress situations ever since (Davidson, 1980).

While it is true that during the selections in the ghettos and in the immediate and extreme reactions to brutalization in concentration camps there were common patterns of behavior and psycho-biological processes, originating in depression and anxiety, the fact is that those similarities overlay highly individualized intrapsychic processes, personal and social histories, and innate factors. To the outsider, looking at the rag-clad, emaciated figures in the ghetto, or surveying the massed victims in grey on the *Appellplatz* in the concentration camps, it would have been impossible to distinguish an intellectual, politically active urban adolescent from an illiterate constricted village boy in the delusional world of the camp. Enriched by our clinical experience and the testimony of survivors, we have become increasingly aware, however, that each survivor's social and intrapsychic life was just as different during the Holocaust as before and after. Some survivors were able to maintain a strong sense of continuity, of self-sameness before, during, and after the war. Others, however, were left with a feeling of personal disorientation toward themselves and others, a feeling of discontinuity of the self in the form of de-realization, as expressed in the repetitive statement "We are not the same." Just as varied were the survivors' capacities for working through and integrating these experiences. We recognize that their early life experiences, developmental histories, family constellations, and emotional bonds within the family specifically shaped the survivor's ego-adaptive patterns and coping mechanisms. Through work with survivors, we have learned to ask specific questions related to these differences: How long did the individual suffer traumatization? Was he alone or with family and friends during the Holocaust? Was he in a camp or in hiding? Were false "Aryan" identification papers used? Was he a witness to mass destruction in the ghetto or the camp? What was his experience in the camp? What work was he assigned? With whom was he associated? What support systems in the form of friends and family and what social bonds did he have? The experience of those who were actively able to resist their oppressors either in the underground or as partisans was different in every respect from the experience of those who were passively victimized in death camps. This determined their personalities and family structures.

While the psychological effects of traumatization upon survivors have been described satisfactorily, patterns of coping, resistance, and recovery have not been articulated as well. In my work, I have studied mourning and survivors' guilt as positive forces for re-individuation and recovery, and thus to understand them in a different, less alienating manner than did my colleagues who see them as a pathological counterpart of the concentration camp syndrome. In studying the different ways in which survivors coped with disaster, with "normal" life, and with re-establishing family ties, I have been repeatedly impressed with the diversity rather than the uniformity of these ego-adaptive and coping mechanisms within the life histories of survivors.

Psychological revival after liberation took place within the context of marriages and the birth and development of children. The themes of separation, dependence, responsibility, trust, attachment, loss, and cohesion were played out within families. These motifs appeared in different guises within the families, as did affective and cognitive styles. What appeared to be psychopathological in origin might later often be appreciated as a step toward psychosocial integration and revival. In the trials of revival, we see the capacity of the survivor to integrate and work through the total experience of the Holocaust by actualizing his capacity to change the survival guilt into a sense of responsibility. In this self-healing process, he retains his own self-cohesiveness and self-sameness, connecting the nuclei of his previous identity and world of past representations and values with the duties and responsibilities of his present world.

There is a profound fear of pathos in the survivor, and therefore there is a tendency for survivors to use grotesque anecdotes in relating their traumatic experiences, in remembering their past. It is expressed in the everyday language of the positive experiences of moving through constructive activity, namely, of the capacity or the will to live, to find meaning and hope, and to develop intense attachments and object relationships, vivid imagery, and creative fantasy formation. In the formal and informal meetings of survivors, I was struck with the way in which they repeatedly recalled their individual and group experiences during the Holocaust. It is a special mixture of understatement, wit, and self-irony with an anecdotal style. There is often a displacement of focus from the tragic, unspeakable reality of the camp to self-irony and small details that make the essence of their survival understandable. For example, one survivor spoke during her therapy of the strong ties that she had with her mother, who saved her during the most dangerous moments of the selection in Auschwitz. She stressed in her story how in the face of the crematorium her mother saved a pot of fat, seeing in it the source of life in the conditions of near-starvation of the camp. Certain that she would survive, she and her mother dug a hole to bury the fat, which they would recover after the selection. With hilarious laughter she told her story, stressing how they recovered the fat, but leaving untold their story of grief and separation from friends and family.

Among survivors, there was a polarity between the drive to master psychologically the overwhelming experiences and the passive submission and repetition of the Holocaust trauma. In telling and working through the experience of the Holocaust, the survivor and his family took an active stance toward mastery and adaptation. In this regard, we cannot minimize the importance of a specific Jewish style of surviving, stressing the importance of life and how to live even in the shadow of death. Among Jewish survivors, there was a need to find a historical connection with previous generations and their suffering. There was a search for a specific Jewish meaning to their suffering and an additional link to the Jewish past. Here I disagree with Bettelheim, who stresses the differences between the Jews of the Holocaust and the Jews of the Inquisition and who rejects the concept of *Kiddush HaShem* (sanctification of God), which was linked with thoughts and the anticipation of the impending death of the Jewish victims of the Holocaust. In the strictest historical sense, Bettelheim is correct in saying that the survivors, unlike the martyrs of the Inquisition, were given no choice between life and death. However, Bettelheim fails to grasp the fact that the defenses and coping styles used by Jews during the Holocaust were never imminent in Jewish history, transmitted from generation to generation. Psychologically, survivors from different geographical areas and from different psychosocial groups or from different ghettos and concentration camps identified with *Kiddush HaShem* because it gave psychological and historical meaning to their experiences during the Holocaust.

People in despair are not engaged in a search for historical truth but rather seek meaning for the confrontation with death and as a defense against the threat of fragmentation and robotization. This search for meaning is apparent both in the style of survival and in the process of recovery of the self after the Holocaust.

Because the survivor aroused ambivalent feelings of fear, astonishment, guilt, pity, and anxiety in every society in which he made a new home, the process of recovery was more difficult. A numbed indifference masked fears that such appalling events could happen again, to any one of us. Man by his very nature evades the intimidations of the catastrophic within himself. The specific transactions between the survivor and the society, connected by ambivalent feelings, as well as the fate of the survivor and his family in contrasting societies (the United States and Israel in towns and on the kibbutzim) are cogent to an understanding of how the structures and the identities of the families of the survivors are shaped by the environment.

After more than thirty years, it may now be safe to say that the majority of survivors have been able to recover their ego capacities and have re-entered the paths their lives might have taken before the Holocaust. I have asked myself why they were able to recover. What prevented their lasting regression? Why were their ego capacities not permanently destroyed or impaired? How is it possible to describe the strengths that at one time seemed to be overshadowed in the struggle to cope with the traumatization and that now emerged after so many years? What is the specific fit between childhood determinants, fantasy, reality, and later life that will cause an adult to succumb or to recover? What role does the family play in the process of recovery?

The families of the survivors developed highly crystallized and condensed family styles and specific agendas around themes such as psychobiological continuity, fears of separation, and fears of unending illness and death. The transactions between the generations have been characterized by an intense interdependence and are expressed through overinvolvement, difficulties with separation, demands for socio-economic achievements, and compliance with external values as well as internally generated standards. Research has shown that we can no longer speak of the transmission of psychopathology from one generation to the next but rather of the transmission of common motifs, mythologies, issues, and sensitivities within families and between generations. These arise from complex processes of identification and introjection and are, of course, subject to events in the course of history.

We have learned much about individuals, families, and societies in the thirty-five years of work with survivors and their families because we have had the unique opportunity to observe the impact of a historical event of unparalleled brutality upon people whose personal involvement in the center of events marked them forever as survivors. Thirty-five years is insignificant in the massive flow of history, but the twentieth century so compresses and distorts the orderly process of historical change that thirty-five years in this century is comparable to hundreds or even thousands of years in previously recorded time.

Paradoxically, the experience of the Holocaust offers a glimpse of hope for the triumph of life over death and destruction. This becomes increasingly more apparent as we study the most recent changes among survivors in Israel and the United States, especially when observing their relations with their children.

Who are the survivors? They have become the historians of their own fates as well as the objects of history. They are monuments to man's destructive power untamed by centuries of European civilization. But they are, as well, symbols of rebirth and of man's efforts to preserve within himself an image of God.

Not by chance do many survivors refer to their cataclysmic experiences of oppression as "the war," rejecting the concept of Holocaust because of its biblical connotation of "totally consumed animal sacrifice." This metaphor is not relevant to their experiences, even though in the free associations of survivors, the parable of Isaac's sacrifice often appears. In the story of the sacrifice of Isaac, the *Akeida*, the survivors often identify both with the sacrifice and the victim. This results in an ambiguity where no clear boundaries in imagery exist. In this imagery, they sometimes identify with Isaac, the sacrificial victim—themselves having been sacrificed by society—and at other times with a pained and agonizing Abraham, himself a victim, commanded by God to sacrifice his beloved son in the service of life. This kind of survival guilt recurs constantly in the survivors' attitudes toward themselves and their relationship with their children and society.

Ultimately the survivor tries to give meaning to his past by using traces of metaphor, fantasy, and childhood memory from before the Holocaust as a defense against the horrible realities of the concentration camps in a search for psychological escape from oppression. The survivor uses the psychological resources of childhood memory as well as the remembered "islands of humanity" in this search for self-assertion and meaning in his life. These are the same defenses that many of the victims used in the concentration camps, where memory and fantasy helped to bring transcendence, respite, and escape from the timeless, arid wasteland to a world beyond the barbed wire.

Recent events have taught us something about the boundaries between fact and fantasy and about the potential within all of us for violence and love, for destruction and rebirth. We have become aware that human beings can overcome extremes of traumatization and can emerge from their experiences with the potential of recovery and reconstitution of their ego capacities. We have learned that the survivors' needs for restitution and love were often ignored because societies overwhelmed with guilt avoided and shunned them. The yearning of the survivor for dialogue and encounter with the other is connected with his hope for restoring and healing his shattered representation of the world in his attempt to redress the balance of his experiences toward the positive. Therefore, the excessive yearning for good experiences exists not only in Jews but also in non-Jews whose image they also yearn to repair. On their part, the survivors discovered that society was unable to respond to their needs for love, rebirth, and restitution and that their utopian dreams would have to be modified by the psychosocial reality of the societies themselves tormented by anxieties, fears of self-destruction and helplessness, and in confrontation with their own aggressive strivings.

This book is an expression of the manner in which the basic personality of the individual survivor meshed with the specific traumatic experiences and psychosocial forces after the Holocaust as they came to the fore in the process of his re-integration. I shall examine and analyze the life of the individual survivor in the context of his specific personal past before the Holocaust, his experiences during the cataclysmic events, his present environment, and his family so that we may understand the interactions between these factors in the individual's life history and in the course of his revival following traumatization.

The chapters of this book are divided into four major areas. The first part, "Oppression and Survival," deals with the variations of experience and trauma during the period of the Holocaust, the psychological consequences for the individual, and the process of survival itself. In part 2, "Society and the Survivor," discussions will focus on the effects of society's relationship with the survivor on his subsequent psychological adaptation, following liberation and immigration, during the years of silence, and the breaking of the silence after the Yom-Kippur War. In the third part of the book, "Survivors and Their Families," the influence of the Holocaust on survivors and their families' integrative and adaptive capacities will be discussed, as well as the differences and the comparisons between the families of survivors living in Israeli kibbutzim and urban settlements in Israel and the United States. Part four, "The Psychotherapeutic Treatment of Survivors and Their Families," will include an examination of specific issues in the psychotherapeutic treatment of survivors and their families, including the effects of severe traumatization, problems of countertransference in work with survivors and their children, the role of survival guilt in the process of mourning and revival, and the dilemma of the survivor who seeks treatment.

Our studies demonstrate that both intrapsychic and external factors were significant determinants of the course of survivors' lives during the thirty-five years after the Holocaust. The processes of post-Holocaust mourning and recovery can then be demonstrated with the survivors, between the generations, and in a historical and psychosocial framework. The rebuilding of self-boundaries, the recovery of identity, and the development of new attachments and of a sense of biological and historical continuity are the hopeful outcomes of the process of mourning, as we will demonstrate here.

PART I

Oppression and Survival

Chapter 2:
On the Eve of the Apocalypse

To recount the history of Europe between the world wars is beyond the scope of this chapter. However, to understand the initial reactions of the Jews as the most persecuted minority of the Nazi oppression, it is important to look at the psychosocial situation existing in Eastern and Central Europe prior to World War II. We may then proceed to examine the initial reaction to the Nazi oppression, drawing either from examples that I witnessed or experienced or from experiences recounted to me by survivors during their therapy.

For nearly one thousand years, Jews had lived sometimes side by side but often intermingled with non-Jews, where their relationship was one of conflict and antagonism on the surface but underneath, of interdependence and attachment. This was expressed in cultural exchanges, language, mythologies, mutual stereotyping of "Goy" and "Jew," and most important, in the intense relations of love and hatred in everyday life. With the intense nationalistic and xenophobic tendencies in the emerging States of Europe following World War I, feelings of suspicion and insecurity grew between them.

Poverty, anti-Semitism, the economic and cultural boycott of the Jews, and the increasing impossibility of emigration were characteristic elements of the sociocultural situation of the Jews of Eastern and Central Europe between the two wars. The result was an intensification of the identity crisis for the Jew, who was faced with the need to resolve the dilemma of being a Jew and identifying with the culture and civilization of his country of which he had been an active participant and contributor. Yet under the influence of the Catholic Church, which in those days was ultra nationalistic, hostile, and rejecting, the mostly Christian population of his "motherland" could not accept him as a Jew. This situation existed in its most extreme form in Poland, whereas the Catholic Church had less influence in France, yet anti-Semitic trends in church doctrine could be found there as well. As for protestant Europe, I am aware that Luther's revolution against Catholicism did not liberate him from the hatred of the Jew, which he incorporated in his own family and the church. More than that, anti-Semitism became an important tool to catch the souls of the new believers. The community, family, and individual needs of the Jew could not be met in the existing social situation, thus creating a need for change.

Some saw this change through migration; others, such as in the Bund Party, in the restructuring of society into a socialist state in which minorities would achieve cultural autonomy. Until the trials of the generals, the intellectuals, and the political leaders in Moscow, some tried to find the solution through embracing the communist revolution. The hopes for emigration were frustrated with the closing of the gates to Palestine and the west, and the east as well, following the Ribbentrop-Molotov pact of nonaggression and friendship between Nazi Germany and Communist Russia.

There was not only a need to change but also to rebuild a new life: "to build and to be rebuilt" was the Zionist slogan. The Zionist ideology provided many Jews with an idealistic framework for the expression of frustration and the achievement of an identity of their own. It also served as an attempt, especially by the young, to depart from the ways of the older generation. The younger generations looked for ideological solidarity and the common strivings connected with this age. They were often highly romanticized either in the form of a return to nature under the impact of the *Wandervogel* movement in nineteenth century Germany or the return to a Tolstoian brand of socialism with its mistrust of the older generation and its values of family, trade, and religion and the accepted communal system of values.

A minority of Jews in Poland believed in the possibility of a harmonious life within the framework of their country. In Central and Western European countries, Jews often identified with the majority and sought to be integrated. In countries such as Poland, Romania, and Hungary, they strove to integrate this loyalty to the Jewish tradition with their strong cultural ties to the homelands. An example was the pediatrician Ludwig Goldschmidt, later known as Janusz Korczak. He tried to overcome the antagonism between the two communities, working as a physician in the proletarian district of Warsaw and at the same time writing in the Pestalozzi tradition of educating children in a progressive style, stressing their rights for freedom and choice. Eventually, he had to succumb to the antagonism between the two groups and was forced to organize two separate orphanages for Jewish and Polish children where he worked as an educator and pediatrician. His book, *King Maciusz the*

First, was a work of the hope of childhood in which children organized an island of peace and love, without wars. In this book, Korczak also resigned himself to the fact that the world of grown-ups, with its aggression, wars, and hostility, would emerge victorious over the world of children, which is governed by wisdom and hope. I remember identifying with "Maciusz" as a child in his triumph and defeat. There are no islands in this world where children can find peace—a truth Korczak realized as he accompanied the children of his orphanage to Treblinka.

The society was in a state of transition, with a partial dissolution of the family, its traditions, and the old coping mechanisms. There was a strong disappointment with western democracies and disillusionment with Russian communism. Some of the more active members of the pioneer movements in the Jewish community had gone to Palestine while hundreds of thousands waited to leave, already emotionally investing in a future outside of their community. It seemed to me that there was no genuine attempt on the part of the Jewish leadership to organize an exodus, as it had done in the times of the Inquisition or the Crusades. There was an avoidance of recognizing the reality of the upcoming danger. I remember the impact on the Jewish masses of the lack of empathy expressed at Roosevelt's conference on refugees at Evian in 1938. All pleas to rescue the Jews of Germany and Poland were rejected, and feelings of isolation and helplessness grew. Yet people still went on vacation in the summer of 1939, denying that the Nazi invasion was imminent and that there would be no escape and no exit.

The Nazi invasion and occupation of Europe totally changed the psychosocial structure of the Jewish community, family, and individual life. From the accounts of eyewitnesses, writings, and diaries, what is most striking was their inability to anticipate not only the degree of destructiveness but also the demonic character of Nazi ideology. The Jews knew of this ideology. We had read Hitler's *Mein Kampf*, Goebbels's propaganda newspaper *Das Reich*, Streicher's *Der Stürmer* with its pornographic assaults on Jews, and Rosenberg's pseudo-philosophy of "German Aryan superiority" and the need for the solution of the "Jewish problem" through deportation or destruction. We were aware of life in Nazi Germany, the anti-Jewish contents of the *Nürnberg Gesetze*. We had read the anti-Nazi *Brown Book*, describing the atrocities of the Nazis in the towns and the concentration camps of Germany. We had heard of the thousands of Jews of Polish citizenship who had been sent over the border to the border town of Zbonszynin in 1938 into no-man's-land between Germany and Poland, losing their homes and friends. After this deportation, my friend and mentor, the Yiddish poet Mordecai Gebirtig from Krakow, wrote the poem "SS 'brent Briderlech" (Lemm, 1992, p. 260), a prophetic vision calling the world to action "against the fire" to save the little *shtetl* and its inhabitants. It was a voice of despair and a cry for help in the anxious, depressed disbelieving shtetls and towns of Eastern Europe on the one hand and the emotional desert and apathy of the Western world on the other. We all heard his message, and it awakened in us a sense of bewilderment, anxiety, and helplessness, coupled with repeated attempts at denial instead of the desired mobilization of resistance.

When the Nazi troops finally invaded our towns and villages, there came a feeling of derealization. "It cannot be true, it must be a dream." To see the Germans in flesh and body and to hear their songs brought on feelings of disbelief and shock. It was ironic that the destruction of the Jews was being called for in a language we loved, the language of Heinrich Heine, the author of *William Tell*, the beloved poem of freedom by Schiller, whom we grew to identify as the "Jewish national bard."

The lack of reaction and very often cooperation with the Nazis of the majority of the population in anti-Jewish actions in everyday life awakened not only pain but also a feeling of total isolation and abandonment, with the concretization and realization of anti-Jewish sentiments. I recall that in 1941, Mordecai Gebirtig wrote the poem "*Es tut weh*" (It Hurts), in which he calls the Polish Christians to action: "How can you, our neighbor, living hundreds of years together, be laughing and be joyful when our common enemy is tormenting us in curse and destruction?"

The question hung suspended in the air. A minority of the Polish intelligentsia and part of the socialist proletariat were able to mobilize the psychological forces to feel empathy and help save their Jewish neighbors who had been left to the SS hoards. But the majority of the Polish population, as I recall, reacted to the anti-Jewish actions in one of two ways: either with manifest greed and satisfaction—influences of years of Nazi propaganda—and already organized in political parties with a clear anti-Jewish manifesto or with active involvement in Jewish destruction. These were mainly youngsters who derived a direct benefit from the Jewish displacement and the "Aryanization" of their property. Yehuda Bauer comments:

> The perennial economic crisis in Poland had a great deal to do with the anti-Semitism rampant among the population. The government saw the Jews as an expendable minority, to be used as a safety valve for the dissatisfied Polish masses. The problem arises, however, whether the anti-Semitism so widespread in Poland can be explained purely by economic factors. True, even the Catholic Church bases its virulent anti-Semitism on supposedly economic grounds. The church in the name of justice to the Polish labourer justified anti-Jewish boycotts. No power will be able to stop the hatred of Poles towards the Jews, but it had to be remembered that a Catholic paper wrote "this hatred is highly beneficial to our Polish trade and to our country." (1978, p. 73f.)

Bauer goes on to note Emanuel Ringelblum's observation in his Warsaw Ghetto diary:

> There was some feeling of identification between the Poles who were just one rung higher on the Nazi scale than the Jews. But there is no doubt that ever-increasing numbers of Polish people benefited by the theft by the Nazis of Jewish property, though a large proportion of the loot remained in Nazi hands. Polish youths, radicalized even before the occupation of the country and now under Nazi influence, turned against the defenceless Jews who did not dare to react to physical attacks and acts of degradation. (Ibid.)

It seemed to me that after the initial psychological shock of war and conquest, a few adaptive tendencies to the total change could be observed. One, dictated by the Jewish system of values, was the attempt to find patterns of life even when life was unbearable. Many social organizations were formed, kitchens aiding orphans, the poor, and the elderly who had been displaced by the Germans. They responded to the age-old call to solidarity: "*Kol Yisrael Chaverim Zeh el Zeh*"—all Jews are brothers and all Israel is responsible for each other, do no separate yourself from the community. But the societal frameworks, like the identity cards issued, had a twofold outcome: in addition to the self-help aspect, they inadvertently helped the Germans to isolate the Jews from the non-Jewish population who aided their *Gleichschaltung*, a Nazi expression for reducing every Jew to the same common denominator of "vermin," as we were called in the semiofficial language of the SS.

In the first months of German occupation of most countries in Eastern and Central Europe, life went on "as if" everything was normal. Massive denial and avoidance of confrontation were employed to counter the total change in biological and psychological existence. I recall my father saying, "I remember the Germans from the first World War," in which he had participated in the Austrian army. "They were gentlemen and defenders of Western civilization. They couldn't change into barbarians. It will pass."

People tried not to change their style of life, continuing to hope for life after the war by accepting the laws and the prohibitions of the Nazis. But in everyday life, we were confronted with progressive diminution of individual freedom and the invasion of privacy. Flats were taken over by the *Volksdeutsche Ukrainian* and other groups that cooperated with the Nazis, and businesses were taken over by the so-called *Treuhänder* Commissars.

I remember my first confrontation with the Germans' total war on the Jews during their invasion of Poland in 1939, in running away from the *mikveh* (ritual bathhouse) in Mieletz, a town 100 miles from Krakow where the Germans burned more than fifty young Jews who happened to be in the neighborhood. Then, in their ominous *Rosh Hashana* action in 1939, they closed the synagogue, ordered all Jews to their homes and robbed every one of radios, gold, jewelry, and other valuables. We denied these signals of the destruction to come and would not heed the writing on the wall. All this was tolerated in the effort to make us invisible in order to save our families and ourselves.

The youths were caught in the conflict between solidarity with the family and their self-ideal as romantic resistance fighters against the Nazi tyranny. Their attempts at resistance had often a broad spectrum of expressions, from more playful to more verbal and to action-oriented ways, connected with their emotional investment in saving friends and relatives from annihilation. They rescued their families from town to town, from ghetto to ghetto, and from hiding to labor camp; gave material support to those in need; organized secret "conspirator" courses of learning; and held secret private evenings of poetry readings against the Nazi tyranny. I myself went through these learning experiences with a group of friends participating in a course in Krakow offered by our philosophy teacher Ben-Zion Rappaport. In those days, Rappaport wrote philosophical tracts of Neoplatonic philosophy relating to the "eternity of Israel." He was certain of the victory of truth over evil but skeptical about our survival. We felt ourselves between despair and naive hope.

What was of psychological importance here was to change the feelings of isolation and hopelessness to those of activity and not to succumb to the Nazi portrayal of the Jew as submissive "vermin." We used every possibility to build a new social unit in the form of pairing small groups of friends when our own families were destroyed. Strong emotional attachments were formed, changing this passivity into activity by sharing our fantasies, our bread, helping each other to move away from dangerous to more secure living quarters, sharing feelings of triumph in overcoming the aggressor by saving endangered families.

The initial reaction to the massive denial and avoidance had both negative and positive effects. The denial did not allow Jews to defend themselves against the Nazis' organized collective destruction, such as the *Aussiedlungsaktionen*, the deportations that took place every few months. Normal "fright-flight" reactions to anxiety did not occur, only flight into fantasy. At the same time, this massive denial allowed us to continue our lives in a semiorganized fashion, with the illusion of a future and continuity of life. I am reminded here of Freud's ideas about alloplastic and autoplastic solutions to internal conflicts and strivings and the meaning of the reality principle. (Freud differentiates between alloplastic and autoplastic solutions of intrapsychic conflict, believing the alloplastic solution to be more reality oriented.) What was the "alloplastic" reality principle-oriented solution in the years 1938 and 1939, when the only possibility of changing the outer reality was to run away? Freud and other privileged Europeans were given this opportunity, but the masses of Jewish families were doomed to stay within the boundaries of the conquered nations where their homelands were changed into prisons.

The inability to accept the change of reality was related to an abrogation of causality caused by the Nazi oppression. I remember my first confrontation with Nazi soldiers on that same *Rosh Hashanah* of 1939, one week after the invasion. I was taken out of the synagogue with other Jews in order to load heavy furniture for the German officers' quarters. I confronted a young soldier with the absurd question, "Why should I feel guilty for being born a Jew?" With this question, I assumed the possibility of some logic and a change of ideological approach and actions in the young Nazi soldier who was reared in the belief that the destruction of the Jews was in the service of the love of his home, family, and nation. My question was a kind of denial of the reality, rejecting the totality of terror that paradoxically had an impact on the young soldier who was silent and then said, "This is war. I can do nothing about it." While the question allowed me to verbalize my doubts and anxieties while still repelling the scapegoating and projection of Nazi ideology, it probably perplexed the soldier. From facing a crowd of anonymous "bad Jews," he was suddenly relating to one person. His allowing me to continue unharmed revealed a remnant of his humanity and his ability to relate to another person as an individual.

Another example of denial was the rumors in the occupied countries that the Nazis didn't mean the physical destruction of the Jews, that this was but an ideological metaphorical expression without consequences. The accidents of destruction they had experienced thus far they interpreted as unplanned impulsive acts of aggression related to war rather than the official policy of destruction. Still, I remember that life went on with a continuous restriction of freedom, rights, and actions, with adults losing their professional identities as providers and citizens. Mothers and fathers lost their role as "protective shields" (Winnicott, 1960) for their children and as possible models for identification, being ridiculed and shamed in their roles as men and women. Yet in the home, among friends, we could share our contempt for the Nazi aggressors and our aggressive feelings in the hundreds of jokes about the Germans. Here we could share our wishes and dreams about plans of the Western democracies to save the Jews by trading Germans for Jews after the defeat of the Nazis by the Russian army.

Slowly, private life diminished, with its possibilities of friendship, strong emotional ties, marriages of love, youth, and political organizations. There were major changes taking place in the community as people began to leave for smaller towns or were selected for the camps by the Nazis, with the help of Jewish functionaries. As the size of the communities was reduced, their resourcefulness for resistance was depleted. More and more friends and family members disappeared as the old social networks, schools, organizations, places of work, and nuclear families were destroyed by the Nazis.

There was no passive acceptance of the Nazi aggression. Old frameworks were replaced by new ones, with strong ties in the form of cohesive pairing and solidarity to one's own group. Paradoxically, in some situations, young people married as an expression of their exaggerated hope in the future as well as an expression of their own families. One survivor of a large family in the Warsaw Ghetto remembers her father telling her to marry a young baker who flirted with her even though her family was very rich and cultivated. The father thought that marrying him would help her chances for survival since this man was very active and mobile and capable of being a good provider.

Physical survival was not always the motivation for marriage after the Nazi occupation and in the ghetto. Many young people fell in love despite the growing oppression as a defense against death and dehumanization and as an expression of defeat of the Nazi ideology and the continuity of the Jewish tradition. An example of a marriage as a defense against dehumanization and acceptance of life as the most cherished value from the eve of the apocalypse until after the miracle of liberation can be found in the following epos of two friends of mine who fell in love during their adolescence. They asked a Hasidic rabbi in the Krakow Ghetto whether it would be permissible and acceptable according to the *Halacha* to marry under these circumstances. The rabbi replied, "It is your obligation, a *Mitzvah*, to marry. Because they [the Germans] wish to destroy life, you should sanctify it—*Kiddush HaChem*." The intense emotional relationship in the marriage continued through the ghetto, escapes, selections, and concentration camps and allowed them to overcome the deaths of their families.

In spite of many escapes and deportations, they managed to stay together. But in 1943, the husband was transported to Buchenwald; and the wife with her mother and sister, to another concentration camp in Germany. In spite of the separation, they managed to send love letters and poems to each other through SS men who received gold and dollars from them in return. This wonder of love continued when, after the war, the young man heard in his native town from one of the survivors that she had seen his wife killed by a German tank during the last days of the

"Death March" from their camp. This eyewitness gave him a bloodstained sheet of poems and letters from his wife, telling him that his wife had entrusted them to her before her death and that the witness had saved them under her shirt against her naked body. In spite of what he had heard, the man intuitively believed that his wife was alive and continued to search for her in all the German camps until he found her one year later in a hospital near Leipzig. She had been severely injured by the German tank that killed her mother and profoundly wounded her sister. Both sisters had survived in the German hospital. The husband and wife believe that only their strong emotional ties and their love made their survival possible. The wife, telling the story of their miraculous reunion years later, said with an ironical smile, "Like Orpheus, he brought me back from hell to life."

Many young people were able to flee to Russian-occupied territory in 1939 and 1940 where there was freedom from racial persecution. One survivor remembers having to fight with her father who begged her to get out of the bunker and go into hiding, saying, "You have a chance to live because of your Aryan features whereas we will be killed." Yet most of them chose to stay with their families out of a feeling of solidarity, the fear of being separated and the inability to accept autonomy of action. Some were afraid to leave their families because they might be destroyed. One survivor remembers:

> I came back from Russian-occupied territory when I dreamt repeatedly that the Nazis killed my mother and I felt that I had to save her and my whole family. When I succeeded in getting back, they were already in the ghetto, some of them already destroyed, and my plans of saving them changed, became an illusion.

Chaika Grossman recalls a similar situation in her diary: the pain of meeting her mother and not being able to tell her that she was about to leave and join the partisans. In another example of the conflict between love and solidarity to parents on the one hand and fidelity to ideology on the other is the case of an adolescent ghetto fighter. Confronted with the situation, he could not mobilize the energy to leave the family or to save them by taking them to the forests. In spite of being an active member of the underground, he decided to remain in the ghetto, saying, "How can I leave when they are dying?"

Both this example and Chaika Grossman's represent the anguish of this most difficult decision: to save one's life while leaving the family to die. For some, this became the dilemma of survivor guilt. Thus, the transition from the initial shock of the invasion was first characterized by an inability to function and act and the wishful thinking of immediate rescue and liberation by the English, French, and Russians, a rather passive attitude of waiting for their saviors. Only gradually did more organized and action-oriented expressions develop within the family and the community. But the disbelief and the denial characteristic of the first months of the war persisted in the ghetto.

Chapter 3:
Life and Death in the Ghetto

The ghetto was a community in despair, fighting for its biological and psychological existence with fewer and fewer chances of survival. It was a social network trying to hold onto some structure and institutions that would help the community and its members. In general, in the situation of extreme Nazi terror, the cohesiveness of the families and the groups grew stronger, but at the same time, I observed dissolution tendencies in those families uprooted by the German *Aussiedlungs* policy of repeated deportation. Part of the community still held onto the transmitted systems of values of solidarity toward the extended family, religion, and ideology as a source of strength. But it was an "as if" community, a "false" community, because the real one had already disintegrated, in spite of the sporadic attempts of its weakened leadership to hold onto some system of values and some privacy, honesty, and solidarity in the face of external aggression.

The ghetto paradoxically gave the illusion of some refuge in a hostile world. Nazi propaganda lured with promises. I remember reading in the Jewish press that people who were able to work and be productive for the German war machine would be able to stay alive in the ghetto. This would not be the case, however, for "unproductive" elements of the society. This promise evoked in many an illusion of some security, and some envisioned remaining in the ghetto until the bitter end of the war. This illusion of stability was particularly popular among the middle class and older population; the young were far more skeptical. This was perhaps due to their daily contact with German cruelty in their working places or due to their ability to resist the psychological lure of the illusion to appeasement in the ghetto.

This produced a situation of tragic conflict between the conservative elements of the *Judenrat* (Jewish Council) and the more radical elements of the Jewish youth organizations and remnants of ideological groups who, from their more critical and uncompromising adolescent approach, preached resistance from the beginning. This conflict was expressed in some form in almost every Jewish community. The resistance itself took a mostly nondramatic form of mutual support; they committed vengeful acts against collaborators and sadistic psychopaths who took advantage of the situation.

The passive resistance grew to an active dimension in different towns of German-occupied Europe, partly documented but not always well known, as in my own town of Krakow. Here the ZOB, a Jewish fighting organization of mostly Zionist idealists, began to take revenge on the Gestapo and German police for their previous actions in the Krakow Ghetto. This culminated in the bombing of two popular German restaurants, killing many. In reality, such actions had no effect on the German policy of destruction or the fate of the war. But it did destroy the growing feeling that the German oppressor was omnipotent, helped in maintaining some self-esteem, and lessened the feeling of total helplessness. The acts of resistance in various forms of self-help and sabotage were also an expression of fidelity to their own self-ideal and gave them a feeling of psycho-historical continuity with their communal psychic life in the chaotic and disorganized world of the ghetto.

Thus, on the one hand, the ghetto was a source of life with expressions of solidarity and brotherhood despite the terror. But on the other hand, it formed a framework for further destruction. This destruction was not only in the form of Nazi aggression but also in the psychopathic behavior on the part of some elements of the ghetto society who regressed in total identification with the aggressor.

Much of the Jewish leadership worked to eliminate the panic: if the Jews did as the Germans wished, it would guarantee their survival. At the beginning of the Krakow Ghetto, there was a newspaper staffed with people of good intentions, naïveté and high levels of denial that rationalized that the labor of the Jews for the Germans was a trial for making the most of their conditions for survival. They hoped that if the German industry and the war effort became dependent on the labor of the Jews for the Germans, it was a trial for making the most of their conditions of survival, overlooking the fact that Nazi ideology saw a triumph of the murderous hatred of Jews even beyond their own pragmatic needs.

These mixed motives of a genuine wish to help, coupled with rationalization and denial, eventually rendered these leaders paralyzed and helpless tools of the Nazi regime. One such man had been a cultural leader in the Jewish community of Krakow before the war, and during the ghetto years, he assumed the manner of a cold, detached bureaucrat, aware that he was suspected of collaborating with the Nazis. In the aftermath of the war, he spoke with me of his anxieties of the total destruction of the Jewish community and of his hope that through his effort he could save a remnant of Jewish life so dear to him. I felt his motivations were complex and his torment sincere, eager to rehabilitate himself in his own eyes. He had managed to save his family and a few others by signing for packages from the Joint Distribution Committee, transferring all but a tiny portion to the Nazis. He was no hero, but he lived through the occupation with the justification that he was continuing the social work in which he was active prior to the war in spite of the drastic changes that had taken place.

Thus, there existed a constant danger of moral disintegration and the temptation to abandon one's old value system. This had a permanent effect on one's relations with friends, family, and society; in the abnormal world of the ghetto, age-old traditions of causality and morality ceased to exist.

One survivor spoke with disappointment and anger about one of his school friends, a young woman of exceptional beauty who became a lover and collaborator of a Gestapo officer. Her "function" was to find Jewish children in the Aryan part of town and take them to the German and Polish police. During treatment, the survivor described his feelings of ambivalence and anguish when he carried out the verdict of the Jewish underground organization by strangling her. I could understand that in his ambivalence, he had seen his former friend as a loner, a narcissistic personality with weak social ties, and an outsider without ideology or religious background. As an adolescent, he had loved the girl and idealized her, although he was aware of her weaknesses and her tendencies to betrayal. This tendency became a tragic reality during the Holocaust when she betrayed her friends to the Gestapo in return for her own survival and better living conditions outside the ghetto. "Her beauty and body image had been the only interest in which she invested," he said as he shared with me the anger and guilt he felt when he carried out the verdict toward a girl whom he once cherished. In therapy, he worked on the ambivalence he felt toward her, his anger at having to give up this idealization, at the same time feeling betrayed and abandoned by her. He felt as if everything he had believed in, valued, and loved had been destroyed. The fear of being betrayed became a dominant theme in his post-Holocaust life, when he continuously feared to be betrayed by his friends and society.

In the ghetto, there was still a possibility for private life and a world in its different spheres, in friendships, in the longing for love, as well as in neurosis. Sexual life was expressed not only in its sublimated and romantic forms but also for some with the attitude of "live today, tomorrow you might die." This was also exploited by the *nouveau riche* and the Jewish police who abused girls who became totally dependent on them for their existence and survival.

The interfamilial conflicts had been diminished in the light of external aggression. But in the confrontation with immediate death, intrapsychic conflicts could be either heightened or diminished. Many survivors who had suffered psychosomatic disorders before the war, such as asthma, high blood pressure, or colitis, showed no symptoms during the war, as if the realization of the prospect of total annihilation caused the anxiety of intrapsychic conflict to diminish. In some cases, the symptoms reappeared following the liberation.

On the other hand, in some of the families, one could see the manifestation of very intense rivalry and aggressive tendencies under the impact of hunger and diminished resources for satisfaction and pleasure. One survivor-patient talked about hunger and his envy toward his sister who was able to get food and satisfy her hunger by working outside the ghetto in a German factory. During the night, he fought with himself over whether to steal his sister's bread, feeling remorse as well as satisfaction. In the treatment situation, it was obvious that the envy he felt toward her as the chosen object of his father's love was reactivated in his adolescent years when having the bread was a question of life or death.

These ambivalent feelings toward the sister were often described in an atmosphere of fog and derealization. He would relate in therapy that "I experienced it as if on another planet." The whole act of taking the bread was "more dream-like than real. I wished it had been a dream."

Most Holocaust survivors in fact remember having experiences of a continuous feeling of de-realization in response to a reality more terrible than their worst nightmares. I recall my own experience: going to work from the ghetto camp, we marched in long columns. Around us were the guards, Polish, Latvian, Ukrainian, and German SS men with their hunting dogs. You could hear the death coming, not the individual death but some collective expression of anonymous, meaningless disappearance. Very often looking at the silhouettes of the people in darkness, I thought it was a nightmare, and I tried to bite my tongue to wake myself from a bad dream. But it was no dream. My weakened comrade beside me fell, beaten by a Ukrainian, and I was stepped on by the anonymous crowd.

Another survivor mentioned in his therapy: "When I am telling you these things today, I sometimes am not sure that these things really happened to me." Such confessions are repeatedly experienced in therapy with survivors, and very often the therapist also shares the feelings of unreality and the sense that it was another world.

In the ghettos and camps of Nazi Europe, the reality principle underwent an extreme distortion, no longer rendering valid the normal cognitive processes and traditions of thinking and causality in human behavior. The individual experiences of one's life and the cultural group experiences and values transmitted through the generations up until the present experience of the Holocaust had no meaning and were no longer helpful in predicting useful reactions with other human beings, especially in relation to the Nazi aggressors. The subjective feelings of de-realization, of experiencing the world as unreal, were accompanied by a subjective feeling of depersonalization. People seemed to change their body image and their representational world due to this extreme nutritional and emotional deprivation.

There were gross distortions and changes in the symbols of ghetto life. Those who once represented justice, law, and order, such as the police and bureaucracy, were changed into the collaborators and murderers of the present, as in the case of the *Judenrat*, the leadership partially appointed by the Nazis. The familiar environment of friends and colleagues became unpredictable. The strong became weak; the moral wicked; and a friend of yesterday became a cruel policeman or a capo beating you during forced labor. There were also changes in the family. One survivor spoke about his emotional upheaval in relation to his family in the ghetto: "My whole world was upset when my usually quiet, withdrawn mother changed into the resourceful, energetic leader of the family, and my active and vivid father changed into a shadowy, anxious passive person whom I despised." These changes were so extensive that many people reacted to them with confusion. "No, this is not life" seems to be the repetitive refrain in Chaim Kaplan's diary of the Warsaw Ghetto (1966). Although he lived in Warsaw for forty years, his beloved city's transformation into a place of abnormality and madness disoriented him completely. "At times," he wrote, "it seems to me I am in an alien land entirely unknown to me. The ghetto was suspended in nothingness." In the other remarkable journal kept by Emanuel Ringelblum, the Zionist leader of Warsaw, we read of the changes in the ghetto society where the sight of people dying in the streets could no longer disturb people. The annihilation policy of Nazi Germany by starvation and disease destroyed the population. Ringelblum (1967) writes: "One is left with the tragic dilemma: What are we to do? Are we to dole out spoonfuls to everyone, the result being that no one will survive? Or are we to give full measure to a few, with only a handful having enough to survive?"

In the memories and associations of the survivors about the extermination actions in the ghettos, where in its ultimate terror the Latvian and Ukrainian SS excelled themselves in killing the old, the disabled, and the children, they speak about hell literally, not metaphorically. George Steiner (1967) argued that Nazism was a concretization and literal staging of medieval hell on earth. His conception was confirmed by many of the experiences of Holocaust survivors. A man who was obsessed by the fear that something terrible would happen to his sister remembered: "An SS-man threw my two-year-old sister against the wall, and I, a 13-year-old Bar mitzvah," he added with self-irony, "did not react, changing into a stone wall myself; I felt that I was then in hell. I died and now I am punished for my sins. 'That is Hell,' I said to myself, and the SS man was one of the devils that I had read about but never believed in—now it had become real."

The people who were deported to the ghetto from widely differing countries such as Germany, France, Greece, and Eastern Europe had the most difficult experience due to their cultural isolation. Many arrived with no relatives or acquaintances and were morally and physically disintegrated. This was true even for those whose prior personality had been strong and resourceful. Most of the people in this group died from hunger or infectious diseases. Their resistance had been diminished by repeated traumatizations and the loss of their family and community frameworks. The result was a collapse of their previous ego autonomy and led to regression.

As mentioned earlier, the population of the ghetto was stratified by the vicissitudes of age. The older generation gradually became aware that they were doomed to death because they did not have the physical stamina to work in the eyes of the Nazis. They tried in every possible way to look younger, but this was not always identical with feeling youthful.

Many survivors today, having now reached the age that their parents had in the ghetto, have identified this age as the time they will die. They have unconsciously identified with their parents and friends who had been in danger of being killed because of their age. I remember that you could see old ladies wandering around in the ghetto with bleached blond hair and rose-colored faces, creating a tragic-comic impression, stressing the tragedy of people who could not be given the grace of aging. It was as if the old Jewish prayer "Al Taschlichenu le'et Zikna" (Don't discard us in our old age when we are weakened, don't leave us) would be prophetically feared and envisioned.

One older survivor remembered that when she came in a transport from the ghetto to Auschwitz and stood before Dr. Mengele, he asked her age. She promptly replied that she was forty (when she was really over fifty) and said, "Herr Doktor, I am strong and healthy and wish to work." She was sent to the right hand side to work, while her daughter was sent to the left into death. She was unable to overcome her anguish at not having gone in the same direction compulsively, asking herself why she hadn't chosen the path of her daughter.

Many of the younger generation who had strong ties to both their families and their peers went through the eternal struggle between fidelity to their family members with whom they accepted the roles of providers and leaders and their need to be faithful to their self ideal and run away from the ghetto to work in the underground or become a partisan. What kind of people ran to the forests from the ghetto, some to become partisans? This decision was very much influenced by geography since the latter possibility existed only in certain parts of Poland, Russia, and Slovakia. In France, Belgium, and Holland, the population and the resistance fighters were friendlier in accepting Jews and recognizing their common goals, not being infected by racist hatred, as had been the case with so many populations and resistance groups in Eastern Europe. There, the decision to fight the Germans and the courage to run away and hide in the woods was mostly influenced by geopolitical factors and not by personality factors as has recently been claimed by some researchers who make a distinction between families of fighters and families of victims. Many survivors lived through different phases of the Holocaust, in ghettos, in work camps, in hiding, and as partisans, making such a clear polarization between the two styles of response impossible.

Among the youth in the ghetto, there was a very broad spectrum of psychosocial stratification and ideological polarization. One could differentiate between three major groups. There were those from the little towns and villages who in their pre-war lives had been more exposed to life struggles and had developed more adaptive tactics of survival than the youngsters who had lived in more protective urban surroundings with high expectations and a romanticized and individualized *Weltanschauung*.

The second group consisted of east European youth who had been influenced by ideologies of the major parties of the prewar world. These were either followers of the Jewish Socialist Bund party that dreamed of Jewish cultural autonomy within a Socialist Poland and of the Zionist youth organization that dreamed of the utopia of building and being rebuilt in the homeland. It was from within the ranks of both ideological camps that most of the ghetto fighters sprang.

The third and least numerous group consisted of Jews who had been transported to the ghetto from Western Europe. These Jews were more assimilated, reared on Western values, many of them ignorant of Jewish values of togetherness and the importance of warmth as a cohesive element. They had broken the bridges of tradition and had rarely been exposed to anti-Semitism. Some felt like "Jews of Hitler," saying that were it not for Hitler, they would not have needed to identify as Jews at all. They therefore could not find affinity and ties with the majority of people in the ghettos. They felt alienated and, in many cases, developed hostile emotions. For them especially, the ghetto was another planet and the cumulative major traumas of displacement and isolation from their homelands and languages, separations from their beloved and alienation from their fellow inhabitants, formed a longitudinal chain of defeat. After the initial shock, there was often a paralysis of action and numbness, a diminished resistance to infection and eventual regression to the *muselman* stage and eventually death (Cohen, 1954; Krystal, 1968).

Of the six million Jews who perished in the Holocaust, one million were below the age of fourteen; perhaps 50,000 children survived. Despite individual differences in their psychosexual development, family background, constitution, and actual experience during the Holocaust, children of all ages displayed an essentially similar reaction to death; among those who survived, psychological regression was a universal phenomenon. Here I would like to concentrate mainly on the distinct and emotional responses of the child to the apocalyptic atmosphere in the ghetto that confronted him increasingly during the Holocaust. The child who was forced to be the passive witness of the massive destruction of his family and community first became aware of himself as a "victim" when he perceived his parents' intensified anxiety and their increased preoccupation with survival. The parents attempted to protect and soothe the child more intensely than before, leading often to an over-investment in family members and a lower level of interpersonal conflicts.

The pressure of having to decide existential questions of life and death resulted in a lessening of the intrapsychic conflicts typical of childhood. In the interest of survival, all anger and aggression of intrapsychic or interfamilial origin had to be redirected outward, toward the actual oppressor and also toward any competing "outside group" (Klein et al., 1963). Aggression was also expressed in the polarization of affect and the splitting of objects in dreams and in the fantasy world of daydreams where loved ones were miraculously rescued and the vicious ones, representing the Nazis, were killed. The maturational processes of children in latency, ages six to ten, became intensified by their responsibilities, often taking over the roles of providers for their family by smuggling food through barbed-wire fences and through the sewers. In many cases, though, there was a discrepancy between their ego capacities for quick solutions and decision-making in dangerous situations. In addition, the intense fidelity toward their gang or to their own family members and the lack of feelings toward others outside of their family circle led in many cases later to lacunae in their superego and moral development. After liberation, these children often became preoccupied with competition and success in the material world and with hoarding possessions that replaced the source of basic security they lost in the Holocaust. To them, only strength and power could provide a sense of security. In this sense, they showed an identification with the aggressor.

A survivor tried to influence his adolescent daughter who, in his eyes, could not defend herself against her peers. "You must kick them. The whole world is made up of gangsters, and you have to behave like a gangster to get respect." Indeed, in his business transactions, he was shrewd and underhand with competitors. This lack of civility was in sharp contrast to his unlimited compassion and sensitivity toward his children who represented all that was good in the world and whom he had "to save." He maintained this split between good and bad and between his private life and the outer world, which for him continued to be a world of gangsters and Nazis.

In other families, the chronic hunger and deprivation led to an intensification of ambivalence, sibling rivalry, and unresolved Oedipal strivings. One survivor-patient who had been a preadolescent during his years of incarceration in one of the ghettos actualized the intense rivalry situation between him and his older brother in his current relations with his wife after the Holocaust, feeling continuously threatened by her dominance and greed. In therapy, it occurred to him that in the present marriage situation, he was reliving the feeling of threat he felt when he had to share food with his older brother who was taking a larger portion, claiming that he was older and needing more nutrition. During one of his sessions, he brought up his unjustified anger toward his wife because she was not giving him the right food and provoking him to verbal and physical attacks. He remembered a scene in the ghetto when he had fought with his murderous impulses and his fear of being killed by his brother. The castration fears he felt occurred again in relation to his wife toward whom he felt admiration, envy, and the fear that she was taking the food and sustenance from him that he deserved.

The progressive annihilation of the ghetto community meant the disappearance of adult figures who had served as a buffer between the child and the outside world and had provided a certain sense of security. The child ultimately recognized the chaos and destruction as a direct threat to his own existence, for his parents were utterly unable to protect him. With the loss of parents, siblings, and the parental image, there grew feelings of guilt, deprivation, and abandonment. The extreme emotional and physical deprivation caused grave doubts and fears about his own body image and self-image. As long as one remained in the familiar environment of the ghetto, one could be strengthened by the group feelings of whatever community still survived. Although it was a community of helplessness and hopelessness, a measure of hope was introduced by the fantasized possibilities of counter-aggression and the restoration of order to the world. Where actual uprisings and resistance took place, they had a positive emotional value and boosted self-esteem and self-acceptance despite their historically negligible effect upon the persecutors (Klein and Reinharz, 1972).

Children and young adolescents in hiding lived in a state of longitudinal semi-sensory deprivation: there was a reduction in motor activity and in meaningful communication with the external world. The child who had never seen flowers, trees, or birds lacked symbols for his internal fantasy life.

Since overt aggression toward the oppressors, without external resources of help, was suicidal, resistance was expressed indirectly. Children engaged in activities such as learning and procuring food—an activity in which they excelled because of their size, mobility, and bravado. They also engaged in underground resistance "play" in mutual support and assistance information. By thus frustrating the persecutors' attempts to dehumanize, they were performing meaningful acts that yielded immediate rewards.

Normal childhood sadomasochistic fantasies paled in comparison with the nightmares of the Holocaust. The unlimited cruelty and destruction inherent in the external world abolished the concept of causality and the security that it had provided. The child could discover a firm cause-and-effect relationship only in the realm of his fantasies. In his dream world, he could control his own existence and retain the human identity that his persecutors were trying to destroy. For the child, "reality" persisted in his recollections of the adults' stories about the lost world, which they only vaguely remembered. The daydreams of the past formed a sharp contrast to the continually traumatic situation of the actual existing world. Thus, the normal value system of the ego ideal was altered and inverted: the ability to fantasize became the hallmark of a still existing ego function. Those children who lost the capacity for fantasy had accepted their dehumanization (Klein, 1973).

For both children and adults, fantasizing and remembering the past served to disconnect the child's ego from the chaotic, overstimulating world of cruelty, death, and hunger. It allowed them to deny and devalue the internal and external traumatic realities of the ghetto through the substitution of game-like activities. A child could deny the danger inherent in smuggling and thieving by pretending that he was playing, but at the same time, he could not engage in typical patterns of role experimentation or libidinal object choice nor could he enjoy a moratorium for the adult roles (provider and mediator with the outside world) into which he was thrust. Eating and shelter fantasies became repeated themes of night dreams as well as daydreams, as did memories of the happy and secure pre-Holocaust period. These games and fantasies were concerned not so much with pleasure as with safety: for children who continually experienced death, the need for security overpowers the pleasure principle (Klein, 1973).

During the prolonged period of traumatization, fantasy-formation functioned as a defense against traumatic overstimulation and as a means of distancing oneself from the external horror of aggression and hopelessness. During the brief, relatively trauma-free intervals, hope was an essential resource in the victim's toleration of painful events. Founded in religious or other ideological motivations, this hope was based on a positive self-evaluation—the feeling that life was deserved—the presence of benign introjects such as pleasant experiences and memories of people who were cherished and who still vividly represented the good, secure world of the past. These warm holding environments of justice and sanity against the background of the actual insane world provided an effective sense of time that could distinguish between past and future. These functions all seemed to derive from satisfactory nurturing experiences of the past.

Whatever ego strength one still possessed had to be utilized in the service of survival. Cohesive pair bonding and the formation of pseudo-families particularly among adolescents led by one strong adolescent who filled the parental function were typical occurrences. Such ties were based upon mutual aid and a deep suspicion and rejection of "outsiders." They were rarely endowed with strong libidinal content, and if so, only for a short time. The observed regression in object relationships, and the impaired reality testing were sometimes in the service of physical survival: the overt expression of intense feelings and emotions, whether toward past or present love objects, could pose a grave danger for survival (Niederland, 1968b). Therefore, the bonding had to be expressed through action-oriented behavior. Positive emotional bonds could be accepted through action, help, and cohesiveness. Abstract words were feared, so they were replaced with concrete action.

For the young and the old in the ghetto, food was not pursued merely to assuage hunger—the rations were never sufficient—but to forge some sort of bridge to life and to find and perform one action that could be endowed with meaning and significance. When human love objects were dwindling, the only actual cathexis was with the slowly chewed hunk of dry bread that symbolized life. Eating was the one activity that could be related to the lost family milieu; every meal was capable of calling up the rituals of family meals in the serene pre-Holocaust past.

New groups of friends formed after their original families had been destroyed, clinging desperately to cherished values and ideals. The attachments and the cohesion of these groups were, to many, a source of support and courage to continue to live in spite of the cruelty surrounding them. Isolated persons who had no one to cry with and share feelings of dissolution soon became victims of depression, which led to withdrawal, apathy, and eventually to death.

As the effects of the nightmare world took their toll, the victim had to suppress all affects not in the direct service of survival. This suppression of both love for the family and hate for the persecutors caused a temporary state of paralysis of action and numbness of feeling. Eventually, all resistance proved futile and the possibility of cathexis, even of food, disappeared. This temporary paralysis and numbness soon became quasi-permanent; the victim sank into a semi-catatonic state of total passivity. As the continual traumas threatened to overwhelm even his greatly heightened stimulus barrier, the only remaining course was to reject absolutely the hostile world outside. This process culminated in the creation of the *muselman*, who, having lost all interest in self-preservation, soon added one more to the total number of corpses.

In my experience, people who adhered to political or religious ideologies had more opportunity for stronger social bonds and object relationships than those with no ideology. The ideology, whether socialist, Zionist, or Hassidic, became a source of strength by making possible the vision of a greater world. It provided a dimension of time and future extending beyond the here and now of the ghetto situation. It also gave a feeling of solidarity and bonding, and more important, it formed a basis for mutual help, a sharing of ideas, and an expression of their hatred toward the Nazi aggressors. During the selections, people helped each other out in the name of their belief in a common past and common future.

The dream of a new beginning in the old-new Fatherland of Palestine, where so many of their friends had succeeded in rebuilding their lives as pioneers, became especially important to the Zionist youngsters. This was expressed in the letters and diaries of survivors, among them the message of Mordecai Anieliwicz during his last days of the ghetto uprising in Warsaw (1943).

I remember also that religious people, confronted with extreme persecution in their everyday lives, with sorrows, and with the possibility of losing their beloved in a selection, in an "action" or an "*Aussiedlung*," asked themselves, "How can God, the incorporation of Mercy and Justice, allow the daily murder of children?" They experienced the catastrophes of Nazi degradation of their own persons, of their beliefs, and of their Jewish God. They were often the favorite objects of humiliation and sadistic rituals of dehumanization of the Nazis; their beards were cut and their *Torah* scrolls destroyed. How did they experience these rituals of organized hatred in the shadow of imminent death? It seems that the possibility of changing passivity into a meaningful religious experience gave them the strength of stoic acceptance of death in the spirit of *Kiddush HaShem* (sanctification of the name of God). The sanctification of God became their most sacred value when it was no longer possible for them to struggle for life. They accepted death in the spirit of Job asking questions but not relinquishing their image of the personal Almighty God, who might yet change their fate. They were able to change their passive acceptance into an experience of activity.

One adolescent survivor-patient related in his therapy such an experience of transformation from an unbeliever into a believer.

> It was Friday evening, as usual, and the Nazis chose this day especially for exterminations which they ominously called "*Umsiedlung*." Our whole ghetto was filled with Ukrainian SS, Polish police and German SS who went from home to home with their Jewish helpers to gather the "selected" Jews for killing. Our uncle M. radiated peace and a special feeling of grace when he said the *Kaddish* and sung the Songs of Sabbath. We heard shootings, crying and the hostile voices of the Germans; we trembled in our anguish and fear. He said to us: "Let us make in dignity our last '*Kabalath Shabbat*'." The normally insecure man grew in our eyes and gave us peace of mind. When the Nazis came into our crowded room, my uncle said to them in German: "Gentlemen, I am ready." When they asked him about his profession and whether he could be useful to them, he answered, "I am a merchant. I am a religious Jew. I can't be useful to you," and he marched out of the room.

From that moment, the patient became a religious Jew, believing in his uncle's sense of duty and way of life. The identification with this uncle, whom he totally incorporated and internalized, helped him later in accepting the loss of his family. During therapy, he became able to change his survivor guilt into feelings of responsibility toward his newly established family and his intense endeavors within the community.

Another survivor in therapy, trying to explain his change from an unobservant adolescent before the war to his extreme religious approach to life, went back to the haunted memories of selection in a little town in Poland.

> We stood for days in the crowded street, without food or water, and every hour the SS brought Jewish men and women from the surrounding villages and towns and killed them. I heard a strong prayer "*Shema Yisrael*" and saw a few old Jews with their ritual garments and their hands outstretched, blessing us on the train before being killed.

This haunting memory of death conflicted with the vision of the blessing of their final moments. It occurred to me during the therapy that this scene helped to organize his whole approach to life and death. His capacity to mobilize hope in the face of death—polarizing libidinal feelings to the comrades during the Holocaust and later to his own family and community—was connected in his mind to that scene in which the Jew was blessing him and his comrades. His post-Holocaust life consisted of a series of attempts to realize this and to "bless" others by sharing these past experiences in schools as a symbol of the revival of life. This stand of blessing and sharing is expressed in his professional work in Israel, which he identified as the remnants of those who survived. "This blessing I took as a command to stay alive and to be as they were: strong and accepting life."

A Jewish policeman from the ghetto, suffering from strong guilt feelings, remembered:

> "I came from a traditionally religious family. When the selections began, I achieved the status of policeman in

> the vain hope of saving my family. One day I was given an order to take the Hassidic rebbe of our family to selection. When I came to his room and said, 'Rebbe,' he said to me, 'Don't speak. I am ready.' When I brought him to the place of the execution, he asked only for a *Talith*, a prayer shawl, and then he blessed me and the other victims. That I cannot forget."

After the war, the man was plagued by severe guilt feelings for having survived. He suffered from paranoid suspicions that his neighbors would know that he had been a policeman and fled from one country to another.

In therapy, it occurred to this man that in accepting the job of policeman, he had hoped to save his parents. Thus, he was not actually fully collaborating with the Nazis but had been human and decent in spite of his terrible function: he had tried to help. Even so, the theme of his guilt remained central in the therapy, and he experienced the therapist as both a savior and a persecutor. In addition, the old rabbi became a representation of forgiveness in the transference situation.

The religious ones could get no answers to their questions. Some tried to find a rationale for their suffering as an expression of God's punishment for their sins, for leaving the commandments or the Jewish way of life. I recall that while working day and night at the railway station clearing snow, I met my Talmud teacher, a man who was punitive and moralistic with both his pupils and family. He told them that it was their failure to adequately fulfill the religious *mitzvoth* that brought about God's punishment in the form of the Germans. When I asked him how righteous, pious Jews were killed and how children were being destroyed and God could remain silent, he answered, "You have forgotten what we learned in the book of Job: 'The righteous man suffers for the wicked one who forgot God.'" I remember my anguish and anger toward this man whom I respected. I saw him in his helplessness, his clinging to old explanations that no longer answered or diminished my anger and anxiety.

Different forms of religious observance were also important for the non-religious population of the ghetto. Holidays often became a symbolic expression of perseverance in the fight against Nazi ideology. When we sang together, the old worlds of melodies gave us the feeling of continuity and belonging to a much greater community, transcending the ghetto's walls.

In my own analysis, I remembered the days at the beginning of the persecution in the ghetto and our celebration of *Simchat Torah*. My father, a very religious man, danced with the *Torah*. The poet Gebirtig, our neighbor and friend, asked him, "How can you dance and pray when our people are being persecuted?" My father said, "We should celebrate the feast of *Torah*, we should have joy. We should continue to express our religion and belief in God as a defiance of Hitler's spirit." As a youngster, I identified more with Gebirtig's question, his defiance of God, his humanism, and his anguish. I could not accept my father's answer. Today I am more able to accept his way of thinking without the ambivalence I felt at the time. His expression of vitality and defiance was a traditional defense against oppression, which had been transmitted from one generation to another in a nation familiar with oppression and suffering. The holidays provided Jews with a particularly strong feeling of time and change, movement, and hope for redemption. Many survivors remember fasting on *Yom Kippur* during the hungry years of the ghetto and concentration camp as an act of free will and ego autonomy in a world where self-expression was constricted.

I remember singing during the evenings in one particular camp; the religious and nonreligious sang together the psalm "*Nafschenu chikketa l Adonai*" (Our souls are waiting for God—He is our shield and our savior). I remember the evenings, sitting on the bunk, singing this song in which everyone expressed his fantasies and longings for freedom. I felt free, transcending into another world, that of free men. As an adolescent before the beginning of the Holocaust, I called myself agnostic while singing the religious songs. I felt a feeling of brotherhood and a strong sense of pride that we now could repeat the world of our ancestors in slavery.

In general, communal singing was a catharsis for emotions of longing and hope. This was particularly true immediately after selections in which family and friends had been deported. Simple, naive songs of longing, love, and vengeance were made up and became popular in the ghetto. Sometimes a popular tango about separation from a beloved took on a special meaning and intensity as a vehicle for the expression of common longings and yearning for reunion with the beloved. I remember the group singing one such song while working.

I know that you will not come
And I must forget you forever. I know that you will not
come back
I must forget your eyes and your smile.
The train is moving, the rails are singing,
You must forget, she will not come back.

Despite the banality of this song, its emotional content took on a special meaning for many, evoking memories, a longing for the past, and paradoxically also hope and tears. These songs also became for many a special island of humanization and narcissistic supplies. This was also true for poems that were written for friends and transmitted from one mouth to another. People told many jokes about the Nazis but also about themselves in the first year of ghetto life when the illusion of some "stability" existed. Many wrote poems rather than prose or fiction; the condensation of emotions in lyric poems, often in the form of psalms, were more successful than prose in expressing the themes of mourning, of separation from loved ones, revenge, despair, anguish, and hope.

Revenge was a major theme in the work of Mordechai Gebirtig and many other now forgotten poets. I remember Gebirtig in a small crowded room on the eve of *Yom Kippur*, reading his poem "The House of Study Is Destroyed" (*Bet ha-Midrasch is Bashumt*), calling God for an answer, following the action in Krakow when synagogues were closed, Jewish homes were robbed, and the Jews pressed into forced labor. People hearing him were moved to reject the notion of acquiescing to this unanticipated reality and to change it by directing thoughts to the future when the cruelty and injustice would be replaced by justice and revenge.

The bells cling and clang as if to say
how long until the slavery will be over
and the revenge will come.

In this song, calling God to action, Gebirtig expressed the anguish of the Jews of the ghetto and their helplessness. Although a Bundist atheist, he used traditional expressions in psalmist style and form in questioning God and used familiar forms and images in an attempt to describe something never before experienced.

Ghetto poets such as Ilona Carmel and Max Gebirtig also often wrote of their longing for nature, for a better world in another place, and of their bitterness toward the world that forgot them. The poets had open ears and eyes to the condition of the children who had never seen a butterfly or did not know how flowers bloomed.

The endless selections reduced the population of the ghetto and depleted the ego-strength of those remaining. Only in very few cases did fragments of families, a father and son, or mother and daughter, stay together despite the selections. These ties were very strong, with both parties in the relationship trying to be saviors, motivated by each other's existence to survive. One woman survivor shared a bunk and working place with her mother and was able to save her by developing from a shy, submissive girl into a very active secure young woman. She and her mother underwent a total change of roles. In their recollections, both of them brought up "small games" or ways in which they had tricked each other to improve the other's chances for survival, such as telling the other they had already had their soup so that the other could have more.

Of course, in many other instances, the neurotic conflicts of envy and unresolved Oedipal conflicts were reactivated by the chaotic situation resulting in a loss of boundaries and regression of superego and ego structures. This led in extreme cases to the abandonment of spouses and siblings. The expression of their ambivalence and latent aggressive strivings toward each other surfaced as normal boundaries and taboos disappeared.

Working in the ghetto was a privilege and a ticket to survival. It meant a chance to stay in the ghetto. From a psychological point of view, working together gave a feeling of *Gemeinschaft* (unity and togetherness) and security. It was a reality-oriented behavior, providing some mobility and the possibility to come into contact with others outside the ghetto. It gave some illusion of action. But it also occasioned confrontation with the hostile emotions of the outside world of non-Jews, the local populations who partly cooperated with the German occupiers. Coming into contact with their hostility awakened feelings of loneliness, isolation, and loss of hope, as one survivor recalled:

> After the selection by the Polish police and German SS of those who had a place to work—the young and

> strong—we went through the gates of the ghetto to the cars which would take us to our work. We hadn't yet recovered from the fear and anxiety of having gone through rows of smiling, kicking policemen and SS in the selection. I was thinking about my beloved mother whom I had left hiding in a bunker because she had no work. We drove through the so-called Aryan section of the town. It was a beautiful September day, a *Babye lato* (literally grandmother's summer—Indian summer). The Poles, looking on our emaciated faces and hearing the shooting, laughed and made grimaces at us while we cried silently, wondering what was happening to our families.

Many of the ghetto inhabitants had strong needs to fight for the intactness of their families in spite of the tremendous danger to themselves. They took on the role of the robust saviors with an enormous amount of courage and an ability to mobilize inner strength and action in the most impossible situations. This not only impressed their fellow victims but also the Nazi aggressors. An eighteen-year-old law student named Anna came back to her home from Western Europe immediately before the outbreak of the war and was captured when the Germans invaded her hometown. She came from an aristocratic Jewish family of generations of leaders, a fact that became an important value through every phase of her life before the war, during the Holocaust, and in her present life.

Her family consisted of children from her father's two marriages. The oldest brother from the first marriage succeeded in escaping to the free world. Her younger brother, like herself from the second marriage, had also been captured with her and her parents under German occupation. From a psychological point of view, Anna had intense Oedipal strivings and idealized her father, who was a leading figure in many fields and a warm, giving person. This was in contrast to her young, inexperienced mother, whom Anna described as having strong narcissistic needs. While she felt her mother to be distant, she found an intellectual and emotional closeness to her father who transmitted his strong ties to the Jewish community to her in an emotional as well as practical way as a leader of the community. During the occupation, he remained a community leader in interacting with the Germans and using his wealth to save people, until he fell ill. Anna then took over these activities.

Her younger brother, a relatively submissive and unsuccessful man, was jailed by the Gestapo in the ghetto, with the intention of sending him to a concentration camp. Her father asked her to intervene with the Gestapo chief in an attempt to save her brother's life. This seemed an impossible task since the previous day, one of Anna's friends had been killed by the same officer on the streets of the ghetto after approaching him. In therapy, Anna described her anguish connected with the possibility of being killed but also the feeling that there was still a chance and that she had a choice and a freedom to act in this extreme situation. She waited for hours for the Gestapo chief, and when he arrived, she asked him to release her brother. His reply was "Don't you know that I killed a Jewish girl only yesterday? How do you have the courage to come here?" His revolver lay on the table before him. She suppressed her fear and replied, "I know, but I have to do it for my father." The next day, her brother was released and came back home. To this day, she does not know why the officer released him.

She was able to save her parents and brother many times after the destruction of the ghetto by transferring them from one bunker to another and hiding them in the Polish parts of the town, influencing her Polish friends to accept her family. Eventually, her parents were caught and killed and her brother sent to a concentration camp. Very often during her actions, she felt that they were a burden and threat to her own life. Nevertheless, she continued the lonely fight to save them with remarkable success. She herself was finally caught as an "Aryan," participating in the Polish uprising and was sent to Auschwitz. There she worked in a factory where she was suspected by the supervisor of sabotaging his work and was beaten by an SS woman in the camp, sustaining a permanent injury. The supervisor developed a special relationship with her, impressed by her courage and non-submissive behavior. He brought her apples and tried to help her after the beating and could not understand why Anna refused to express her gratitude to him. She answered, "If I thanked you, you would be temporarily relieved but I would feel permanently ashamed."

On one occasion, Anna went to the same supervisor after seeing an old woman whom she knew was being worked to death. She asked him, "Why are you giving her work that will kill her in a few days? If you wish to kill her, why not do it immediately?" The supervisor, enraged though impressed by her directness and courage, shouted, "I will kill you." In the end, Anna was not killed, and the old woman was released.

After liberation, she continued her pattern of being a "savior," finding her brother in one of the DP camps in a *muselman* state of depression and withdrawal. Not being able to have her own children as a result of the injuries she sustained during the war, she adopted a child. Her accident-prone daughter played the role of a victim, always needing help from Anna, who was not able to let her develop the capacity for autonomy and courage which she had so remarkably developed herself. She had been unconsciously re-enacting the role of the savior in her object relationships, mobilizing her intense emotions to help people whom she experienced as victims. In spite of her courage and integrity, she could not liberate herself from this role as savior, eventually leading her to seek help in the form of psychotherapy.

The attempt to maintain a family and social structure characterized the first phases of ghetto life. During this phase, a partial denial of the vast changes in reality was possible. In children, denial allowed some kind of semblance of everyday life, allowed them to play, to smuggle, to hide, and to run from danger. It provided a method of coping with the aggression and hostility against the perpetrators of their changed world.

For adults too, denial provided a social moratorium and partial denial became a psychological necessity since it allowed for hope. As described in Elie Wiesel's *Night* and so many other autobiographical stories, there was a selective narcissistic reasoning at work: "It may be happening in other ghettos and communities, but it can't happen here, to my family." Thus, while denial made possible the continuity of everyday misery and hope, it also prevented the anticipation of the events to come, the mobilization of public opinion to action against the evil and precluded any meaningful resistance.

Chapter 4:
Life in Hiding and False Identity

Some individuals and families decided to hide or try to live as so-called Aryans or non-Jews, "equal to the other population." We must understand the subjective psychological difficulty in reaching such a decision within the context of the "religious" obsession of the Germans and their collaborators to find Jews. They developed a kind of paranoid alertness as to who was a Jew. This was particularly true not only of the Germans but the anti-Semitic segments of the population of the occupied territories of Poland, Russia, Ukraine, Slovakia, and Croatia, where the hunting of Jews became a lucrative profession.

The difficulties in making the decision to live away from the Jewish population as an Aryan non-Jew was connected with both psychological and reality factors. Most important were the strong ties, the solidarity, and the fidelity still existing between family members and close friends. The second most important factor was the German policy of massive reprisals of twenty deaths for every person missing from the ghetto. This also applied to the non-Jewish families who gave assistance to the Jews. The policy of collective punishment led to a profound estrangement between the Jews and the non-Jewish population. The psychological and ideological problem of the population who did not give help to the Jews was connected with the fear of retaliation as well as the fear of God's punishment for their complicity with the Germans in relation to the Jews and their own guilt. They therefore accepted the representation of the Jews as "Christ-killer" and "enemy of humanity" to rationalize their inability for courage and their collaboration in the killings. The Nazi anti-Semitic propaganda was successful in diminishing what existing feelings of solidarity the two groups may have enjoyed before the occupation.

The Jews received some help and spontaneous support from small but important minorities in Holland, Denmark, Norway, and from a large part of the population of France, where a traditional openness and liberalism gave the population courage to live up to their ideal of freedom and decency in human relations. In addition, between ten and thirty thousand Jews were protected by individual Poles. Whether as an act of solidarity with Jewish comrades from socialist camps, as part of the Polish intelligentsia, or based on humanitarian or religious beliefs, those who hid Jews risked the death verdict in accordance with the German law. Many individuals and families were sent to concentration camps for the crime of hiding Jews. We also know from oral histories of Jews who lived in hiding, of organizations such as the socialist PPS, which offered active help to Jews who had connections. These episodes of help pale in comparison with the organized solidarity in Holland or Denmark, where the entire population helped the Jews, which should perhaps be seen as expressions of heroism, if taken within the context of the general hatred of Jews in those dark days. These historical acts of grace were experienced again and again as a source of hope for the survivors and their families and helped them to resist succumbing to hatred and despair.

The situation of hiding depended on the host population as well as on physical conditions but especially on whether the person was alone or with a family or friends. The ability to establish interpersonal relationships with the host family was a very important factor in survival. Most of the hosts in Eastern Europe were motivated not only by humanitarian factors but also by financial rewards. Thus, survival in many cases depended on whether one had financial resources to pay for help. This produced a strain from the outset between the Jew and his host family and led to feelings of distrust from both sides in their transactions. In many cases Jews were rejected when their financial resources were depleted. This was especially true in the villages and towns where Polish and Ukrainian psychopaths, so-called *Schmalzowniks*, specialized in discovering Jews in the city streets and apartments, developing different "techniques." The accepted technique to discover the male Jew was to order him to lower his trousers and see whether he was circumcised. Discovering a Jewish woman was more difficult. One technique was to put women into a situation of danger and to hear their reaction. The girl's cry of "Mama" instead of "Matka" or "Boska" (God's mother) was taken as a sign of being Jewish. Ironically, the Christian credo of love was used as a tool in the discovery and murder of their lord's original people. They would also discover whether women had any knowledge of Christian catechism and prayers or if the style of their language was too sophisticated. Once discovered, the *Schmalzownik* usually took bribes, but if the Jews had no resources, they were turned in to the Gestapo.

One survivor lived for many years in tremendous anxiety of being discovered, expecting every day that in the street someone might order him "trousers down." He experienced this twice and lost a fortune in diamonds as bribes to save his life. He spent his last diamonds on an operation to make him look uncircumcised. The man later suffered from impotence after the liberation and had difficulties in accepting his Jewish identity, wandering between Israel and Europe, feeling nowhere secure and at home.

There was a broad spectrum of experiences of people living on Aryan papers. Men and women who had non-Jewish features were more fortunate, but sometimes their sad eyes too discovered them. Sometimes their reaction to witnessing Jewish destruction gave them away, lacking the greedy and aggressive feelings of the native population. From a psychological point of view, these victims had to invest their total attention to the task of living up to an image of the Christian Aryan. The difficulty of this task was compounded by the fact that they were often from a different social class and possessing a different *Weltanschauung*, body image, and patterns of behavior.

One survivor told me in her therapy how she lived for two years as a Christian on false identity papers. She related in fantasy to her "imaginary" Aryan family, which she began playfully to believe in. She created a family, imagining the roles of the different members: a beloved father who was a Polish officer and now a camp prisoner, a strong protective brother who was also a prisoner of war, lovely protective uncles and a good warm mother in France. All were alive and thinking about her. She lived in this fantasy world while her real dead family became less vivid. The terror of death and the feeling of loneliness and isolation of the Jews awakened in her a need for total identification with her Aryan surrounding world, especially since she believed she was the only surviving Jew.

Other victims were more fortunate, hiding together with members of their family or meeting old friends living as well on Aryan papers and keeping in touch with them. This gave them a feeling of solidarity and mutual help in situations of danger. In some persons, the eternal fear of discovery day and night led to a need not only for imitation of the Aryan but also a strong motive for negative identification with the non-Jews. Mostly it was an identification not with the representational world of Christianity but with a deep-rooted fear, which later led to psychological problems, as in the case of the modern Marranos, which will be described in the chapter on families of survivors. In others, hearing the aggressive and hostile remarks and being the objects of destruction not only of the Nazis but of the general population awoke in them strong feelings of hatred toward the anti-Semites, coupled with solidarity with their fellow Jews and a deep religious longing for Judaism.

One very religious survivor suffered from a tendency of suspicion in his interpersonal relations related to his survival experiences. He had been an adolescent when he lost his family in the Holocaust. In his therapy, he recalled how he had changed from an observant agnostic to an extremely religious man. Living on Aryan papers, he survived a *Lapanka* (a search by the German and Polish police) from which he ran away and miraculously survived. He came to a church where he began zealously to recite the old Jewish prayers he had learned from his grandfather. Here he promised to identify fully with the Jewish religion as a protest against the Christian world, which he felt allowed and participated in the killings. The promise mobilized and intensified his desire to leave Christian Europe, and he ran away through many countries of Europe and arrived eventually in Palestine. Here he actualized his Judaic longings by becoming extremely religious as well as nationalistic in his striving for total security and by rejecting his past dependence and false identification as an Aryan.

A contrasting example of survival is that of the *case célèbre* of Brother Bruno, who came from a traditional Jewish family background and had been a member of a Zionist organization as an adolescent with a religious Zionistic *Weltanschauung*, with the goal to come to Palestine as a pioneer. When his nuclear family was destroyed, he succeeded in living as a *volksdeutscher Kommissar* in eastern Poland and in this function saved many Jews from destruction by warning them when the extermination began. When he was discovered as a Jew, he ran away to the monastery of his native town, Krakow, where he found refuge. There he went through the process of conversion, with deep mystical religious experiences that influenced him after liberation to choose not only to live as a Catholic but to dedicate his life as a monk to the service of God. Yet he felt an identification with Judaism and was given permission by the church to move to Israel and live among his brothers. He later became a *case célèbre* in his fight to be a full Jew according to the Law of the Return to Zion, in spite of his Christian religion.

Both cases serve as illustrations of intense religious experiences awakened in the midst of total destruction when their biological and psychological existence had been threatened. In the first case, the non-supportive, non-empathic environment awakened aggressive hostile feelings and longings for the old secure world of childhood mythology and belief, represented by the beloved grandfather, where there was causality, stable boundaries, and belonging. Whereas in the latter case, the isolation in the monastery and the empathic environment of the monks after continuous experiences of miraculously escaping the danger awakened in him a need to merge in a mystical experience. These experiences expressed his symbiotic longings for security with the all-loving and embracing mother religion.

As mentioned earlier, it was easier to live within the population of Western Europe because of the more tolerant and accepting atmosphere. This was especially true for those individuals who had strong ties with nearby comrades connected with the resistance movements as in France and Belgium. Still the *Quislings* (collaborators of the Norwegian puppet government who collaborated with the Germans), the collaborators of the Laval government in occupied France and the native Nazis of Holland (well documented in many diaries such as *The Diary of Anne Frank*) and Belgium, caused tremendous difficulties for people who had to be on the move from place to place to avoid capture and death. Many of them reacted with a total rejection of Judaism and continued to live as modern *Marannos* (Christianized Jews during the Spanish Inquisition) after liberation. They rejected their identity of Judaism because of the fear of a possible repetition of the persecution. Some of these victims achieved a paranoid intensity in their denial of their own Judaism and their eternal fear of being discovered. They changed their Jewish identity into a painful secret that could not be shared even with their spouses or their children. In some cases, this "shameful" family secret was revealed when there was a need for psychiatric consultation.

Seven-year-old Christine Mary came for a psychiatric consultation because of a school phobia. The child had a constant fear that something would happen to her, especially at school, and needed to be escorted to school by her mother and often had to have her mother stay with her. During the therapy, tremendous quarrels occurred between the parents, with verbal and non-verbal threats that something terrible was going to happen in the family. This led to an investigation of the family situation that brought to light the dangerous family secret. The parents were the only survivors of their original families and had lived on Aryan papers in their native town, with a chronic anxiety of being discovered. After the war, they decided to continue their lives as Aryans, even after attaining refuge in Western Europe. The parents' ambivalent feelings for their own families was expressed in the fact that when Christine was born, she was given the name of Mary after her grandmother whose name was Miriam. The father developed a paranoid preoccupation at the same time, with the possibility of persecution, believing that "Hitler and other Nazis were living in Argentina and could return." During the interviews, it was revealed that his relationship with his original family was ambivalent, with an underlying tone of desertion. The child received continuous double messages about her identity as Christine Mary as well as fearing the ghosts of the past who were threatening her life. The problems of identity connected with the ambivalence toward the parents' family of origin and the possibility of a false solution of living as Aryans unfortunately led to the child's expression of the shared psychopathology of the family.

The pairing of support behavior and friendship between survivors made it possible for many who lived on Aryan papers to go to Germany as *Fremdarbeiter* (foreign workers), where there was less danger of their being discovered as Jews. Here the feeling of security allowed some normalization of their interpersonal relationships and a return to psychological homeostasis. Only then was it possible for them to fully realize their losses and permit themselves to express bereavement, which had been impossible during the dangerous situation of the ghetto.

A special group I wish to mention are those adolescents and children without parents who ran away from the ghettos or were given to non-Jewish families for hiding by their parents, in some cases, to quite unknown families where they lived as a member of the family. Some were also sent to monasteries. Many cannot forget the rejection and the running from place to place in search of some dwelling to rest for the night. Their eternal feelings of alienation, shame, and degradation return again and again in their lives.

One survivor, nineteen years old at the beginning of her Holocaust experience, remembered a recurrent theme in her dreams. She would be running through the streets of her town from door to door, a kind of dark labyrinth where all the doors were closed. This repetitive motif was connected with her intense reality experiences, when as a ten-year-old girl, she was smuggled through the sewer system out of her town to the Aryan section, with the hope of being accepted by the Christian part of the family. Her aunt had married an Aryan Christian. But she was not accepted by the family because of their fears of being discovered and destroyed. Day and night, she hid in vacant bombarded houses, persecuted by real dangers and her own fears. She eventually found refuge in a monastery, pretending to be an orphan from the east. Her inner life was a complex fabric of distrust, fear, and anxiety that she would forget her Christian prayers taught to her by her father in the ghetto, longing for her parents, the fear that they were dead and later on the knowledge that they had died. Her aunt told her that her parents had been destroyed in the Warsaw Ghetto with the rest of the Jews for having killed Christ. All those memories came up again and again in her psychotherapy, making her own relationship with her daughter difficult in her overprotectiveness toward her as well as her preoccupation with the past. In the motivation for choosing her profession as a pediatrician for disabled children and in her creative works as a sculptor, she came again and again to her need for protection of the injured child in herself.

For many of the younger children, ages two to eight, who lost their parents and in some cases were adopted by Christian families, physical survival unfortunately did not mean psychological survival. Their parents transmitted anxieties and fears to them during the persecution period. They suffered from the separation from their nuclear family as well as the extended family, the lack of narcissistic resources very often connected with their displacement from one family to another, and the lack of stable object relations during the time of hiding and later on. Their recovery after liberation by their original families or by Jewish organizations awakened in them the continuous traumatizations and identity confusion. In Eriksonian terms, they were injured in all stages of psychosocial development. They were unable to negotiate the fundamental tasks of development, from the establishment of basic trust to particular problems in the spheres of identity and intimacy.

A patient named Sophia, born in 1939, was left by her parents with a Christian family two years later, before their deportation, with the hope of recovering her after liberation. The parents never returned. An aunt did return and tried to recover Sophia from the Christian woman who had cared for her. The woman did not wish to give up Sophia. After a long legal struggle, the aunt was able to get custody of the child. Sophia, who was five years old by this time, did not want to be taken by her aunt, expressing her fear of being eaten by the Jewish witch. It happened that the Christian woman had been psychotic and had totally isolated Sophia from other children and subjected her to alternating spells of love and severe beatings. She developed a strong symbiotic relationship with this woman and feared separating from her. The aunt eventually took Sophia to a Scandinavian country where she sought peace of mind for the two of them. Here Sophia withdrew more and more into her world of fantasy, unable to participate at school, often engaging in brooding and aggressive spells toward the aunt—beating her and fearing she could kill her—whom she "sometimes saw as a savior and at other times as the witch who should be killed." Psychotherapy did not achieve basic changes, and when she immigrated to Israel at the age of eighteen, she manifested a psychosis with strong suicidal and homicidal attempts against her aunt, requiring hospitalization. In the therapy and her artistic paintings she expressed her hate and love toward the aunt in a polarized way, becoming a representation of her mother. Her fragmented ego could not integrate her strong longings and strong aggressive tendencies towards the same object. This schizophrenic girl was the victim of the demonic forces of the Holocaust which she projected onto her aunt, the only survivor of the family, who became herself a victim again.

Slightly more hopeful is the case of the young man whose parents left him at the same age of two years with a Christian family of his native town. The mother later returned from the concentration camp to find out after many months that the child had ended up in a Christian orphanage after the Christian family had given him up for fear of being discovered. The son, at the age of six years, not only developed an institutional syndrome of kicking and aggressiveness but also expressed so total a hatred toward the Jews that the mother hid her Jewish identity from him for many years. Only gradually has the boy developed more of a feeling of closeness with her. After one year, she did reveal that she was Jewish, and he exclaimed, "But you are so good, how can you be Jewish?" Today this youngster, once afflicted by racial hatred and in spite of cognitive achievements as a scientist, has difficulties in object relationships and a tendency to use defenses of projective identification in situations of anxiety. For example, when he cannot accept his aggressive feelings toward women, he projects them in a very intense way toward his love object, feeling persecuted by his wife.

The third case is of a woman, a young lawyer born in 1940, who was separated from her mother when she was selected for death from the ghetto. Both she and her father were saved by a Christian woman whom the father married after the war. Because of the danger of *Razzien* (the searches by the Nazis and police), the two-year-old child spent hours and days in a closet and was conditioned not to speak or cry because if discovered, she could be beaten and killed. In spite of the good relationship with her family after the liberation, she developed logorrhea, a compulsive need to talk, especially in anxiety situations.

In general, the hiding situation generated a specific relationship within the framework of the people who were together, with their strong interdependence—so well described by Anne Frank—and also by an oversensitivity in relationships to each other. This often developed into animosity and hostility, especially between strangers or between members of extended families. It seems that in religious families, being together in semi-sensory deprivation situations, crowded and hungry, the possibility of praying together and of ritualizing mourning diminished the aggressive feelings toward each other and gave them the rationalization for their own survival or to be witnesses for *Klal Yisroel* (the people of Israel). Feelings of hope and despair were mixed together, and a strong leadership was helpful in diminishing the intra-familial tensions that existed because of the specific conditions of physical deprivation and anxiety.

In the writings of survivors, we read of the guilt they felt, having stayed alive while their friends and neighbors were killed. Yet the possibility of sharing, verbalizing, cooperating together, and the friendships they formed were an important factor in their transactions with their host who had to be placated to renew in him the motivation to support them in hiding. A scientist, living as a youngster with his extended family in hiding in one of the European countries, thought that his present extreme need for autonomy and privacy, as well as his tendency to dominate and his intolerance of submission in relationships, were connected with his long years in hiding. This man developed a strong cathexis of boundaries in his home and work situation, with a great sensitivity to intrusion into his privacy. At home, he could not tolerate intimacy or his children coming to his room, or crowds, or situations of close physical contact, because it reminded him of the crowded, unventilated room in hiding, with its odor of unclean bodies. In therapy, he described his rages toward his father when he had seen him being submissive toward the host, paternalizing and stressing his "Christian tolerance" toward them but also their dependence on him. He experienced his father as a weak, fearful coward and developed through the years features of intolerance toward others and a very sharp, critical, and analytic orientation to situations. He became a pessimistic man, always finding himself sitting in a place that was strategic for running away.

Another example is of a Jewish writer who before the war had been an active, independent man. He lived in hiding for three years during his early adulthood with his wife-to-be. The intensity of their relationship in the years after liberation made it impossible for him to separate from her and his children, for he was reminded of the years of hiding when he experienced the death of two members of his family who left the cellar during the evening to relieve themselves. This intense yet harmonious man developed a strong interdependence with his wife, and they remained inseparable. During hiding, they developed a mutual relationship that was to be the pattern of their whole life. He played the "feeling" role in the relationship, the spirit who expressed feelings of hope, despair, prayer, and mourning for the whole family. She, on the other hand, played the "doing" role, having an active orientation in the family's transactions with the world, beginning with the transactions in hiding with the host population. This complementary behavior, which was at first a defensive response to the influence of life dangers, later continued autonomously after the danger had ceased and formed an integral part of the dynamics between the parents and the children.

Chapter 5:
The Disintegration of the Ghetto and the World of the Concentration Camp

The long period of traumatization, beginning in the ghetto, involved constant confrontation with the destruction of family, extreme danger, and the experience of death of loved ones and put tremendous stress on the victim's psyche. The theme of separation from one's family is central in the therapy of survivors.

I remember I was taken with many other young people to a labor camp where we built the *Ostbahn*, which was to connect Berlin, Kiev, and Moscow. The conditions, as usual, were terrible, the supervisors of the work excelling in their brutality no less than the Ukrainian SS. Rumors of the destruction transports of families to death camps awakened in me the desire to see my family and try and save them. Therefore, I ran away from the workplace at night through the fields and forests to return home, back to my parents, who still lived in the little town where Jews were doomed to destruction. I tried to find a hiding place for them with a Polish neighbor family but was not successful. I remember the last night before the destruction of the Jewish community. I felt that this was the last meeting between us. Every one of us tried to support the other, but the tears of my mother awoke in me a tremendous certainty that this was our last supper together and that the family as such would cease to exist. We were crying in silence, looking at each other and saying good-bye to one another. Father blessed me, knowing that the blessing could have a magical power. Still, every one of us tried to be brave. I had to leave at midnight so that I would be back at work by six o'clock in the morning.

The ominous quality of this last supper contained aspects of denial of death and the disintegration of the family. It was this denial of the inevitable that formed the motivation for returning to be together with my family.

In the ghetto, there was a continuous fight to hold on to some subjective feeling of freedom as expressed in strong ties to the family, mastery of anxiety through attempts to move from place to place, running away from a terrible ghetto to a "better" ghetto, also the continuity of intense friendships, the occasional reading of a beloved book or writing poems. It is important, in the light of the descriptions of the victims as helpless, regressed crowds, to stress their attempts to hold to a framework in which there still would be object relationships, fidelity and empathy. Those were values cherished from childhood, internalized from one generation to the next, and intensified by the persecution. But the Nazis repeatedly tried to destroy every emerging form of relations between victims by continuous and frequent displacements, transports, and selections of who will live and who will die. This led to disintegration of social bonds and to regression in many aspects of interpersonal relationships as well as "robotization" (Meerloo, 1962) of some ego functions. In spite of this, the basic expressions of belonging and strong emotional ties to family and loved ones remained intact for many. This intensified the experience of separation from and loss of the family, becoming unforgettable, fixated imprints in the psyches of the victims.

I remember that my mother stayed in the ghetto when I was taken to the labor camp that was built on the grounds of the Jewish cemetery. At the beginning, I had a chance to visit her on my way back from work at the *Wehrmacht* army factory to the labor camp on the pretext of needing disinfection in the *mikveh* (ritual bath) every two weeks. The German soldiers, who occasionally were human and understanding, allowed us to visit the remnants of the family and to bring them food. This occasion was one when we could support each other and bring some food that we obtained through the exchange of clothes on the Polish side. When I came to the ghetto on one particular day, the gates were closed and the whole ghetto was surrounded by SS police and their helpers of destruction. I cannot forget standing near the barbed wire and looking at my mother in the window behind the barbed wire fence, with butter in my hands that I wished to give her. I called to her in anguish, not accepting the verdict of death. I tried to shout to her that she should try to come out of the ghetto and join the working gang who were selected for one of the workshops and transferred from the ghetto to a concentration camp. I tried helplessly to save her, denying that it was our last meeting.

It was not only the fact of the acknowledgment of one's helplessness in confrontation with the destructiveness of the Nazis. It was not only that but also the feeling of being alone with nobody to cry with. I don't know if it is possible to express the emotions in words to look upon somebody close who will not die but be murdered without explanation, without knowing the reason why. This question reverberated in my mind when I looked into the eyes of my mother.

The so-called liquidation of the ghetto—in the technical terms of the German language distorted by the Nazis—meant the end of life and the killing of children and the destroying of lives of women and men in their prime. This very often awoke regressive trends in the victims, including doubts about continuing the fight for life and strong doubts about the meaning of life. I recall that in the beginning of the ghetto, there were still people like my teacher—philosopher Ben-Zion Rappaport—who could write philosophical tracts in the Neoplatonic tradition, in which he dealt with the basic questions of life. By the end of the ghetto and the beginning of the concentration camps, the victims' cognitive processes were connected to concrete questions of survival and death. I still remember a lecture in Ben-Zion Rappaport's flat. Reading Plato's *Republic*, he expressed doubts that philosophers could be good leaders and save mankind. He said that now there was no place for philosophers and that the demagogues of Plato's days had never dreamed about the beast in man as we now experienced it.

It is therefore naïve to differentiate between victim-heroes who were faithful to the ideal autonomy and the regressed, polarized robot-like victims. It seems that every one of the victims went through different phases in which they sometimes showed regressive behavior as a defense against the destruction and were oriented toward their own physical survival, showing interest primarily in their own food and security. At other times, the same victims could achieve altruistic self-ideal–oriented attitudes in relation to comrades as well as expressing courage in the face of the Nazi aggressors.

There were many examples of resistance in everyday life, such as indirect actions against the Germans in the form of sabotage, mutual aid between victims, and intense friendships that gave meaning and truth to life. Meeting a friend in the ghetto or concentration camp who was glad to see you and gave you a few friendly words could change a whole style of coping from regressive behavior to mastery. Yet repeated separations from family and friends as well as repeated displacements from camp to camp could destroy one's sense of extreme passivity and regression to psychic organization in relation to the outside world and to the self.

A patient-survivor who was an adolescent during the Holocaust remembers:

> First, I came to a camp where people knew each other and helped. But then I was transferred and felt my strength leaving me, not having support. In the camp I met two other colleagues from school. They were privileged inmates, working as mechanics before the war and they had been in the same youth organization as I. I worked with them in a stone quarry where the usual survival time was one to two weeks. I knew that I did not have many days to live; because of exhaustion and emaciation I would not be able to carry the stones and I would be shot as so many others. So, meeting these friends was identical with survival because due to their influence I was transferred to a more secure place. Another time both of them saved me when I was beaten by a Capo who punished me—I do not know why. From being with them I regained my interest in life. From total apathy I became interested in learning about Nazi Germany defeats. One comrade had good relations with a master-supervisor who had been friendly and talked about German defeats and the invasion of Americans and Russians and this news awakened in me again the wish to live.

The wish for physical survival was the leitmotif of every behavior, every fantasy. As hunger and physical deprivation intensified, regressive forms of behavior took over and the primitive quality of life increased.

Survival in such conditions depended as much or more on the victims' psychic strength and adaptive powers as on physical endurance. There were many factors that affected the capacity for adaptation and survival. Differences in the types of experience, psychological health prior to the war, and cohesiveness of group experience in the ghetto and the camps were significant influences.

Those who were deported directly to camps without anticipation or previous confrontation with Nazi brutality often lacked the coping styles and the group cohesion found in those who were in the ghetto beforehand. In spite of suffering in the ghetto community life, autonomy and some freedom of decision in the lives of the individuals existed, albeit within painful surroundings. The walls of the ghetto had offered some illusion of comfort and security, but the barbed wire and naked anonymity of the camps could not do so. There was no family through which to relate to the environment; a number replaced even one's name. One was stripped of both personal and group identity. In such a world, there was a lessening of the intrapsychic and interpersonal conflict situations. Instead, there grew a feeling of total terror. Two basic tendencies could be observed: on the one hand, the inmate's denial of his own mortality despite the pervading atmosphere of death—the smoke rising from the crematoria, the ever-present gallows, and the acrid smell of burning corpses—and on the other hand, the longing for death as the liberator from these infernal horrors. With death so real and irreparable, one could not relate to it as mysterious, unique, fearful, and personal for more than a brief period. When death occurs by the tens of thousands, when its quantitative aspect is its dominant qualitative aspect, it imprints itself as familiar, banal, anonymous, and senseless.

Mortality was therefore highest in those groups that lacked moral support, and those who were transported from France, Holland, and Belgium to the camps in Poland experienced intense shock. The danger of moral disintegration was constant in the abnormal world of the ghetto and the concentration camp. The age-old traditions of causality and morality ceased to exist.

The camp conditions meant an inordinately heavy strain on the ego's capacity to deal with external and internal danger as well as a massive onslaught on the inmates' sense of freedom, independence, and mastery. This, together with the loss of loved ones and the sudden dissolution of an external familiar world, induced regression in ego functioning, variously described as states of "primitivization" and "withdrawal," accompanied by defensive operations such as numbness and a sense of unreality. Conflicts around issues of trust, aggression, passivity, and impulse control that had been in a state of equilibrium and integration before threatened to become overwhelming, due to the regression of ego functions.

Two additional factors have to be considered, however, to understand the dynamics of the situation fully. First, it was usually an adult ego experiencing the external and internal traumatic situation. This adult ego with its developed perceptive sense, though in many ways possessing greater resilience, could not as easily take flight into infantile mechanisms of defense such as childhood amnesia or a total denial of reality. The traumatic state that existed was not simply an exacerbation of infantile conflict but an experience that was qualitatively different from it because an adult, adolescent, or latency child (in any case, not an infant) was experiencing it.

The second distinct factor in the situation, and probably the most important one of all, was the *reality* of the external traumatic experience. Whereas infantile conflict reflects mostly situations in fantasy, in the concentration camps, such fantasies actually became true. Sadomasochistic fantasies, for example, have a far-reaching impact on defensive structures and character formation in children. The camp inmate, in his state of regression, experienced not only the stimulation of such fantasies but also the shattering effect of their actual realization. He had to deal not only with all that was stirred up inside him but also with the undeniable fact that all this was really happening. Fantasy had none of its safeguards in the camp situation, although many inmates attempted to cling to the notion that what was happening to them, what they saw happening to others—which they experienced by identification—was not real and that they would wake up from this nightmare because it was not kept in the realm of fantasy but was fully realized. Obviously, there were long-lasting severe impacts of such a psychotic-like situation on the inmate's ability to perform the task of reality testing. Once fantasies have become fully true, there is no way to tell what is "thought" and what is "reality"; the former is as dangerous as the latter. Jerzy Kosinski's book *The Painted Bird* (1965) is a most powerful narrative that illustrates such blurring between fact and fiction in the experience of his hero. In addition, fantasying in itself became dangerous and was therefore restricted and impoverished. Pleasurable passive drifting was avoided. What took its place in conscious awareness was either blandness or apathy regarding matters of mastery and righteousness in everyday life situations.

Reality testing was further strained by the past and by the ambivalent ties with the captors. The "friendly Nazi," a symbol of paralyzing extremes, while serving as a temporary life-saving device, was nevertheless a delusion. Deep down, the inmate knew of the impending chaos and destruction and of the stark brutality of his opponent, maintaining complete self-deception and denial in the face of all that constituted a severe assault on one's sense of reality, and this produced a continued and debilitating effect on a variety of ego functions.

In the same vein, the phenomenon of the identification with the aggressor was *not* an identification with the aggressor per se but with one who had mastery and power in order to avoid the sense of utter helplessness and castration, yet it exacted an enormous price from those who adopted this strategy.

Those inmates who had friends, particularly family ties such as father and son or mother and daughter, had the strongest defenses against the resignation that usually brought death. A survivor-patient named Paulina recalled that when she looked upon her mother's emaciated face, she resolved that she would not allow her mother to decline to the state of a *muselman*. She began to *handeln* (trade), making soup from kohlrabi and greens she found in the fields and selling it for bread for her mother. She also sold remnants of clothes of inmates to Polish civilians who worked in the factory. The determination to assure her mother's survival provided Paulina with the inner strength and resourcefulness that saved both their lives. Without the bonding and the sense that she had someone to live for, her will to live might not have endured.

Every inmate developed infectious diseases in the form of typhus and dysentery. Our lives depended on support from friends because going to the so-called sickrooms was often equivalent to accepting the verdict of death. From a psychological point of view, the capacity to identify and empathize with a sick comrade was necessary in order to save one's own humanity and not regress to the stage of a *muselman*. It was not only a function of the superego but also an expression of ego strength because without this interdependence, there could be no survival.

In the ghettos and concentration camps, the inmates usually experienced the holidays in a very intense way. We felt connected with the symbols of redemption during *Rosh Hashanah* and *Passover*, recalled the meaning of holidays, returned to their spiritual resources, and internalized a mythology about returning from the house of slavery to freedom. On the one hand, we felt strong ties to Judaism and our tradition, reciting, "We have been slaves of Pharaoh in Egypt," and identifying with the tradition and hope of the slaves who eventually would be redeemed and freed. Together with this was the anger that we had been abandoned and forgotten. It seemed that our fate was of no concern to anyone.

An inability to find an affinity with other camp inmates could lead to isolation and ostracism. One example reported by a survivor in his therapy was of a youngster from Germany, a so-called half-Jew or *Mischling*, who, confronted for the first time with intense self-hatred and self-denial, pathetically wished again and again to become an Aryan. He would proudly and arrogantly proclaim to the other inmates, who were "East European pariah swine" in his eyes, that his half-brother was fighting on the Eastern front against the Russian barbarians. His claim for special privileges and his feeling of racial superiority aroused such rage and aggression that the other inmates, including the patient, killed him during an air raid without feeling remorse. Only later did he begin to feel guilt and remorse during his recovery and growth in the years after liberation.

Inmates also attempted to maintain a connection with the outer world by trying to pick up bits of information about the progression of the war. Listening to clandestine radios was a source of reinforcement and hope. Yet news of German defeats at the hands of the Russians was much more an expression of a wish fulfillment than reality and in many groups fuelled the conflict between those who preferred to deny the grim reality of the situation and those who saw it as the hardest.

New arrivals to the camps were confronted with two conflicting messages. The older, experienced victims told them to forget about their families, to try not to think of them, and to have no feelings in order to survive. Yet for many, it was only the internalization of the family that held them human and allowed them to retain their self-images in defiance of the Nazi tactics, which tried by all means to take the individuality away from the victims.

I remember standing on the bunk every night. I spoke to my family in fantasy and said the prayers that I used to say in my home. It was a kind of connection with the world that I loved and which was still important to me and allowed me to cry at times.

Inmates were tormented by the question of whether one was entitled to live when one's own family had been murdered. The feeling of having abandoned one's family was not always grounded in fact, but being separated from a loved one who was to be killed by the Nazis awoke overwhelming feelings of remorse. Literature on this period stresses that people chose to live even when their loved ones died. But the fact that they were not able to save their families produced feelings of helplessness and guilt. This question of continuing to live when others died recurred after selections, after survivors "miraculously" remained alive by some luck or some action which by chance succeeded. By moving to one side rather than another, one was free to live for another short interval, free of selection and death until the next trial, which would undoubtedly come. And then one remembered the dead. A middle-aged man who was the lone survivor of his family felt the need to sit at home for one year to write memoirs of his life during the Holocaust when his children left home to study abroad. During therapy, he spoke of friends of his who had recently died and worried about being the only survivor of this peer group. He then realized that all his real friends had already died in the Warsaw Ghetto. He had organized them in an underground resistance group, which was discovered by the Germans; all his friends were killed, and only he, in a confrontation with the Gestapo officer, was able to bribe him to save his life. In the crowded wagon on the train to Auschwitz, he wished to kill himself but dreamed of his mother who was saying to him in Yiddish, "Stay alive. Do it for me." He saw this dream as a message that his duty was to continue his life.

A patient survivor of Auschwitz had a job there, writing false reports to the secretary, having been chosen for this work because of her knowledge of languages, her Aryan appearance, and her youth. She was the only survivor of a family of six brothers and was haunted by the question "Why me?" She was confronted with this question again and again when she had the occasional opportunity to save someone from the list of those designated for gassing by changing names. She was constantly faced with the dilemma about whom to choose to live from among her friends and extended family. In her post-Holocaust life, paralyzed by ambivalence and an inability to make choices, especially in relation to her children, she developed symptoms of phobias of travelling and going far away from home, fearing always that something terrible would happen. This woman developed intense anxiety the day after she accepted restitution money from the Germans; she felt haunted by the vision of people who had died while she had stayed alive. She could not allow herself restitution and in the end gave the money to an orphanage that housed children of those who had been killed by the Nazis. In therapy, she experienced an intense working through of her survival guilt and realized that she was not the guilty one. She could then come in touch with her own restitution processes, rediscovering the ability to love.

Many survivors were in similarly unbearable situations, confronted with the choice of saving their own lives or dying with their beloved. A woman patient-survivor described her pain and difficulty in being rejected by fellow workers in her present life. She remembered the first confrontation of being rejected and ostracized by her own group in the concentration camp when she was selected to stay by the capo due to her intelligence and beauty. Others were transported to probable death in gas chambers, while staying meant the stability of work and food. Her comrades looked at her accusingly, and one of them said, "How can you stay when we are going?" These words echo constantly in her thoughts.

Parents were forced to watch their children die while they were allowed to live. Two concepts came to bear on this agonizing condition. In the past, *Kiddush HaShem* (sanctification of the name) meant to die for God rather than leave the religion, as was the case in Spain and the crusades in the Middle Ages. In the Holocaust, some accepted their deaths as having some meaning. Others, including the survivor, had to grapple with the second concept of *Kiddush HaShem*, choosing life, however difficult to bear that might be. Jews chose to live as witnesses to the crimes and to seek revenge and restitution in the form of continuing their lives and the creation of new life.

During the selection in Auschwitz, a young man of twenty-two was separated from his wife and their six-month-old child when he was ordered by Dr. Mengele to go on one side and his wife on the other. Remembering it during therapy, he recalled feeling bewildered and confused, not knowing the meaning of the choice. He was preoccupied with guilt about his wife and child, insecure about his role as husband and father. Only many years following the liberation, living in the United States, did he finally feel secure enough about himself as a man and provider to decide to marry again. Immediately after the birth of his daughter, he began to feel guilt and was haunted by ruminative depressive thoughts: *Why didn't I go with them?* The working through of the situation brought to his awareness that the act of killing was not his doing and that not even his staying alive was fully a result of his will.

Victims were often unable to fully use the cognitive processes of their egos after the strains of being transported. Being in a state of confusion prevented them from totally falling apart, lest they feel the pain and become psychotic.

In spite of the common problems of all concentration camp inmates, there remained a social stratification of experience based on nationality, differences in functions (whether or not they were part of a group of privileged inmates), age group, values, cultural and psychosocial background, and the nature and duration of their concentration camp experiences. Germaine Tillion, a non-Jewish inmate of Ravensbrück, a women's concentration camp, observed that the "resistance to death seemed to vary" along national group lines (1975, p. 23), but survival depended less on nationality and more on being part of a group where they could share, give, pray, and sing together. I remember one special group of youngsters who were the *Hassidim* in the Krakow Ghetto, who in their intense religious approach to life vigorously held themselves to the performance of the 613 *mitzvoth* (commandments). With the defenses of massive denial and avoidance, they adhered to their religious way of life and continued to study *Talmud*. They recited in the cellars of the ghetto, "I believe in the coming of the Messiah in spite of the fact that he will come too late." To many of them, this Maimonidian credo became a moral and religious duty, and they continued their prewar way of life with the study of the *Torah* and the teaching of the law, even to the gates of Belzec and Auschwitz.

Yet the experiences of Jewish victims were unique in many ways, especially from a psychological point of view, in that they were the targets of a scientific destruction, not as individuals but as representatives of a nation, culture, and civilization. They had nowhere to go, and no one was concerned about them.

If on the other hand there were some family members who had escaped from the Nazi destruction, this was of immense importance as a motive for survival. Inmates would carry on an internal dialogue, longing and fantasizing about a possible reunion with their beloved. A survivor remembered having a brother who had left his country to go to a kibbutz in Israel. This gave him enormous courage and belief in a reunion with him. Paradoxically, he was afraid that his brother was in danger in the war situation in Palestine when he heard about the German invasion of North Africa. This capacity to care within the camp and to fantasize about the free world was an expression of the continuity of the self and identity as well as the ability to change passivity to activity, which again inspired motivation for continual efforts at survival.

In spite of the diversity of the Holocaust experiences, one can differentiate three general patterns of survival: by individual and group mastery, survival by regression, and mixed survival tactics. There were those who regressed to more primitive modes of object relations; narrowness of interest (only food); primitiveness of thought processes and of patterns in relation to one's language, appearance, and dress; and diminishing narcissistic investment in one's body.

Survival by individual and group mastery was connected with the pre-Holocaust experiences of the individual. If one could be embedded within a family from which one could draw support and in which every member of the group fulfilled varying needs, one could maintain a sense of uniqueness. Food, song, and shelter were shared; anxieties and fears could be ventilated; there were common memories of better times. All of this reinforced the reassuring message that even in times of great danger, one was not alone. This acted as an island of humaneness and emotional connection within the ocean of hatred and primitivization of object relationships.

Individual mastery also involved tactics of overinvestment in the body, cleaning it almost ritualistically when water was available, with a magical thinking that this cleaning would give a healthier appearance and this would increase one's chances of survival. One learned different kinds of body movements, such as walking in the best way to conserve energy and tactics to imitate work when the capo was not watching. "Organizing" against the Nazis, mainly in the form of stealing, became important achievements from a psychological point of view. Stealing or sabotaging factory property was connected with joy and revenge and was perfectly acceptable to the individual and group superego. It involved taking risks, anticipating the consequences, and exploring pros and cons. Mobility and quick decision-making in the dangerous situations of selection and hiding were also vital for physical and psychological survival.

Survival mastery was also connected with fleeing from one camp to another, in situations when this was still possible, yet this involved the self-deception that conditions could be better elsewhere. I remember running to five different labor camps in the Krakow area or another such escape with my parents and brother. We fled from Krakow to a small town where there was still no established ghetto and again from there (following a Gestapo action in which many Jews were killed or deported to camps) to another town where it was rumored that the *Landeshauptmann* (mayor) had a Jewish lover and was a more "benevolent" protector of the Jews and where the police and Gestapo could be bribed. Of course, there were differences between the conditions in different places, but they existed more in our fantasy than in reality. Too often, Jews felt that through their work and cooperation with the Germans, they could guarantee their lives. This wishful thinking was one of the most dangerous of weapons.

Throughout the trials of the period, the ability to relate to individuals and develop constant object relationships and having friends with common ideologies was of the utmost importance in upholding morale and strengthening the individual in his motivation to live. The mutual support and developing high sensitivity to the dangers of everyday life and the capacity to quickly think through and act on one's opinions all remained crucial factors in increasing the slim chances of survival.

PART II

Society and the Survivor

CHAPTER 6:
THE SURVIVOR IN THE IMMEDIATE AFTERMATH OF THE HOLOCAUST (1945–1948)

This chapter relates to the lives of the survivors during the initial period after the liberation of the countries destroyed by the Nazi occupation and the war and to the bombed and tattered areas of Eastern Europe and the displaced persons camps in Germany, where the bulk of the survivors lived out of their suitcases and waited for the visas that would allow them to emigrate overseas or to Palestine, the country of their dreams, the idealized Motherland, the gates of which were closed by the English.

The mood of the general population was characterized by traumatization and emotional upheaval, millions grieving their beloved, the collaborators of the Nazis fearful and anxious, millions of Germans shocked by their defeat and the inability to mourn their *Führer*. Other countries were gripped by the fear of a Soviet invasion and, with ambivalent feelings toward their liberators, lived between hope and resignation. All traditional beliefs and values were forever shattered and basic trust in individuals, the family, themselves, and God was also deeply shaken. There was only the total preoccupation with the struggle for physical survival and daily existence, rebuilding the most elementary necessities of shelter and food.

In such an atmosphere, the Jewish survivors felt these insecurities to an extreme degree. The destruction of their entire world—parents, children, and friends—awoke in them the question of how to live with the massive losses. Not only loved ones but familiar structures, the streets, the faces, and the landscapes from childhood were gone. There was also often the loss of language with which to express emotions that brought further disconnection from the world of beloved representations and that diminished the verbal capacity for sublimated and complex expressions of grief.

The first period was characterized by physical exhaustion and diminished resistance to disease, which led to the psychological sensation of living in a fog: an inability to use the cognitive apparatus in order to understand what was happening in the outer world. This psychosomatic state engendered passivity, an inability to express emotions of anger, joy, or vengeance, still living with the self-image of someone who has no right to live. Many survivors remembered their inability to cry and to enjoy their freedom since it had come too late and was connected with the deaths of so many others. From one point of view, the survivor felt that the world owed him something: that it should see him as a hero who had conquered death. Many shared the fantasies of a world of absolute love, justice, and harmony, which would come as a result of their suffering.

In this interval between death and life, there was the lethargy of mind and action of many who had lived on the verge of being *muselmen* in the stage between death and life. The relation to the American, British, and Russian liberating troops was one of total idealization. Those who had lived as Aryans continued to be suspicious and lived with their false identity. Their suspicions were largely justified, not only by their experiences during the Holocaust but after liberation as well. In returning to Hungary, Poland, Czechoslovakia, and Russia, the survivors were met with disbelief, followed by anger and the fear of vengeance.

The long bouts of infectious diseases, such as dysentery, abdominal typhus, tuberculosis, long years of amenorrhea in girls and women, as well as longitudinal loss of potency in men, shattered their body images as men and women and awakened in them doubts as to whether they could be loved again. These thoughts were especially characteristic of adolescents whose preoccupation with appearance was in many cases connected with the wish to return to their "faces," which had been treasured and loved by parents and family.

A beautiful girl of sixteen, the queen of her class, became preoccupied in the DP camps with how to save her beautiful body and face. This was connected with the knowledge that these "treasures" she possessed had given her the security to live on Aryan papers, to flirt, and to still feel strong in relation to the "men-wolves" whom she controlled with her exceptional beauty. She felt reassured by the knowledge that she was desired and accepted by the world of men and envied by women. A few months after liberation, she was involved in a minor automobile accident in which her face was slightly injured. This brought on exaggerated fears and a major depression with anxiety that she would never again be loved.

A young man of seventeen, suffering from a rash on his buttocks as a result of a vitamin deficiency, reacted with the fear that a woman who would discover his scars when naked would never love him. He was afraid that his skin changes would expose all of his bad inner feelings, which in turn would awaken rejection in women.

Those survivors who did not return to their homelands experienced another loss—of the countries once experienced as motherlands and fatherlands, now cemeteries associated with hatred, anger, and disappointment with the host populations. The neighbor of yesterday had been, if not an accomplice to murder, at least an indifferent onlooker at the time of the selections and the deportations. Many survivors recalled this again and again with bitterness or pained smiles but also treasured and sustained the memories, the tears, the kind words, and the small gifts of food that a few of their former neighbors had shared with them. These isolated experiences of humanity reawakened feelings of unity and belonging in the survivors.

In the first period after the Holocaust, there was an intense attempt to return to their old homes in order to try and find family members, often despite the firm knowledge that they had been killed. This denial of death was so intense that the Jewish search for a remnant of the community was commonplace. Confrontation with the destruction of the community and the death of loved ones promoted feelings of rage and anger that allowed neither revenge nor mourning. Survivors remembered the parting words of their friends and colleagues to take revenge. In the words of Gebirtig, "*SS wet kumen a tog fun nekome*" (The day of revenge will come). They remembered their own fantasies of revenge, but their anger was then expressed in words alone, cursing the Nazis and the SS. Consciousness of rage somehow did not allow for collective hate or vengeance, in sharp contrast to the anti-Semitic stereotype of the Jew taking vengeance in the Old Testament style of "an eye for an eye" or expressed by Shakespeare in Shylock's passion for his "pound of flesh." We may understand the incapacity for vengeance in fact or fantasy as being interwoven with the process of mourning and the awakening of survivor guilt. Survivor guilt was connected with the inability to take revenge and ambivalence toward the perpetrator; the survivor often directed the hatred and aggression toward himself instead, with disbelief that he had the power or right to take justice into his own hands. There was also the feeling that the perpetrators should be *judged* in a world where a sense of justice and order was re-established. This ambivalence led to avoidance against taking vengeance personally.

At the same time, the first phase of the survivors' coping was characterized by action, but of a different kind—wandering from country to country, community to community, from one DP camp to another, with the vain hope of finding security and familiar figures from the past. Images of their beloved began to appear in their daydreams and fantasies. Their eyes searched constantly, hoping to catch sight of them in the street. This characteristic phenomenon of searching for familiar faces was connected with an identification with the lost objects and with feelings weighed down by them. One patient said, "I have my father and mother on my shoulders. They were giants, but I am so small. How can I carry the burden?" In therapy, patients expressed feelings that in spite of the separation through death, they experienced their families as with them. They remembered their parents as eternally young and their friends as beautiful heroes, and so they cherished them in their memories. The inability to relinquish these images was connected with a vague feeling of still being with them, of being accused of not taking revenge. We observed in many cases that these ambiguous feelings were an expression of unfinished mourning; the perished beloved ones became introjects who punished, accused, and rejected as parents from whom one could not totally separate nor accept their deaths. The inability to mourn and take revenge during this period was therefore intimately and directly connected.

In many fantasies of the survivors, the Nazi aggression was associated with a sadistic sexual violation since the SS often called the female camp inmates "whores." Some survivors denied any sadness or loneliness by acting out with sexually aggressive behavior toward German women as an attempt to "avenge," in their words, their mothers and sisters who in their minds had been destroyed by the Nazis. In the therapy of these individuals, not only a regression of the superego could be observed but also a temporary regression of the long repressed psychosexual drives. They had regressed to the anal-sadistic stage, identifying with the aggressor, especially those young adults who had been adolescents during the Holocaust and had had to repress all aggressive and sexual drives. Also observed was a tendency to behave in an adolescent manner, with a polarization of affects, extreme ventilation of emotions, changes in mood and style, from ascetic self-flagellation (connected with survivor guilt for being too passive, not saving their parents, having stayed alive) to loss of control, impulsive and aggressive behavior toward their peers, and manic fantasies of omnipotence, fantasies of being a savior in which they were saved and were saving others.

For the religious, the inability to mourn was also associated with the inability to say *Kaddish*, which they rationalized by claiming ignorance of the time and the place of their parents' and siblings' deaths. This inability to accept the deaths and to mourn was accompanied by unsuccessful attempts at introjections of parental representations, with the expressions of repetitive self-punishment, psychosomatic complaints, fear of being "intoxicated by hatred," and accident-prone behavior. Many experienced repeated accidents or confrontations with border police or guards in an attempt to now overcome their passivity and triumph over the official authorities. These attempts were largely unsuccessful, due to the compulsion to be the helpless victim.

Others tried to adopt an attitude of "Let us forget and enjoy life", but they failed. This attitude was connected with an avoidance or denial of their losses, again an inability to mourn. Interpersonal relations in these cases were characterized by superficiality, an inability to sustain long commitments and stable relationships, and an eternal search for the idealized object representation in the partner. The disappointment that the new partner did not have the same idealized qualities of the lost object was expressed in therapy by "She is not as good as my mother" or "He is not as strong and loving as my father." These people, who experienced the destruction of everything they have loved and believed in, lived in an emotional and social vacuum in which they could express neither emotion nor love. For many, clinging to another partner meant an attempt to escape from the loneliness.

It was as if time had stood still and the missed adolescence and the eternal struggles were reawakened in them as before the Holocaust. One could therefore experience the cohesiveness in groups of survivors that was experienced as an extended family, with an exaggerated search for a partner and the inability to be alone. On the one hand, there was a general atmosphere of clinging to the old rituals among the survivors, associated with memories of home, although the religious belief was lost. On the other hand, the same people could exhibit a bold cynicism toward tradition, laws, and society in their countries or in Germany, which they viewed as corrupt and criminal.

The pogrom in Kielce, Poland, in 1946 marked a turning point in the confrontation of the remnants of infiltrated Nazi hate combined with traditional Polish anti-Semitism. It disillusioned those survivors who had wished to participate in the rebuilding of socialist Poland and led to an emotional upheaval as a result of the conflicts between the old socialist ideals and ideology and the adolescent self-idealization of being the ones to liberate the Poles together with the Jews. The atmosphere of anti-Semitic hatred after the liberation from the common Nazi enemy was for many the final straw. The whole *Zeitgeist* was connected with temporary arrangements, temporary relationships, living out of suitcases, but with a total commitment and investment in the future, which was idealized and distant. People living in German DP camps or in their previous homes in Czechoslovakia, Poland, Romania, or Russia and the occupied territories of Ukraine and Lithuania re-experienced the hatred of their surroundings that intensified their desire to leave the gigantic graveyard of Europe. In western European countries such as France and Holland, the remnants of Jews also experienced disappointment in meeting their former neighbors, with their suspicions and non-empathetic attitudes. They had anticipated a hero's welcome but experienced neutral and often hostile behavior from the people who were afraid that they would now have to return apartments, jobs, and belongings that had been stolen by the collaborators and Quislings. Particularly in France, many had identified with the Petain ideology, and the traditional anti-Semitism influenced the attitude of a significant part of the population to the returning survivors.

The psychological atmosphere of the survivors was therefore largely connected with anticipating the emigration and what would follow. Many survivors ignored the existing boundaries between their efforts to save what remnants of their people they could. They crossed borders compulsively and continually as if to compensate for the immobility and lack of freedom that was imposed on them during the Holocaust. There was almost playfulness in the undoing of the helplessness of survivor guilt in the confrontation with danger that they could still manage in the border crossings, with the cheating of the uniformed border guards and feelings of triumph in bringing colleagues and families out of Poland and the other occupied territories. One patient told me with satisfaction of how within six months of his liberation he crossed the borders of Czechoslovakia and Poland eight times and brought many friends, relatives, and unknown fellow Jews to Germany, always under difficult circumstances, false papers, and covers. It gave him a feeling of being a savior and of undoing the guilt he suffered for not having saved his loved ones during the deportation when his parents were taken and killed before his eyes.

Most survivors waited with their luggage in the camps for the possibility of an overseas visa to the United States or England, where they could find a framework of strength and security. For these people, the idea of a Jewish homeland brought associations of further enclosure and of another form of the ghetto. Others participated actively in the Zionist movement, disillusioned with the possibility of living together with non-Jews as equal citizens of Europe. The Yiddish song "*Ich kume a Heim*" (I'm coming home) became popular and expressed a longing for a familiar atmosphere. The song "*Ich vil nicht zein a Ger*" (I don't want to be a stranger) expressed the discontent with the DP camps and being an eternal wanderer. Zionism provided a goal for expressing the legitimate anger against the nations of the world, particularly toward Great Britain, which with the White Book had stifled the possibility of unlimited immigration to Palestine. England was thus viewed as punitive and identified with the image of an aggressor, not allowing the Jews to "return home."

Palestine was seen as an idealized fantasyland where survivors could fulfill their needs for basic trust, security, and an all-embracing love—the real primary motherland. This fantasy was a continuation of those fantasies experienced during the Holocaust—the image of Palestine was of a colorful utopian land where a cohesive love and a new beginning could be found, without hatred or aggression, an image that provided survivors with strength and a purpose to survive.

Chapter 7:
Encounter: The Survivor versus Society

From the beginning of recorded history, we can observe the meeting between society and human beings who have experienced disasters and survived. A wide range of interpersonal relations and a variety of intense emotional responses are manifest on both sides. The theme of survival is seen in the Old Testament story of Noah as the only survivor of the flood as well as the savior-survivor relationship classically presented in the story of Abraham and the "sinful survivors" of Sodom. And there is the story of Lot's wife, who kept looking back and eventually, as a result, was transformed into a pillar of salt.

Mankind has always been fascinated by the possibility of life after a cataclysm, and the survivor became a symbol in manifold expressions of his rebirth and regaining a new life but also as the "guilty one" who survived destruction of his world and kin by the graceful mercy of the Lord. By staying alive, the survivor is required to accept the price of survival—the existential guilt projected onto him by the non-survivor, the observer.

It seems that society as such—individuals and groups—is afraid of the survivor who awakens guilt and fear in them, guilt for not having actively intervened and fear of the possibility of experiencing the same fate. Hence the fascination and the repulsion connected with Holocaust survivors that manifested themselves in two generations of silence and avoidance and were followed by the sudden flood of popularization and banalization in the media and the parlor talk of society.

First, the survivor was seen as a kind of toxic object that could contaminate society with the extremity of his horrific experiences. He was a disturber of peace and feelings of security. He represented the possibility of chaos and disintegration of society, which is avoided and denied by every false and illusory means. One way of dealing with the survivor in ancient times was as a "messenger of evil tidings." In Greek mythology, this messenger was often sacrificed to the gods; in short, killed. Similarly, in Jewish history, when the messenger of Saul brought news of Jonathan's death, King David punished him.

The survivor was also seen as a lunatic or a *nebbish*, arousing pity without empathy. In such a way, ambivalence toward the survivors is changed into something more acceptable to society. The Judeo-Christian tradition of charity and reparation can be seen as an expression of guilt. In Jewish families in Europe, the United States, and Israel, the conflicting ambivalent feelings between loyalty and fidelity to one's own murdered families left in Nazi Europe were very often connected with guilt feelings and vague fears of vengeance. Thus, the desire to make reparations of some sort functioned as an avoidance of the real confrontation with survivors themselves.

In Israel, society tried to come to terms with the Holocaust and its survivors in different ways. For many years, Israeli society stressed the heroism of the struggle and resistance in the ghettos rather than dealing with the concept of survival as a positive value. Heroic resistance and the partisans' active fighting were overstressed as a leitmotif of the Holocaust rather than relating to motivations and trials of survivors as individuals and groups. The actual fact of survival and the reality of different modes of survival were thus denied. This can be seen in the ritualized Holocaust Memorial Day and in the symbolic name given to a kibbutz in Israel established after the war by survivors—kibbutz of the ghetto fighters. This was an integral part of the desired self-image and a challenge to Israeli society.

Furthermore, only after thirty-five years as a state can we begin to relate to the Holocaust without idealizing survival as representing only "fighting and resistance," as the only accepted legitimate form of survival. An important expression of this change of attitude now, after thirty-five years, is seen in the first systematic preparation of a curriculum and teaching the Holocaust in Israeli high schools and universities and the establishment of special faculties and institutes for Holocaust studies (Ettinger and Arieli, 1969/1970), treating the subject without ritualization and avoidance.

The tendency throughout the years has been to ritualize and memorialize the Holocaust as an historic event without relating to the survivors. In many circles, the survivors were seen as "bad, guilt-ridden, envious, jealous, greedy for compensation, imposters, overbearing," etc. As individuals, they aroused in non-survivors a diversity of feelings from shame, pity, and guilt to anger and irritation, very much as non-Jews saw Jews. This attitude was connected with the fact that the original European non-survivor population in Israel had left their families behind in Europe before the Holocaust and very often in a personal conflict situation. These families left behind were murdered in the camps while they enjoyed normal lives, though they were helpless and passive in the face of the tragedy.

Confrontation with survivors awakened in them guilt and ambivalent feelings toward their murdered families. In actual fact, the motivation to leave Europe and come as pioneers to Palestine was connected with their conflicted and ambivalent feelings toward their families, the Diaspora communities, and the way of life they had rejected as not gratifying their basic needs. The need to create a new pioneering society was a manifestation of this dissatisfaction, with the rejection of the way of life of the parents in the *shtetls* of Central and Eastern Europe.

The children of these parents who had left Europe before the Holocaust for Palestine as pioneers and confronted after the Holocaust with the survivors on their arrival in Israel often took the stance of blaming them. They saw them as being responsible for their fate by not having come to Palestine before the Holocaust, as their parents had done, and some even went as far as to say paradoxically that their fate was a punishment. This again is a manifestation of projection of the unresolved guilt of their parents toward their murdered families whom they had left behind in Europe.

The survivors pouring in from the DP camps of Europe appeared in the eyes of their brothers in Palestine as actively preparing to fight for the survival of the new reborn Jewish state, as unfortunate remnants of a generation that had passively accepted its fate. The image was that of a shameful remnant speaking Yiddish, the language of the despised European Diaspora and thus also representing a throwback to the generation of their fathers whom they had rejected. In psychodynamic terms, we see here the badly disguised internal representation of the Jew as a bad object of self-hatred and self-condemnation projected onto the survivors.

In Israel, the return of the survivors from the countries of death brought back the long repressed conflicts and ambivalent feelings of many of the non-survivors from similar backgrounds toward their childhood homes and families. This is a theme frequently encountered in the family therapy of survivors when one survivor projects his own guilt and anger as well as rescue fantasies onto his own spouse. In "mixed" marriages between survivor and non-survivor, the wishes for compensation are expressed by the survivor in intense ways, arousing anger and hostility and resulting in sadomasochistic relationships.

The deep need of the Jewish people to save and rescue connected with guilt was expressed on a social level in the momentous organization of "*Escape-Briha*." In this epic phenomenon, tens of thousands of survivors were rescued and smuggled from Eastern European countries via DP camps to Palestine as a kind of posthumous act of saving, which served rehabilitation of the self-image of the guilty non-participant observer. The need to rescue the Jewish remnants from Eastern Europe was fully vindicated in the pogroms set up by the Polish and Ukrainian local populations with anti-Jewish propaganda during the Nazi occupation. In the chaotic situation of Eastern Europe, survivors were occasionally even tragically suspected of being collaborators of the Nazis.

The survivors, on the other hand, accepted the idealized *Sabra* image of the active, tough supermen, the "sons of freedom," but this acceptance was not without envy and jealousy for not having had the same experiences of upbringing in freedom.

These mutual false images changed only through a painful longitudinal process that integrated the two groups, with common achievements and joy, pioneering and fighting together in wars and, of special significance, the common losses and common mourning. The high point in this process was the Yom Kippur War in which a new identity was forged for Israeli society, neither hero nor victim but rather the antithesis of a hero-victim bondage.

On the one hand, *Sabra* Israelis were contemptuous of the Diaspora behavior and the language (Yiddish) of their brothers from the concentration camps. On the other hand, the fact of their being survivors was often overlooked and avoided, and they were welcomed as equal citizens sharing in the common struggle of the state for survival and building up. The reality of Israel's plight of being surrounded by enemies served as a justification and rationalization of this paradoxical and ambivalent position with regard to the survivors. This avoidance of recognizing the Holocaust background of the survivors in everyday life was evident, for example, in the lack of official registration of their survivor identity on their arrival in Israel.

The leadership of the *Jischuv* (Jewish Community in Palestine) felt guilt and failure in the face of ineffective action. The horror of the experiences and fantastic losses of the Jewish people in the Holocaust led to the shocks of confrontation with the total and overwhelming defeat of the Jewish people and massive collective denial and avoidance of the general population in Palestine, which they shared with the Diaspora communities in the West (Goldman, 1979).

The reaction of Israeli writers to the Holocaust and to survivors during the first twenty years, which only very few people could relate to the Holocaust, was a consequence of their own inability to mourn. The exception was the poet Abraham Schlonski (1971) and others. Only during the last decade began the slow confrontation with the painful identification with the victim, particularly in Yoram Kaniuk's description of the whole of Israel as a madhouse in *Adam as Dog* (1968). Amos Oz in *Under This Blazing Light* (1979) referred to the problems of the Holocaust and the survivors in an allegorical form but not without a great deal of ambivalence. Both related to the desolation, the pain, and the madness of the survivors and their effects on society. The only real confrontation with survivors that was written by a survivor was that of Aaron Appelfeld (1979), who described in a complex, understated way the experiences of the survivor during the Holocaust and his relationship with the nonsurvivor during the time of the struggle for independence in Israel. He wrote of the confrontation of the survivor with the harsh *Sabra*, transforming the experience of his own cultural inferiority into a rich psychological study of the demeaning trials of Israeli society in *Badenheim*.

Another aspect of post-Holocaust traumatization was the accepted notion of the Holocaust victims as sheep passively going to their deaths. This was the feeling of many *Sabras* during the Independence War—a feeling of active superiority over the survivor. In their eyes and in their active stance, it was a socially "improper behavior" on the part of the survivor. In the eyes of the people, whose slogan was "never again," the survivor was invested with a negative valence as a passive, traumatized pariah who could perhaps be rehabilitated as a "desert generation" but whose children could gain the freedom and the normalcy from their acceptance into Israeli society. These transactions led to the acceptance of a kind of "shamed secret" among the survivors and the ritualization of the Holocaust rather than an ability to empathize with the survivor's experience. Ironically, only the Eichmann trial and the Yom Kippur War awakened society's previously denied feelings, finally allowing mourning and an identification with the survivors of the Holocaust catastrophe, consequently leading to the self-affirmation of society itself as survivors of the catastrophe.

Premature diplomatic relations with Germany, accepted by the majority of the *Jischuv*, were also experienced by the survivors as traumatic, awakening in them disturbing memories of the past and a deep sense of alienation from the society. This alienation was reminiscent of their feelings of having been forgotten and sacrificed in the isolation of the ghettos. In time, these feelings changed as they confronted the new reality of Germany and the efforts of its people, particularly Brandt's acceptance of the collective shame of his country toward the survivor. A process of working through began in which anger was differentiated—directed toward the Nazis rather than to individual Germans.

The process of the ritualization of the Holocaust was experienced as traumatic and demanding—marking off one day a year that was experienced by the masses in Israel as a kind of fossil and paradigm of Jewish persecution in general. This feature changed somewhat during the last two decades, promoted mainly by the Eichmann trial—the first major confrontation with the reality of the Holocaust, allowing for some identification on the part of Israelis with the survivors. It was also the temporal distance from the event that enabled greater psychological closeness to the Holocaust, especially for the younger generations who began to study the Holocaust from elementary school to post-graduate studies. During the last two decades, more and more non-survivors accepted the study of the Holocaust as a legitimate instrument to achieve their own Jewish or Israeli identity.

In many respects, the survivors were seen by Israelis as having refused to leave the "fleshpots" of the Diaspora in spite of humiliation, persecution, and imitative assimilation. In America, the Jews, as a result of their guilt and pragmatic values, related to the survivors at the same time in such a way as to help them help themselves but without allowing them to mourn adequately. They asked of the survivors, "Why are you crying? You came to the Golden Land and now you should forget your past problems of pain, suffering, and evil." In America, the survivors built their own communities in the spirit of *Landsmannschaften*, without identifying themselves with American Jewry, yet idealizing Israel and its struggle for emancipation. They still had the feeling of themselves as being the uprooted shuffling debris of traumatic experiences, focusing with pride on their children in an attempt to revive a feeling of their own moral superiority—their children would be better off than the others.

Still, there was a historical difference in the transformation of their identity in America as opposed to Israel in spite of their common background and experience. In Israel, the survivors arrived at a time when their own personal fantasies of rebirth coincided with the fantasized and realized establishment of the old/new homeland. The vicissitudes in the historical development of Israel with its many wars led to a greater sense of a common fate of the survivors as Jews who were confronted with the repetitive danger of death and annihilation, if not of themselves, then of their sons. In therapy with Israeli survivors, the repetitive motif of the hero was often heard who, confronted with death, was born again and was now confronted with the threat of the death of his own son. In addition, in Israel, more than in America, the Holocaust became more and more a part of the cultural and national heritage, which could not be avoided, confronted with the daily associations to the Holocaust in the media and the newspapers. Different from Israel, the children of the survivors in the United States, with greater stabilization of their family life, had much more ability to mourn the losses in a way that their parents were unable to do. They often saw themselves as children of survivors, while in Israel, the survivors' children accepted the common fate and identity of Israel and were more often faced with the mourning for those who fell in the wars.

I observed a kind of painful bitterness in survivors when asked by a non-survivor, "Why did you go to the slaughter like sheep?" This was the repetitive question asked by those who were shocked that survivors were passive victims in confrontation with the mass murders by the Nazis. This expression of ignorance on the part of the Israeli population was a consequence of the official curriculum of the school system where little was taught about the daily existence and the individual motivations for survival during the Holocaust. The survivor emotionally accepted the question as an accusation and rejection, awakening in him the eternal questions toward the population: "Where were you when we were being murdered. How could you enjoy life as if nothing was happening when you had the information of what was happening to your families in Europe? How could you organize a festival in kibbutz *Gehlia* while the remnants of the Warsaw Ghetto were fighting for their lives and the pride in the eternity of Israel?"—as it was expressed in the last letter of Mordecai Anieliwicz to the leaders of the kibbutzim in Palestine (1943).

Such confrontations have been typical of many of the dialogues between the survivors and the non-survivors, in which unconscious feelings of envy and greed were associated on the part of the non-survivors toward the survivors who received indemnification money from the German government. The fantasies often were that the survivors were becoming wealthy and established, different from themselves. Paradoxically, the small reparation was given to the survivor only when he could show that he was physically or emotionally injured, which was often experienced as a painful admission that Hitler's goal was achieved in their psychological destruction.

A painful chapter of retraumatization of the survivor is that of the process of restitution and indemnification. These experiences of restitution were part of a chain of post-Holocaust traumatizations, as many survivors reacted to the formal examination during the restitution process with anguish, based as they were on anachronistic theories of traumatization (Kretschmer, Bonhoeffer, and Schneider) of ignorant psychiatrists in the United States, Israel, and Germany. Because of the lack of empathy on the part of the psychiatrists, the survivors reacted with psychotic-like states, feeling in these encounters a repetition of their persecution. The psychiatrists, due to their own guilt and the need for a socially neutral position vis-à-vis the survivor, resorted to formal conceptualizations of the nature of traumatization, which gave them security and enabled them to avoid their identification with the victim. They covered up their feelings of shame and anger, which awakened in them the need for denial and an absolute objectivity in their approach to the problems of the survivors.

American Jewry related to the survivor with mixed feelings. On the one hand, there was an uncanny identification with the survivor as the ghost who came from the world of the beloved *shtetl*, but also the ghost coming from the *Gehlia*. This accounted for their psychological solidarity with the survivor but also for the banalization of the refugee with whom they had a familiarity and cultural and emotional intimacy. They could not grasp the polarized differences between the two prototypes of the survivor as the one running away from the pogroms but having an intact community and the man returning from another planet whose whole world had vanished. Therefore, in America, the shameful secret was the unspoken compromise not to relate to the emotional conflict between the two communities. Also in America, the survivor became a symbol of what they were afraid of in themselves—the victim fearing destruction.

The motivation of many survivors coming to Israel was the expectation of normalcy—that they would be given the guarantee of security, if not for themselves, then for their children. Paradoxically, Israel was the only country where survivors had awakened in them the old insecurities and patterns of surviving with the investment of old boundaries between themselves and the outer world—"We have to be strong and fight so that we can live." Thus, their dreams during the Holocaust of returning to a world devoid of hatred and war, where humanity had learned its lessons, were not fulfilled. They became disillusioned by the repeated wars with the Arabs and the deaths of so many children, robbing them of their naive hope for a world of justice and peace and the disappearance of the need for one country to scapegoat another.

In some survivors, the feeling of being special played a role in the complex feelings associated with their answering the question, "Why did I survive?" Some felt that they survived because their parents loved them. In their magical thinking, they believed that if it had not been for their parents' prayers, they would have died. We hear this rationale from the non-religious as well as the religious survivors: "Someone prayed that I should live."

Among the hundreds of survivors that I interviewed and who were in therapy with me, there were common emotions related to their survival—the bitterness and the pain felt in the relation of the society to the survivor. They were often asked the question, "Why did you stay alive?" with a kind of suspicion that they had done something wrong or immoral in order to survive: "You betrayed your family and community in order to stay alive."

Alexander Solzhenitsyn describes the Russian prisoners of war returning to society, faced with the feeling that they were traitors—that they should have died, not come back—and awakened in them unrest and guilt. The survivor is like the ghost coming back from the grave, awakening in society a feeling of discomfort and guilt and awakening in them the question, "What did I do for my family which stayed in Europe?" The reaction of the community was in a way an effort to rigidify their defenses to further avoid their survivor guilt.

I remember Ben Gurion speak about the fight against the White Book and the British at the Congress of *Sherit Habeta* ("The Remnants of

Those Who Saved Themselves") in January 1946. He did not express one word of sympathy toward the survivors of the Holocaust. This great man could not share the grief and the bereavement; he denied any mourning, serving as an example to a whole nation that turned the Holocaust into a shameful secret, not to cry about the past but to look toward the future. This psychological mystery had an important impact on the situation that was to follow. He could not understand that only through mourning was there the possibility of liberating the forces for emotional investment, for building, for sharing, and for joy. The pairing of this denial with the mobilization of the forces to fight has led to the "as if" situation in Israel today. A nation invested everything in fighting and action at the expense of being. He did not allow the people to mourn, in spite of the phrase "We are the special nation," and therefore the first expression of real mourning did not begin until the Yom Kippur War—a late and delayed mourning, and I should add, a kind of pathological mourning.

We observed the disappointment and bitterness of the survivor in America as well as in Israel, having been called a *Pleita*—a displaced person—a label associated with negative feelings. When asked the question, "Who are you?" the collective reaction of the survivors was frequently "I am a survivor." Often the whole identity was connected with survival. Later they might speak of being Israeli, American, or Jewish. But the most important feature of their identity was that of being a survivor—with both negative and positive valences toward this identity, which therefore influenced the survivor's approach to life and to society. Working with survivors in psychoanalysis who have important roles in society—professionals, high-ranking officials, and industrialists—we see the importance of being successful, of not being a burden, and of having overcome death. But it is also important for them not to rise to the highest strata of society. This may be a reflection of a coping mechanism, which was important during the Holocaust: not to expose oneself too much so as not to put oneself in a situation of danger. Thus, survivors attempted to place themselves within the spectrum of the society in which they were neither on top nor on the lower levels. In the ghetto and the concentration camp, it was important not to be exposed, not to exhibit one's special features because on account of them one could be killed. One's chances of survival were better when one was a part of an anonymous whole.

Another collective observation of the survivor was the expectation of a special life after the Holocaust. There were many restitution fantasies about life after the war—of becoming an exceptional person. Often you heard these persons claiming to have two birthdays—one being their own natural birthday and the other the day of their liberation, their rebirth. Associated with the fantasies of rebirth was the expectation of having a wonderful fulfilling life where society would be good, where there would be no wars, aggressors, fascism, or interpersonal aggression. They were tremendously disappointed when later they found their life to be a struggle. Although the wars in Israel were experienced as such a disappointment, it did however give them a chance to fight with weapons for their new country, for their home, and for their children. In such a way, it gave them an opportunity for restitution.

Now we observe a different situation, with survivors in mid- and later-life struggling with the reality of their children leaving home—their children who have been such a positive part of themselves. The old feelings of having been left return. Often heard is the expression of disappointment that this was not the kind of world for which one had hoped; when this hope diminished with the confrontation with the reality of their situation that awakened in them the "normal miseries of life."

Chapter 8:
The Impact of the Psychosocial Environment: The Holocaust and the Yom Kippur War

Every age seems to pose its own characteristic questions, which every individual tries to answer in accordance with his *Weltanschauung*, personality, and profession. But the question, "Why the Holocaust?" has been relegated for decades to a corner of consciousness because of its extraordinarily complex humane, social, historical, and existential components and its universal aspects. We are still unable to approach or study those fateful years of the Nazi regime without the most intense emotions. The Holocaust is a repulsive and disgusting symbol, and it is for this reason that the world has refrained from relating to it with either intellectual or emotional honesty.

From a psychohistorical viewpoint, the few attempts to analyze and understand the behavior of the European Jew during the Holocaust have not been successful. The primary reason for that failure has been the inadequate consideration of the unconscious emotional motivations of the role and the behavior of the Nazi aggressor. Even more crucial has been the lack of basic knowledge and emotional awareness of the Eastern and Central European Jews as the objects of total aggression.

Such was the case with Bettelheim, who suggested that the Jewish leaders' refusal to recognize the Nazi reality—the persistent denial of its meaning, so pregnant with disaster—was the factor responsible for the inadequate reaction to the plan to annihilate the Jews. Hannah Arendt (1963) was another Jewish scientist who not only emphasized the passive role played by the Jewish community leaders and organizations in the success of Hitler's plans to exterminate the Jews. She also hurt the sensibilities of survivors by attempting to understand Eichmann, the incarnation of Nazism as a man. Gershom Scholem (1963), in his letter to Hannah Arendt, stressed her own emotional ambivalence toward Jewry and Zionism as the source of her approach to the Holocaust.

It is important to stress that finding inaccuracies in a thesis does not invalidate the thesis entirely. Freud's assumption of the concept of psychic energy, one of the fundamental principles of the psychoanalytic theory, had its source in the rational *Zeitgeist* and in Helmholtz's inspirational effect on science at the beginning of the twentieth century. These assumptions regarding the existence of dynamic and static energy operant in mental processes have contributed greatly to the understanding of emotional processes and thereby to the psychoanalytic process and clinical observations, in spite of the problems they raised.

Although it is difficult to judge such theses about attitudes of individuals, families, and groups under oppression, specifically the Jews in the Holocaust, such theses do have value. They not only relate to various psychosocial causes that might facilitate an historical assessment but also shed light on the psychic processes of the individual, the family, the group, and the nation, in the past and the present. Because the Holocaust has had strong ongoing effects on both Jews and non-Jews, understanding the psychosocial background of the greatest catastrophe of all mankind, the catastrophe in which the Jewish nation became the scapegoat of the projection of internal bad self-representations for the European nations is of utmost importance.

This attempt to understand the psychosocial background of the Holocaust must be made in spite of the fact that in interpreting the events of the Holocaust, one exposes oneself to the pressures of one's own present conflict situations with their fantasized and real threats of extermination. Such threats and intrapsychic conflicts place psychological and emotional demands on the interpreter to view the past according to his present self-ideal. There is therefore a tendency in us to avoid and deny certain painful confrontations between our own inner life and the historical realities of the Holocaust as well as present-life situations in Israel and the Jewish Diaspora. It is for this reason that attempts at analogies are psychologically stressful. The repetitious use of the term *Holocaust* by prominent leaders in Israel in dealing with political confrontations with the Arab neighbor was especially painful and traumatizing for survivors.

The ongoing effects of the Holocaust on the Jewish people are seen particularly clearly in the conscious and unconscious behaviors of the Israeli people—both Holocaust survivors and the general population. An attempt must therefore be made to understand the basic emotional problems of the Jewish population during and after the Holocaust and connect that with the psychosocial causes of Israeli attitudes—both individual and societal—toward the Holocaust.

Observations based on clinical work and on formal and informal meetings with various people who have experienced either the Holocaust or the wars of Israel as well as with outside observers, both Jews and non-Jews, have revealed various basic psychohistorical and dynamic aspects of the Holocaust, which have had an intense effect on the Israeli people. The unrest and the anxiety in Israel about individual futures as well as the future of the nation and of mankind seem to be not wholly connected to the political reality of Israel but also with feelings of anxiety and basic loss of security, which have been repressed deep within all Israelis as a result of their fear of identifying with a downtrodden nation. There seems to be a fear that the sorrow and the distress incurred by such identifications might cause them to develop a defeatist ideology such as that of various defeated nations, including their own, at various periods of history (e.g., the Messianic movements of Frank and Shabtai Zvi, as well as the Morranos, both of which made their appearances after periods of Jewish genocide).

During the Yom Kippur War, Israeli soldiers were concerned with the relationship to the Holocaust, whether consciously or unconsciously. The Israeli population as a whole is still concerned with the Holocaust—even more so since the Yom Kippur War than during previous years—and this concern finds expression in Israeli psychological and psychopathological make-ups, in individual experiences, in interpersonal relationships, and in public lives.

The depression manifested in the atmosphere of crisis and lack of Israeli self-confidence years after the Yom Kippur War is not connected solely with the actual political and economic situation of Israel but also stems, at least partially, from an entire generation's denial and avoidance of the problems of the Holocaust. These defenses were probably due to an overwhelming fear of identifying with the defeated nation at a time when the Israeli people needed to call forth all their positive psychological forces—libidinal, vital, and inner sources of hope in order to build the new Israeli society.

In an attempt to better understand these forces and relationships, I will describe what I term the *Holocaust complex* or the *Holocaust syndrome*, that complex of feelings and/or emotions related to the occurrence and the fear of the recurrence of the Holocaust.

For nearly fifty years, neither the survivors of the Holocaust, throughout the Diaspora, nor the Israeli nation was able to relate to what had happened to their people in Europe. Such a confrontation, however, is a vital first step in the lengthy process of working through the experience and its consequences.

In 1973, the Yom Kippur War, despite its being different from the Holocaust in both essence and degree, caused a narcissistic trauma to the Israelis who experienced it as an additional cataclysmic experience. It caused the Israelis to gradually face, confront, and work through their actual, immediate losses and mourning, as well as those of the Holocaust, which until then had been avoided or repressed.

Attempts to understand the reasons for the defeats and the failures of Israel during the Yom Kippur War necessitated the confrontation with emotional forces that most individuals and groups preferred to consciously ignore or unconsciously resist with the defense mechanisms of repression, denial, and avoidance, just as, in contrast, the German nation found it difficult for many years to accept a collective blame and shame. Heuss, the first postwar president of the German Republic and himself a liberal intellectual, differentiated between collective guilt and collective shame, saying that the German people were not willing to accept a collective guilt, although they did accept a collective shame. For a long time, the Jewish people could not consciously realize the collective feeling of a national disaster as an expression of common destiny.

In contrast to the "relative psychosocial mental health" of the German public today and its uncommonly swift return to a normal social and political course of human society, the inability of Israelis to experience the real destruction of the Holocaust, to truly mourn the dead on an individual and collective level, kept them from experiencing personal and national security.

The inability of the German public to accept guilt seems to me to be related to their inability to mourn, as Mitscherlich described in his book *The Inability to Mourn* (1967). He describes the stagnation of German psychic life and creativity as resulting from this inability. In comparing the two groups that "experienced" the Holocaust, it is evident that the German public as a whole (with certain exceptions) and after their massive expression of aggression and hostility—and after their *Nibelungian* catharsis—made use of collective denial, avoidance, and repression of guilt. These defenses, in addition to their inability to confront their own fathers who perpetrated the aggression, seem only now to have late effects on the German psychosocial reality. It is particularly expressed in the psychological conflicts of the postwar generation and their pronounced fears and obsessive anxieties about the atom bomb as if it were a late punishment for their fathers' guilt. Modern German terrorism seems to be a displacement of aggression from their own murderous fathers to the society at large, with the ultimate false self-realization of their image as fighters for absolute justice as the expression of their primitive, archaic superego in the acting out of their aggressive drives.

These mechanisms of suppression, denial, and removal of conflict were in the service of the collective ego, as we would expect, in order to avoid collective guilt and shame, which would then go hand in hand with a need for self-punishment, and in order to refine aggression in the direction of mastery, a trait that seems to be entrenched in the collective German character.

It seems obvious that the collective "superego" of the German people underwent far-reaching changes during the course of the Holocaust. The psychological mechanisms responsible for these processes were twofold: the projective identification with the projection of the internal bad object onto the Jew as an object of aggression and an exchange of the human object of aggression (the Jew) for the dehumanized, inhuman one. In Nazi jargon, the Jews were referred to as "vermin" in such a way as to justify the outbursts of aggressive drives.

Epidemiological and statistical studies of the relatively low incidence of depressive states and attempted suicides in Germany, especially in that part of the population involved in war crimes, indicated that payment of monetary compensation, with its symbolic meaning, eradicated the need for individual processes of involvement and guilt feelings by enabling the German people to deny and avoid the issues of responsibility and guilt. Furthermore, it is obvious that the Germans fantasized collective identification with the *Führer*-aggressor during the Nazi regime as a means of survival. Thus, they had the conscious belief of being protected from the Bolshevik plutocratic Jewish aggressors in the outer world and unconsciously from the omniscient *Führer*, who could destroy them if they were not obedient.

With the changing world perspectives during the last decade, there are a greater number of voices in the German intellectual community who are willing to relate to and confront themselves with the complex problem of guilt in relation to the Holocaust and thus liberate themselves from lingering images of the past. The themes of mourning, bereavement, and restoration, as suggested by Martin Wangh (1968), are dealt with in different ways by the German psychoanalytic societies, often with serious and painful attempts at delayed mourning. Studies of children of Nazis in the psychoanalytic literature have also shed light on the inner world of today's middle-aged men and women who have accepted their responsibility.

By contrast, the mechanisms of denial, avoidance, and repression did not effectively benefit the Jewish people as a collective unit (the object of the aggression), for they provided no relief from their distress and the feeling of insecurity—in spite of Israel's national successes. Israel's successes and victories, both peaceful and military, as it gradually built up and fulfilled its self-ideal, provided neither a complete catharsis nor a means of re-establishing basic trust and fundamental principles. It is this fact that at least partly explains the appearance of hesitation and obsessive self-doubt during and after the Yom Kippur War and still does so today. These doubts are expressed in the media and manifested in the "internal wars of the Jews," which seem to be a part of the Jewish psycho-historical reality throughout the ages.

During more than forty years of Israel's existence, the Holocaust was a part of life that Israelis felt ashamed of, needed to forget, and avoided to get in touch with. Thus, even to this day, the Jewish people throughout the Diaspora, and especially in Israel, have been unable to decide whether or not to learn about the Holocaust should be an essential part of education and be taught in schools and if so, how. The root of this avoidance syndrome is Israel's need to build up its life and to repress those factors that might damage its enthusiasm and faith. This endeavor has caused a lack of memory of the Holocaust in the family constellation, in literature, state education, and all other modern means at the disposal of the nation. The Holocaust, therefore, became a nasty subject which, at its best, was transmitted through rituals and ceremonies, most of which are devoid of specific emotional content that would stimulate the participant to relate to, mourn, and identify with its existential meaning.

Toynbee (1975) proposed that Judaism is a "historical fossil"; in Israel, the Holocaust had become not only a "fossil" but also a "shameful secret"; it had undergone a process of banalization. The way the Holocaust had been related to within Israeli society—so different from the way Israel presented its problems to the rest of the world—clarifies the basic conflict of a nation that was undergoing a process of "rebirth" without having freed itself from an unconscious level of the "the Holocaust complex." The image of the Holocaust survivor was that of a refugee about whom there were questions and suspicions, both conscious and unconscious. "How is it that you were the one to survive?" "How could you remain human after what you went through?"

References to the period of the Holocaust in Israeli literature and folklore are mostly autobiographic sketches that only touch on descriptions of the cruelty of the aggressor, aspects of active heroism, revolt, and fighting that produced the "Heroism Myth" (the archetype of the active hero indifferent to the "passive" survivor).

In contrast to the myths of heroism during the Holocaust, the ability to survive and remain alive was considered to be the passive expression of servility and mal-adaptation to slavery. During the years after the Holocaust, when Israel gained its independence and the population rejoiced in its overabundance of self-security and self-acceptance, the myths of shameful defeat and "the lamb being led to the slaughter" became a part of the imagery of the survivor in the eyes of Israeli society. The rare references in Israeli literature (e.g., in the works of Gur, Megged, and Bartov) put greater emphasis on the negative aspects of Israeli reality, expressed by anxiety, pity, the attitudes of "blood (money) for blood," and the problem of the Israeli-born *Sabra* in identifying with his Holocaust survivor brothers. These writers deal with the inability of the *Sabra* and the survivor to communicate and consistently tend to overidealize the *Sabra* and his active struggle.

Another treatment of the subject, that of Appelfeld, is, on the other hand, an expression of protest against the over-emphasis of the "activist life" and the idealization of the War of Independence. In his work, however, the survivor is described as a man who tries to "escape" from the Holocaust and to identify himself with Israeli society but fails.

In the field of medicine and psychiatry, these attitudes toward the Holocaust found expression in both clinical work and research. In the 1950s, the examination, anamnestic data, and medical summaries barely recognized the etiological effect of the Holocaust experience on physical and mental illnesses. By contrast, in the 1960s, more attention was focused in clinical work and research on both the psychopathology of survivors of the Holocaust and the transmission of this pathology to the next generation. This newly developed scientific eagerness to learn about the problem of massive traumatization of the individual and the family has led many clinicians and researchers to give pre-eminence to the psychopathology, which is expressed by psychosocial regression during and after the Holocaust and by various symptoms that can be classified under the general heading of the post-KZ syndrome.

Whereas these psychopathological aspects have been emphasized, almost no attention has been given to the remarkable ways in which man is able to re-awaken himself and call upon healthy libidinal forces after a period of lengthy regression. In all psychiatric research, there has been almost no reference to the psychological strengths and achievements manifested in the fight for survival during and after the Holocaust, which alone enabled the inmate and later the survivor to remain alive. The lengthy chain of intrapsychic and existential struggles comprised complex processes of regression in the service of the ego as well as the use of fantasy as an ego-adaptive mechanism and means of defense against the chaotic situation that existed at the time of the Holocaust. These processes enabled a return to the internalized past as a source of shelter and security as well as hope for the future. These central aspects of hope that activated and mobilized vital forces were primary factors in the struggle against insecurity and a lack of basic trust. These intrapsychic strongholds enabled men, women, youth, and children to maintain their personal images and human characters in the face of a reality that surpassed the most sadomasochistic fantasies in the history of mankind.

These positive psychic processes also enabled Holocaust survivors to carry out their "rebirth fantasies" in reality, the importance of which should be emphasized in any discussion of the intrapsychic life of human beings during periods of both intrapsychic and external danger. My research in 1966–1967 and thereafter and theoretical works from 1970 onward have dealt with the place of fantasy and hope as mechanisms of re-adaptation and re-integration.

Clinical and therapeutic observations have shown that in spite of the basic and qualitative differences between the experience of the Holocaust and that of any present-day state of danger (whether during the Yom Kippur War or afterward), the automatic associations of Israelis—both as individuals wounded in battle and as a collective public—are with the threat of national extermination. This fear is evidenced by the Israelis' lack of faith in their ability to tolerate complex situations that have no immediate resolutions and that cannot be considered decisive and indisputable victories. This intolerance is fostered by the ideology that after the "deluge" of the Holocaust, any further collapses and failures cannot be tolerated and that Jews must therefore always fight, win, and conquer rather than take the passive role of the "sacrificial lamb." This education succeeded in providing us with a new generation of proud people who excel in their ability to successfully cope with stress situations of short durations. However, in the process of developing this ability, an even more valuable faculty had been lost—the ability to begin life anew, "to build and be built," and to develop psychological mechanisms that enable one to withstand continuous states of pressure, illness, injury, and loss while still maintaining faith in life.

In their phylogenetic and ontogenetic development, the Jews have always emphasized the value of life: "Choose life" (5. Mose 30, 19) was the source of the psychobiological survival of Holocaust survivors. It was the source of their ability—once physically free to renew themselves mentally and physically—to resume the development of the self, the self–ideal, and a new psychosocial framework, despite the specific regressive style of psychological adaptation, which they adopted during their years of internment as their means of survival.

During the Holocaust, one of the stumbling blocks of the Jewish nation was its adherence to an ideology that was no longer operative but gave some meaning to their experiences. Rather than face reality in an operative way, the Jewish leadership—due to the extreme psychological pressures of the Holocaust—adhered to pre-existing ideological and religious models that contained elements of omnipotence, magic, and Messianic sentiments ("I faithfully believe in the coming of the Messiah, and even though he tries us hard, I await him every day") or to a utopian socialist view of the "brotherhood of nations" model and the faith in men, all of whom were "created in the image of God." All of these models, as human history teaches us, were inappropriate to the actual situation during the Holocaust. As a result, the Jews had to live out their lives with no higher direction or purpose than their immediate biological survival as individuals and occasionally also groups.

The point of view that the myth of heroism and that of being resigned to sacrifice ("the sacrificial lamb") are diametrically opposed is incorrect both factually and historically. It has become evident that during the Holocaust, one's particular mode of response was entirely dependent upon personal, familial, geographical, and circumstantial factors. Moreover, most people who experienced the Holocaust went through various stages of oppression (ghetto, underground, partisans, work camps, and extermination camps), each with its own adaptive measures. Thus, the two responses of active rebellion and passive adaptation through withdrawal and regression were not opposite poles but rather interwoven and interchangeable.

Similarly, today, although the nurturing of a one-sided ideology that stresses extremes of emotional and physical activism may be suited to certain situations, it could prove to be inappropriate for long-term adaptation to situations of conflict and continuous pressure (Selye, 1950). The lesson to be learned from the past is the value of long-term psychosocial adaptation to long-term stress situations, with the development of specific ego-adaptive mechanisms for active short-term efforts. Such long-term adaptation that does not mobilize all of one's resources is in the service of continuous survival and allows for the regeneration of libidinal and creative processes of psychological development, rebirth, and renewal of the individual, family, and group. Furthermore, it is clear that in the Holocaust and in the war, both in active mastery, in fantasy and reality, and in interpersonal relationships as opposed to isolation and passivity, constitute a crucial factor in the release from the defeatist feeling of failure and hopelessness in individuals and groups.

In at least part of the Israeli population, the destruction of the myths about the Holocaust is already well under way. Today, due to a process that began during the Eichmann trial and reached its peak in the Yom Kippur War, it is not only the survivor who carries within himself the grief and awareness of the Holocaust. Both the trial and the War had a profound influence on the breakdown of the mutual alienation and isolation that existed between the Holocaust survivors and the rest of the Israeli population. Until then, that part of the Israeli population that had not experienced the Holocaust had kept an emotional and social distance between themselves and the survivors, partly because of their guilt feelings, apprehension, and unrecognized fears and partly because of a feeling of "moral superiority" as a new generation of active fighters. The gap between the two groups has since lessened as a result of the clarification of several myths, as well as an emphasis on the common fate of all Jewish people. In spite of the basic differences between the Holocaust and the Yom Kippur War, the latter transformed the relationship of world Jewry, and especially Israeli Jewry, to the Holocaust. The Yom Kippur War made the Holocaust not only a memory or an historical fact but, in the minds of many, an actual renewed possibility. The incubation of this process was hastened in the period of alert prior to the Six-Day War, but what happened for the first time in the Yom Kippur War since the creation of the state was a fantasized as well as a real possibility of defeat, with no particular expression of concern on the part of the rest of the world. It was this isolation that reawakened in Israelis the fear of helplessness, destruction, and extermination, basic affective states that until now psychiatrists in Israel have ignored. This time, however, the fears were eased by mutual feelings of belonging, partnership, and continuity of identity, which found expression in the attainment of the basic affect of hope in the individual as well as in the Israeli people as a group. Both the Holocaust and the Yom Kippur War, in spite of the essential differences between them, produced a common experience of national catharsis, which is still being experienced in its negative as well as positive aspects.

The negative aspect is the regressive response to danger manifested by fantasized and real feelings of isolation and heightened feelings of anxiety, leading to feelings of loneliness, omnipotence, magic powers, and aggression. Along with these feelings are avoidance of real mourning and bereavement and absence of hope, all of which lead to aggressive fantasies toward the outer world with chauvinistic solutions, creating a vicious circle of avoidance, hopelessness, and aggression, as it was experienced during the recent war in Lebanon.

On the other hand, the positive response to danger is the realistic, developmental one formed by common experiences of real and fantasized danger, common losses, and hopes, common experiences of death in the family, of friends, and in the nation (which in Israel was an extended family); common mastery; and common bereavements. Sharing these experiences brought about an awareness of the existential and historical aspects of the Holocaust, thereby causing both the survivors and the rest of the population to refute the stereotype of Holocaust victims being ghosts, heroes, saints, or sheep being led to the slaughter.

As a result of withstanding and adapting to the continuing pressures of the wars and the accompanying threat of extinction, collective patterns of emotional expressions of grief and mourning have developed in Israel, which, though personal in their source, are experienced by the group as a whole.

Our clinical and therapeutic work with people who have undergone traumatic experiences of catastrophic proportions, both in the Holocaust and in the Yom Kippur War, have indicated that the boundaries between destructive fantasies of one's internal reality and those experiences—either during the external realities of the War or the Holocaust—are not always clearly defined. The reason for this lack of distinction is that at times of personal and social catastrophes at various stages of our personal development and of the society, nation, and generation in which we live, each one of us needs to struggle with the "survivor" and the "aggressor" within himself. We are all survivors of various developmental crises during the course of our lives and some of us carry scars within our egos that are ineradicable. Despite this fact of previous regressions, we possess within us a potential for development and growth at later stages, a fact that psychiatrists, with their tendency to concentrate on psychopathological processes, sometimes forget. This capacity exists not only in individuals but also in groups and nations in which trauma, by its very nature, mobilized emotional strength and the development of appropriate ego-adaptive mechanisms. It is also important to stress that the self is influenced by actual object relationships and transcendental experiences and by the intense emotional experience of ego-mastery during war and peace and expectations and hopes for peace. The aggressive impulse is often not only an expression of destruction projected from ourselves onto the external world or merely an expression of the death wishes of the Thanatos instinct; it can also be an expression of self-assertion in the service of the ego—a means of release from a situation of helplessness and its concomitant hopelessness. When an element of hope and responsibility appears, whether this occurs within the psychosocial reality or within the psychotherapy itself, it is precisely at this point that we see a sublimated expression of aggression in the service of self-assertion and in the building of the personal, group, or national boundaries. It is this sublimated aggression that facilitates the emergence from a state of helplessness and hopelessness. Therefore, it is possible to see that aggression in the service of the ego and integrated in the self is expressed in situations following war or massive trauma by massive criticism of leaders, psychosocial structures, and ideologies that proved useless in solving current problems. Such criticism is expressed in psychoanalysis during the phases of re-integration or, in a psychosocial framework, in crisis situations. It is also expressed in individual psychosocial developmental phases of individuals, such as adolescence, or in group processes within the longitudinal history of mankind. Such expressions are legitimate early signs of renewal of positive ego forces of the individual and of the group. Thus, it is also probable that the post-Holocaust search for different ideologies and meanings that are suited to the new reality, as opposed to past realities, was an attempt to renew the collective superego in its value system via an assertive and executive approach to reality. This approach to reality was in opposition to the self-ideal of the Diaspora Jew as an introspective intellectual.

The structure of society allows for the expression of aggression in formalized and acceptable ways. Societal institutions such as political parties, the army, and demonstrations, as well as extreme criticism of past leaders all serve the need for idealization and projective identification of good and bad internal objects. The society and its institutions, including spontaneous political movements, provide people who have undergone massive traumatization with a representation and a means for expressing frustrations, hopes, and needs in order to eventually restore their basic security and trust. There seems to be a hidden collaboration, a collusion of anonymity—to use Michael Balint's term—in which the public institution or organization provides, through participation in its framework, a partial expression of the aggressive needs and behavioral patterns of the individual. These behavioral patterns may facilitate adaptation, defense, and also the release of repressed pressures and drives. There seem to be various ontogenetic factors and determinants for the expression of suppressed aggression of this type. Here, one may mention Waelder's idea that open aggression occurs precisely when external conditions of pressure and compulsion are partially or totally absent from the individual or the group and when the group has begun to receive a greater share of enjoyment and gratification.

In the same way in which each society develops social ceremonies designed to cope with crises and changes in life, so the Holocaust survivors in Israel developed means of dealing with their traumatic experiences. The open expression or group and community handling of the reality of the Holocaust in the lives of the survivors have enabled them to share the burden of their memories, lessened their feelings of inappropriate fear and secrecy, and enabled them to educate the new generation to accept their identity as children of Holocaust survivors without shame.

It must be stressed that these activities are not compulsive or exhibitionistic repetitions. Rather, they are a healthy way of coping with a traumatic reality within the framework of a renewed adaptation to life.

These group or community meetings have a strong liberating effect on the participants by giving them the opportunity to feel partnership with each other and continuity with their people. Such group experiences validate anew the positive value of life as part of the Jewish tradition in which survival and living are not a source of shame and guilt but positive commands: "and therefore choose life."

These group and community experiences, which are new to the Israeli public, have led to the exertion of community pressure on the state and its institutions to accept the existential significance of the Holocaust rather than relate to it as a negative symbol.

The ability to share a common sorrow engenders the ability to share hope and the fantasies of rebirth, expressions of healthy individual and group ego strengths. In times of catastrophe, entrenched fantasies seem to satisfy human needs and yearnings for basic security in spite of the knowledge that such fantasies are diametrically opposed to actual phenomena. The satisfaction of such fantasies derives from affects connected with repressed memories of childhood that have undergone idealization. Although there is some awareness of the unreality of these fantasies, that awareness does not disturb the feeling of security and the lessening of suffering. In times of crisis, it is also possible to see in the workings of fantasy signs of active and well-functioning ego processes that enable one to differentiate between the internal world of fantasy in which rules govern causality and reality in the memories of the pre-Holocaust and pre-War past and the external chaotic reality of aggression and suffering during the Holocaust and during the war.

Considering the intensity of their traumatic experiences, one may say that the survivors of the Holocaust have attained an adequate adaptation to their new lives. Nevertheless, the Holocaust remains in their conscious and unconscious lives, in their dreams and memories, and in their speech and associations. Moreover, it seems that "the Holocaust syndrome" is now a general experience of a large section of the Israeli population, which is evidenced in experiences of loss and mourning of the past and hope for the future. There is also a renewal process of individual and collective identification with the losses of the Holocaust, but along with this goes skepticism about the world outside Israel.

An interesting situation has arisen in Israel where the group, including the nation, identifies with the individual survivor of the war or the Holocaust. This process of group identification with the individual contains transactional qualities that provide simultaneous satisfaction for the individual and the group. It appears that this emotional process of national catharsis is still going on and will continue into the coming generation. This process, which includes the adaptation of the Holocaust survivors and the rest of the population to each other, is the basis for the resolution of the conflict where the guilt is attributed to either the survivors or the non-survivors. It stands for the anxiety in non-survivors—"It can also happen to us"—in regard to the Holocaust.

Although the process of mutual identification is in an early stage of development at this point, the present-day Israeli already has an awareness of the Holocaust that is sharper than during World War II or the years following it.

The Holocaust complex contains not only the negative ramifications of a lack of faith but also other aspects—mainly the heightened appreciation of the value of life. Acceptance of the Holocaust and the continuation of mourning as a common experience is enabling the present-day Israeli community to experience a sense of historical continuity and in times of danger to summon up libidinal links within its groups without resorting to extremes of hatred toward their external enemies. The ability of Israel's new generation to relate honestly to its casualties, to mourn them, and then to gather inner strength again is a continuation of the successful attempts of their parents to work through the mourning of their generation. The children are thereby continuing to experience the mourning for the past while at the same time embracing and representing the hope for the future.

In order to fully understand the Holocaust complex or syndrome, which plays an integral part in Israeli life, experts in the study of human behavior, including psychoanalysts, sociologist, economists, and political scientists, are needed to search out and explore all the aspects of the Holocaust. Knowledge and understanding of the various external as well as internal forces operating during that time will eliminate the defense mechanisms of shame, denial, and distortion that have resulted from repression and alienation. Widening the scope of our knowledge by means of self-scrutiny will enable us to reduce the repressed areas and the resultant defensive measures and thereby lessen the tendency toward self-hatred on the one hand and the magic approach of chauvinism and denial of reality on the other.

PART III

Survivors and Their Families

Chapter 9:
Psychological Issues in Families of Survivors in Israel

As I look back to the survivors who stood on the *Appellplatz*, many questions occur to me in regard to their motivation for re-establishing old family ties and beginning new families, following the Holocaust. I try to focus on individual survivors and find out what motivated them to embark on new familial relationships at a time when, from all appearances, all social structures had deteriorated. I ask myself, what were the essential ingredients in the compulsion for the psycho-historical continuation of the family so richly embodied in Jewish values? What kind of relationships were these survivors able to engage in, and what chance did these families have of surviving? What effects did the marriages that followed the Holocaust have on future generations of these families? Are there specific kinds of problems related to this group of families as a whole, and if so, how do we distinguish them from those found in the non-survivor population? Are the theoretical constructs and methodologies used in working with families from the non-survivor population applicable in the work with these families? To what extent do the post-Holocaust behaviors, attitudes, and unique problems of the survivor and his family constitute a complex *Gestalt*, which characterizes the entire family? And most importantly, who are these survivors and in what ways were the marriages and births of children connected with the theme of survival itself?

My initial answers to some of these questions during the first years of my research differ from those I now propose. At first, I was convinced that escaping into a marriage, the survivor could evade the overwhelming feeling of mourning and bereavement for the family members who were lost during the Holocaust. I now see that through this "escape" they expressed their inability to mourn, but this was only one component of a much larger issue. The family provided the framework and defined the boundaries in which to continue the individual process of revival. The family framework allowed the process of re-individuation—after living for so many years as one in an anonymous crowd, with no privacy, no walls, no concept of what is "mine," and no physical boundaries for intimacy—by giving the individual the freedom to discover the old self and allow for interpersonal relationships. The emotional confrontations that took place in the families were painful, as they reactivated Oedipal and pre-Oedipal conflicts, but the family was the only setting in which the process of re-individuation could take place.

The urge to establish new family ties can be seen as an almost instinctual drive in the process of revival and the revival of the "family self." For many survivors, their internalized concept of the family was the only link to the past. The emergence of this revitalized concept in the post-Holocaust survivor's life provided the foundation for a sense of continuity with the past and the hope for a future life.

Before delving into the lives of the families of survivors, however, I feel it would be helpful to outline the theoretical concepts and define the terms in which this material will be discussed. Let us begin by exploring the concept of the family ego and its effects on family relationships.

The Family Ego

The family is a highly specific group that lives together for a long time in both internal and external realities (Klein and Erlich, 1978). Throughout the course of this shared living, the family develops a family ego that can be characterized as a number of closely related psychological functions specifically and authentically characterized and delimiting a given family. The family ego is integral to what the family presents as its self-image. It also determines what is acceptable as family memory, including attention to events of the recent past as well as the sense of the family's continuity with former generations. The family ego helps to define the family's capability for and adequacy of judgment in relation to individual family members and its role in the community at large.

The family ego is not represented by any one individual at a given time and is not the sum of all individual egos in the family. Rather it is a discrete function within the family that evolves out of the interactions between the family members. It represents three important levels of perception: (1) how the family sees itself, (2) how others see the family, and (3) how the family conceives that others see it. As such, the family ego is not a static construct but rather one in which family members fulfill, in an active, dynamic manner varying needs of the family in a specific, shared, or overlapping fashion.

The unique features of the ego structures of the two founding partners of the family form the cornerstone around which the family ego is established and which continues to shape it subsequently. This "autonomous sphere" of the family ego is a product of the partners' individual and shared life experiences, ways of perceiving and integrating internal and external realities, their capacities for neutralizing instinctual drives, and their styles of intrapsychic and interpersonal communication and defense mechanisms. The legacy that the founding partners leave is that even in the event that they separate or in some other way are removed from the family, the foundation they have formed and established remains a constant, highly specific, and dynamically active structure both in them and in their children.

Immigration and the Family Ego

Since we are concerned here with the family ego structure of survivor families, it is important to look at the effects of immigration on the development and the continuity of the family ego. Issues and crises around the "state of the family ego" are poignantly observable in an immigrant society and country. Immigration is clearly an event that presents deep challenges and dangers for the family as few other events do. It sets into motion powerful extra-familial forces that, in turn, create intra-familial strain: the changing role of the parents, especially the decline in the authority of the father that results from his lessened status and effectiveness in the changed circumstances; the rise of the younger generation, their ascendency in the new society and in the family due to their greater adaptability; the decline of authority in the family and the clashes around values and loyalties; and the final devaluation of the "old" culture and nuclear family by the suffusion of the family with new members, representatives of the "new" culture, through friendship and marriage are all factors contributing to the conflicts in immigrant families.

Although these are expectable and normative processes, they may help to intensify, catalyze, or revive conflicts in the family that, under other circumstances, would have remained dormant.

Just as the individual ego is geared toward living in an average expectable environment (Hartmann, 1939), so is the family ego. The close, finely tuned relationship between the family ego and its environment—physical, cultural, and psychological—may be a powerful determinant of the limitations, internal capacities and strengths, and the particular coloration or profile we observe in a given family. The family ego draws on familiar, at times intuitively grasped and occasionally even measurable, dimensions of strength and weakness in the family. These may be innate, acquired, internalized, or tacked on, as the case may be. Attributes such as the level of education, the capacity for insight or psychological-mindedness, the physical health and infirmity, and the social, political and economic power determine, to a certain extent, the outlines of what a given family can identify with and synthesize as its own and what it rejects as abominable, sick, or foreign to itself. More importantly, these characteristics determine the conditions or limitations with which successful integration of family experiences can proceed and beyond which fragmentation, disintegration, or expulsion must beset the family ego.

These considerations help to point out why immigration can be regarded as a trauma that taxes the family ego deeply and heavily. It does so primarily by interfering in a drastic and, at times, cruel manner with that finely tuned interaction between the family ego and the average expectable environment toward which it is geared through the forceful alteration of the latter.

We observe two basic paths or tendencies when adaptive capacity of the family ego falters under these circumstances. In the first pattern, the family's inner strains are propelled and projected onto external forces and events. This, in turn, contributes to the disintegration of the family unit. The breakdown may, in this pattern, also come through action of individual family members who break out on their own and bring into the family new members who may be in opposition to members of the nuclear or extended family.

In the second pattern, over-consolidation and excessive cohesiveness result. Family members stay closer together in order to ward off the external, hostile, and threatening world. The defensive significance of this kind of cohesiveness can be seen in the usual lack of adequate feelings of warmth, permissiveness, and elasticity that generally mark the state of "togetherness." Instead, rigidity, intolerance, and even coercion to follow the family line emerge. Constriction of object ties and interests in the environment takes place, and in the case of immigrant families, this frequently leads to the family's eventual return to its old country of origin or to the search for new family love objects in the form of a new country of immigration. The ties of the family to the old country and the family of origin often find expression around familial symbolizations such as "Fatherland" or "Motherland" as archetypes. The very same archetypes or their opposites are also used to project commonly shared fantasies, expectations, and disappointments about the new country. Thus, the old or new countries may be alternatively pictured and experienced as good, providing, and nurturing maternal objects or as depriving ones; as strong, protective fathers; or as weak, confused and impotent ones. In these projections, the family ego expresses its particular strains through the use of such processes.

In some cases, families that were held together under oppressive political regimes, such as for instance those of recent immigrants to Israel from the Soviet Union, are empirically seen to fall apart through separation and divorce at a fairly high rate, once in a new environment of greater social and political freedom. This is another instance of the fine interweaving of the family ego and environmental forces. As in the case of the individual ego, the family ego may derive support and be heavily indebted to external forces that act to preserve the ego in a state of seemingly good synthesis. This state may never be seen differently as long as the environmental or external forces continue to shore up the ego. The true picture may unfold only if and when the external framework is removed.

Adolescence and the Family Ego

Immigration is only one potential crisis situation that serves to highlight the subtle interaction between family dynamics and the function of the family ego and, in particular, the latter's reliance on synthetic processes for its survival. Other potential traumatizations may similarly serve to illustrate the point through their exacerbation of the normative process. The crisis of adolescence that receives so much attention and emphasis in our culture is essentially a crisis of the entire family and not of a lone individual within it.

The adolescent identity crisis (Erikson, 1959) can be viewed as the attempt to deal freshly and courageously with issues the parents no longer dare deal with. The aggressive, sexual, and melancholic upheavals of adolescence place a heavy burden on the capacity of the family to accept and integrate, to control and set free, to stay together and separate, to invest their energies in one another, and to alter such investments. All these emotional storms and shifts form a genuine expression of the conflictual and long-term forces that press for resolution within the family while simultaneously also representing different or novel adaptive solutions to old, unresolved conflicts.

Here we may indeed discern, perhaps even more clearly, the task of the family ego to integrate experience as well as individuals or its failure to do so. The preservation of both is a function of the family ego, much the same as the individual ego safeguards the experiential wholeness but also the physical integrity of the self.

Where the capacity for ego synthesis is overburdened beyond its tolerance, we may witness the physical separation of individuals—as in the adolescent's trials of escape from the family with its subtle or overt assistance. In another outcome, the family unit itself may split up through separation or divorce, with all its positive and negative aspects—without the integration or synthetization of the experience in the service of differentiation of members and the individuation of the adolescent. The inevitable crisis of separation can be experienced and resolved either positively or negatively. A schematic representation of a positive resolution or mastery may be some variety of "We all went through this upheaval together and now we can separate well." The mode of separation, however, both that of the adolescent and that of the parents, is a reflection and function of the family's capacity for integrating, accepting, and sharing the traumatic life circumstances while maintaining the sense of belonging and togetherness, even after separation.

In those cases where adolescence brings about separation without the adequate synthetization of the experience in the family, meaningful relationships between the generations may be seriously disturbed, to be healed only after a very long time or possibly never.

A further momentous challenge presented by adolescence to the family ego is directed at the family ego's flexibility in shifting, sublimating, and releasing the old libidinal investments in object relations as well as its capacity for reconstruction and neutralizing aggression. The quality and the intensity of the object ties that have been forged through the vicissitudes of infancy, early childhood, and latency must be changed, with interfamilial alliances to be newly established or recharged between parents and adolescent, parents and other children, and parents themselves. Furthermore, the adolescent's burgeoning sexual drive and revived Oedipal strivings lower, in sudden and potentially troublesome ways, the family ego's threshold for sexual fantasy and action. This sudden change in threshold comes, of course, after a period in which incestuous feelings within the family were in relative quiescence and sublimation during latency. Such changes pose serious problems for the family ego, its flexibility in shifting cathexes, mobilizing defenses, and neutralizing and sublimating rising drive levels within the family.

The nature and the quality of the adolescent's newly established separateness thus depends rather heavily on the family's capacity for integration and accommodation of divergent and potentially traumatic experiences such as separation. Through internalization of object relationships as well as direct learning of associated behavioral patterns, this experience will in turn influence the adolescent's own capacity for dealing with similar experiences. Parenthetically, we are aware that the complex internalization of triangular object relations, of both Oedipal and pre-Oedipal origin, and their imprint on the resolution of the adolescent crisis involves the whole family. It will clearly be a decisive component and a specific contribution that the adolescent will bring to the family and will eventually establish in his own right. In other words, it will become a formative and influential aspect of that family's ego. We may, perhaps, see here a partial mechanism for the transmission and determination of the nature and the quality of the function of the family ego over the generations.

I now come back to these victims who stood on the *Appellplatz* and subsequently became the founding fathers and mothers of their own families and who, since most left their countries of origin, became immigrants in another land.

In understanding the function and the dynamics within the Nazi Holocaust survivor family, consideration must be given to the psychosocial structure and history of each spouse before the Holocaust, the severity of their traumatization during the Holocaust, their experiences in the phase after liberation and immigration, as well as the difficulty of transition to the new societies in which they settled.

The Conspiracy of Silence

In general, the survivors' war accounts were too horrifying for most people to listen to or believe. Even people who were consciously and compassionately interested played down their interest, partly rationalizing their avoidance with the belief that their questions would inflict further hurt. In addition, guilt for having knowingly neglected to do anything to prevent Nazi atrocities and/or for having been spared their fate by living outside Europe at the time led many bystanders to regard the survivor as pointing an accusing finger at them. Reactions such as "That is the past . . . let bygones be bygones" or "Be grateful and happy for getting to this country . . . look at the positive side of things" ensured the survivor's silence with regard to the Holocaust.

The survivors were also faced with the pervasively held myth that they had actively or passively participated in their own destiny by "going like sheep to the slaughter" and with the suspicion that they had performed immoral acts in order to survive. Insensitivity, ignorance and anxiety led to callous attempts at humor, crude comments, disbelief, and denial that the Holocaust ever happened.

This conspiracy of silence had a number of consequences for the survivor families. Their potential socio-cultural support systems had significant gaps during the initial phase after emigration from the DP camps to the United States or Israel. Moreover, those who re-united with their surviving relatives in the hope of sharing with them their sense of loss, grief, and rage and to re-establish some semblance of familial continuity felt betrayed when their relatives also participated in the conspiracy. Not only did this intensify their sense of isolation but also it made their task of mourning almost impossible. The outwardly imposed silence proved particularly painful to those who had survived the war and were determined to "bear witness."

Survivors were left with two major options. One was to seek out and cling to fellow survivors. Some established their own societies and organizations with membership based either on common war experiences or on a common place of residence before the war. Others chose to live in the same neighborhoods. Maintaining bonds of loyalty and mutual help proved of utmost importance for survival during the war and immediately afterward. Many survivors kept these interpersonal ties intact even when dispersed in different countries. Regrettably, these partial solutions often amounted to the re-establishment of a "ghetto" mentality, which maintained and even deepened the survivors' sense of isolation and mistrust of society.

The second option for survivors was to withdraw completely into their newly established families, using their children as a captive audience. One wife complained in therapy: "My husband started to constantly drill the child with his war preoccupations from the moment he could understand syllables." Children of such families, although remembering fragments of their parents' and "lost families" war histories, attest to the emotional climate of the Holocaust, which was present in the family both verbally and nonverbally ("through osmosis"). A double-bind message was often conveyed, involving the security of the home and the dangers that could suddenly occur.

Some survivors used the conspiracy of silence as a defense against the overwhelming anxiety that flooded their memories and lives. This often led to a reaction-formation style and a preoccupation with protecting children from pain and ensuring that they were exaggeratedly healthy and "hyper-normal" citizens in the new adopted countries. The parents equated sickness with death and tried to convey the image that "everything was all right" even when real sickness existed.

Such parents had intolerance for the complexities of life, believing that everything should be simple. They were haunted by thoughts that something terrible could happen to them and their families at any time.

The experience of survival created specific psychosocial patterns of relating that I characterized as the "survivor family ego identity." Such a concept is not a mere listing of psychoneurotic symptoms of overt pathological interactions. Rather, it encompasses a protean picture of the family life-style with its conflicts and resolutions.

Over a period of years, I have worked with my survivor families at mental health clinics and mental hospitals in the United States, Europe, and Israel and interviewed others in non-clinical settings. The case material presented hereafter derives from these clinical studies and interviews.

In the clinical material, there is evidence of varying degrees of psychopathology in the survivor families. The problems presented by these families run the gamut of the psychological spectrum. Given its very context, those families seen in clinical settings are those in which the strains of the family have reached crisis proportions, and this particular clinical population is in no way intended to represent the entire survivor population. Indeed, despite the massive psychic traumatization of the Holocaust, the majority of the families of survivors are surprisingly well adapted, with high achievements and integration with their communities. Many examples of such families can be found among survivors who immigrated to Israel and raised their families in kibbutzim communities (Krystal, 1971).

Whether the resolutions of the conflicts attributable to the Holocaust trauma are successful or unsuccessful is, to a large extent, a function of the strength of the survivor family ego and especially the synthetic function of their ego.

Elsewhere in this book, I have pointed out the danger of making generalized statements regarding the health or the pathology of survivors. This holds true of survivor families as well. Nevertheless, certain issues emerged as dominant themes in the make-up of the family ego identity of survivor families. These include (1) over-protectiveness on the part of parents for their children (and children for their parents), (2) compulsive behavior in relation to caring for children, (3) obsessions regarding the health of family members, (4) high expectations for achievement, and (5) fear of separation.

It is true that many of these factors can be observed in non-survivor immigrant families as well. In discussing the problems of Holocaust survivors as parents, it is important to note that they were influenced by particular values as well as by their traumatic experiences. Jewish immigrant parents are known for their over-protectiveness, their high expectations of their children, their valuing of education, and their attempts to supply their children with material pleasures that they may have lacked in their own childhood. The tone and urgency with which they are expressed in survivor families, however, distinguishes these families from non-survivors and calls for an elaboration of what we have called the survivor family ego identity.

One striking feature of survivor parents seen in a clinical setting is that most of them did not seek help for themselves but rather for their children. Survivors had little motivation for changing themselves but were motivated to help their children, illustrating the degree to which survivor parents, as a group, invested their sense of well-being in their children's well-being.

Beginning New Families

Each survivor emerged from the Holocaust with an internalized concept of the family. Often this concept could not be tested against reality because survivors lost spouses, offspring, parents, siblings, and extended family members. In addition, those survivors who were children during the persecution had had limited opportunity to experience their families. For many of these individuals, the family concept was linked to feelings of abandonment, disappointment, helplessness, unexpressed aggression, and idealization.

The dynamic process of survival that began with the individual's desire, ability, and perhaps "luck" to endure the persecution continued into the stage of liberation and into all the subsequent phases of being passed along and re-integration into society.

Today, the majority of the survivors of the Nazi Holocaust reside in Israel, Canada, and the United States, with the remainder in Europe, South America, and South Africa. They, as a group, are seen in outpatient and in-patient hospitals much more frequently than other sectors of the population (Rakoff, 1969). In addition, in the more severely affected families of this population, there seems to be an overabundance of physical illness, real or fantasized, among the parent generation and its children.

Many Holocaust survivors married within the first three years after liberation. Much of the motivation for these marriages and for subsequent child bearing was directly connected with the fantasy and the hope for individual and family survival. In the ghettos and the work camps, friendships, pairing, and in some rare cases sporadic sexual relationships were possible. Marriage itself, however, was unusual during the Holocaust because of the undeniable and inescapable theme of survival.

The wish on the part of survivors to revive their dead families was expressed by re-establishing new family units following liberation. In its extreme form, this trend had a psychopathological dimension. Evidence of a repetition compulsion of the victim-aggressor bind and a survival lifestyle were seen. This was observed in the work with some survivor families in clinical settings in New York and in Israel. In these clinical populations, survivors repeated the theme of victim-aggressor in marital conflicts in their new family relationships, thus re-enacting images and feeling states derived from the Holocaust. By sustaining these sadomasochistic roles, families brought to the surface the usually subconscious confrontation with death. In many families, this had a pathological influence upon the children who either accepted the threat of killing or destroying or, via reaction formation, fought against this representation. An example of the struggle against such a representation was seen in a patient whose mother repeatedly accused her "You are my Hitler" when she did not eat or help in cleaning. In fantasy, the patient killed her mother or withdrew into a depression and stayed in bed for days as a defense against her death wishes against her mother. During a family session of another family, the parents accused their twenty-eight-year-old son, who was seen as a failure, of being their "second Holocaust," implying that it was much worse than their first.

To understand the dynamics of the present-day survivor family, it is essential to know the circumstances under which the couple married and how the family was first formed. There are three basic categories: (1) couples who married before or during the war and were reunited after a separation; (2) those who married immediately after liberation in the displaced persons camps; (3) those who married after a transitional phase many years after liberation.

Regardless of when survivors married, the motivation for these marriages was as varied as the personalities of the partners themselves. One motive for marriage was an intense need to cling together for mutual protection against the environment and to overcome discontinuities with life-affirming acts. For some, marriage was a symbolic act of defiance against Nazi oppression and the Nazi threat to Jewish cultural values and traditions. Another motive for marriage resulted from the dependence of one partner on the other for physical survival. During the Holocaust, many fathers, feeling weak and helpless, asked their daughters to marry men who were physically stronger and could defend their daughters, even though the women were not attracted to them, but the motivations were correlated with physical survival. One such example is that of a sixteen-year-old girl from the Warsaw Ghetto who married a man because of her father's insistence. The prospective husband was a tailor who could get work outside the ghetto and thereby bring in food. Following the liberation, such marriages were more often than not conflict-ridden. In this particular case, the woman realized that she was the emotionally stronger of the two partners and more intelligent than her husband. She felt unable to sever the relationship, however, because she feared "punishment" from her dead father who perished during the Holocaust.

Many marriages occurred immediately after liberation in the displaced persons camps and were a step toward overcoming discontinuity in the survivors' lives. These marriages were consciously or unconsciously connected with rebirth fantasies. Some of these couples had been married before the war and had lost their spouses and children. These sole survivors strove for a continuation of their pre-war lives by remarrying immediately. Others who had been looking for a marriage partner prior to the war returned to that stage after liberation. In general, these individuals could no longer bear to be alone. They had a need to change the self-images that had been forced upon them in the concentration and labor camps where they had been unloved, uncared for, and anonymous numbers without any positive emotional investments. Even though the peers in the concentration and labor camps could cling together for survival and perhaps help each other in small ways, there was no emotional investment between them. There was no emotional energy and no place for love, and there were no real love objects. The essential concern was that of survival.

Theoretically, we see in these families that originated in the camps an abandonment of the pleasure principle as the basic guideline choice of partner and rather a return to and emphasis on the "safety principle" (Sandler, 1960) mentioned earlier. This safety principle determined the survivor's perception of his world. He could not tolerate any interruption of his investment in safety for the pursuit or expression of pleasure.

The marriages after the war were an attempt to fuse safety with pleasure and to leave behind the anonymity that accompanied dehumanization. This transition was accompanied by an increase in prestige in the DP camp society. The married individual could begin to differentiate his functions and develop his self-image.

Following liberation, marriage helped to lessen the feeling of alienation in new surroundings in which survivors found themselves. In the post-liberation stage, the survivor's social and psychic apparatus was redeveloping as part of the process from de-humanization to re-socialization. The marriages were a result of this reorganization of the survivor's social and personal functioning. They furnished him with an opportunity to give and receive, to be a provider and caretaker. Through marriage, the survivors' partners became actively involved in giving and sharing rather than passively receiving and accepting restitution from the outside world.

The importance of the marriage was underscored by the fact that survivors placed all their faith in their new husbands or wives. Agencies, even if they were benevolent, such as UNRA, were mistrusted. Survivors could not trust rabbis either since they had lost their aura of omnipotence when the survivors discovered that they suffered the same fate as their communities. Survivors had no need for doctors or psychiatrists since they could do nothing to protect their own lives by satisfying the need for such basics as food and clothing and to create a new life through marriage.

Many unsuccessful marriages were a consequence of the fact that there was no real courtship and not much choosing and weighing of the qualities of the potential spouse. This was partly due to the limitation of freedom implicit in the context of the war. In ghettos, concentration and labor camps and DP camps, the choices were restricted. The most important requirement was that the survivor feels that his potential spouse could help him to continue to survive and to make him or her feel safe and protected. In some cases, the relief of finding anyone who came from the same town or had known one's relatives led to a quick marriage. In other cases, survivors married the remnants of their own decimated families, such as a brother-in-law or a sister-in-law.

With regard to ethnic, religious, and personal groupings, the choices of marital partners were probably not very different from those that would have been made had there been no Holocaust. However, there was an exception in that there were numerous instances of young women marrying older men who had already fathered children that had perished. These women looked for a man who would be a protector and provider but at the same time represented, in fantasy, the lost little brother or dead father whom she wished to bring back to life. The reverse was true for men who married women whom they saw as mothers who would take care of them.

The other group of survivors that postponed marriage underwent a post-liberation phase that was different from those who married immediately. They delayed marriage by placing themselves in a psychosocial moratorium; their time was spent studying, teaching, and interacting. They were planning for their future as well as striving to continue that which had been disrupted, whether it was their studies or their psychosexual development. There were many who spent these years trying to emigrate from the countries where they had been persecuted. Some went to Israel to fulfill ideals, to return with the scattered family, or to simply live in a land where they knew they would be safe from persecution. Others went to countries such as the United States or Australia, where they had fantasies of opportunities for new lives and new families. Belief in the rich "Uncle Sam" who resided in the United States was common among those survivors who came to the USA, seeking a secure framework, free of persecution (Niederland, 1961).

Because the ego strengths and weaknesses of the partners varied, so did the successes of the marriages. Although some of the marriages may have been satisfying in the context of survival, they were generally not successful in "normal" life. Whereas at a time of extreme stress and trauma, security and familiarity fulfilled their greatest need, with the passage of time and the diminishing of pain, some survivors found that their primary motivation for choosing a spouse was not enough to fulfill other emerging psychosocial and intellectual needs. The need for cohesion, pairing, and togetherness, which were so important at the beginning of the marriage, dissipated as the partners changed over the years. The spouse, who at first had represented the normalcy of life before the Holocaust later became the projected, haunted symbol of the Holocaust itself. Initially, the partner embodied the vision, mythology, and language—in other words, the "sweetness of life"—of the pre-Holocaust world. He or she was the "friend" with whom the survivor would escape. In such families, the life axis narrowed to that of survivor and persecutor. Neither partner could experiment with different roles and changing self-representations due to the rigidity of their Holocaust experiences and the resulting motive for marriage.

The most important motivation for marriage among the survivor population was the same as that for any non-survivor population—namely, love. That feelings of tenderness, warmth, and intimacy between survivors could surface at a time when such feelings were generally repressed makes these marriages all the more remarkable.

In many instances, strong attachments were developed during the adolescent years of the couple and they were either married before the Holocaust or in the early years of the war. These marriages were based on common socio-cultural backgrounds and common ideals that are so important during the adolescent years. These ties became increasingly important as other family members perished. Their bond became the couple's only link with the lost world. It is only appropriate that I relate the following poignant account of one such marriage. Had it been the only such instance—and it was not—it would serve to illustrate the profound importance of family ties for the survivor during the Holocaust and following it.

Rachel and Daniel met in high school two years before the war began. Their friendship developed and was based, in part, on their commitment to Zionism. Their hope was "to build a new world in which to be reborn, a world free of anti-Semitism, hatred and oppression, a world in which one could begin anew." They wanted to run away from the world of the "ancient regime" of oppression and social injustice.

After displacement from their hometown, they lived for a while on Aryan papers. Many times Poles, in whose house they stayed for short periods of time, suspected Rachel and Daniel of being Jewish and blackmailed them, threatening to turn them in if not paid. Eventually they chose to live in the ghetto "together with their own." In the ghetto, they would not have to experience the "humiliation of being rejected by Poles, who only yesterday had been friends." During the years in the ghetto, most of their family members died.

The emotional bond between Rachel and Daniel intensified as a result of the disparity of what they saw between the death and the hatred in the outside world and the warmth and the hope for new beginnings that they saw in each other. They were married during the years spent together in the ghetto and their mutual support and help gave them the strength to continue their struggle for survival.

Despite the fact that Daniel was a socialist and young scientist, his Hasidic background resurfaced and he asked the Hasidic rabbi in the ghetto for a blessing of the marriage. The Holocaust inspired him to continue the traditions of previous generations as a protest against Germany's vow to destroy "not only Jews but their spiritual heritage." This act served as a kind of irrational magic for Daniel during the Holocaust and was a source of reassurance that he and Rachel would not be destroyed.

Soon after the marriage, Daniel and Rachel were separated by the "liquidation" of the ghettos and were "resettled" in different camps. Daniel was sent to Buchenwald, and Rachel to a different concentration camp in Germany. During their years of internment, they were able to communicate sporadically via German SS officers who would, for the price of one of the pieces of gold that Daniel had hidden in his rectum, deliver letters back and forth between camps. It was ironic that during such a time, these SS men served as *postillions d'amour*. Not only letters but also poems were sent back and forth between Rachel and Daniel.

Two days before the liberation, Rachel was "mortally wounded" by a German tank on her death march from the concentration camp. She was able to give the poems she had written during the long days of separation to a comrade survivor before she succumbed, asking her to give them to Daniel.

After returning to her native town, the woman was able to give the poems to Daniel and tell him of Rachel's death. In one of the poems, Rachel had written of the fantasized reunion she longed for.

Daniel despaired over the news of Rachel's death, but something in him believed that Rachel could not be dead. He began a search of all hospitals and DP camps in Germany and finally found his wife a year later.

The marriage, to this day, is one of loving tenderness and complementary relations between the couple and their two children. This family ego, with its system of values, warmth, solidarity, and high standards of morality that are incorporated into the everyday lifestyles of the family members in the interactions with each other and the outside world, gives the family a sense of moral ethos, a self-ideal, and a sense of self-sameness.

One common family objective cherished by each family member has been to remember the past experiences of love and belonging and to try to integrate them into their present lives. "We can't run away from the memories but we are not 'professional' witnesses of the past. This is our background interwoven with our real life." This "epic of love" reminds one of the myth of Orpheus and Eurydice, but with a significant difference. Daniel and Rachel have been able to look back to *L'Univers Concentrationnaire* of human destruction and realize that they were not destroyed as man and woman. They were able to achieve inner strength and retain their humanity by reaching out to one another. Moreover, their children accept their parents' past as an important part of the inner family ego identity.

The following vignettes relate family histories, sharply contrasting with that of Rachel and Daniel. They typify the degree of psychopathology of the family ego and family identities seen in survivor families or families that were unable to work through the losses, separations, and the collective death. Their family histories were collected in clinical work with these families and will be used to illustrate the manner in which the dominant themes in the make-up of the family ego (i.e., over-protectiveness, compulsive behavior, obsession with health, high expectations for achievement, and fear of separation) are played out in the survivor family.

Sonia and Abraham R. came to the United States from Germany in 1952, after barely escaping death in Nazi concentration camps. Both spouses had lost their entire families during the Holocaust. They had been married during the war in a ghetto, only to be separated and sent to different camps. They were reunited, by chance, following liberation. The trauma of having lost her entire family influenced Sonia's decision to begin a new family immediately following liberation. She felt that "I could not cope with my mourning for my lost family in any way other than having a child." Abraham felt that at the time they had little to offer a child, and that Sonia's longing for her family would not be assuaged by the birth of a child. She persisted in voicing her desire for a child, and Abraham finally agreed. Joseph, their son, was born in a DP camp. After the birth of her son, Sonia was able to give up the fantasy that she had been "damaged" by the Nazis to some extent.

Six months after Joseph's birth, Abraham became ill. He was unable to work, so Sonia was compelled to go out of the home and earn a living. For five years, her husband was ill at home while his wife worked. Sonia experienced much guilt over her forced inability to be with her son, but her ambivalence as regards parenting the child was expressed in her reassurance that Joseph was being cared for by a "very fine German woman" who doted on him and spoiled him. The irony was that the ideal representation of the mother was a German woman. She developed a strong resentment toward the woman who was able to "mother" her son and felt both envy and anger. She developed a great ambivalence because of her ability to "mother" Joseph. On the other hand, she felt hostile because the woman represented the "Germans who took my ability to mother."

Sonia often felt the need to be mothered because of her loneliness. She and her husband felt they had not received sufficient help from the social agencies—"They gave us money, not love." Even after coming to the United States, the family was plagued with illness.

Joseph's early development was complicated by several illnesses involving his speech and ability to walk. His early years were characterized by his being very accident-prone. As a result, he missed school a lot and was prevented from participating in many normal sports.

Because the father became ill (and was even hospitalized at one point) during Joseph's early developmental years, there is some suggestion that the father-son rivalry was acted out via these infirmities. Sonia initiated contact with the therapist because Joseph was a poor student and had recently failed all his subjects. It was apparent early in the treatment that Sonia's attempts to replace her dead family with the child had influenced the whole cycle of the mother-child relationship, with difficulties of separation and differentiation from as early as the symbiotic stage and through later development. Despite Joseph's complete recovery from his childhood illnesses, Sonia was convinced that her son was "epileptic." There were problems with the other children, Sara and David, as well.

She had an enormous stake in proving that "in spite of everything," her family was "normal" despite the many illnesses of her husband and son. Her disappointment in Joseph and her frustration with him were very great. She wondered, however, whether she might have contributed to what she called his "nervousness."

There was an air of apprehension in the family which negated any possibility of pleasure in the present, for they were always awaiting another disaster. On the one hand, the mother's ambivalence toward her son caused her to punish Joseph severely by hitting him with a broom or whatever was handy when she lost control, and on the other hand, she over-protected him.

Abraham was afraid to admit openly to the conflicts between him and his wife. Although he occasionally lashed out at her, he felt guilty and had a sense that he had disappointed her. He stammered badly and was defending himself against everything and everybody.

These survivor families are generally overly concerned with the opinion of the outside world because of their self-esteem. They emphasized the fact that they were "normal" despite the numerous injuries suffered during the Holocaust. They tended toward somatization and could more readily accept a physical illness than a psychological one. Their denial and avoidance was a result of their belief that should they accept the fact that they or their offspring had psychological problems, it would mean that "Hitler was victorious."

Jacob B. had lost his first wife and their two children in Auschwitz. Eva B. met and married Jacob in a DP camp, following liberation. She had lost her parents and extended family in concentration camps while she was in hiding in non-Jewish homes during the war. Her motivation for marrying Jacob was based in large part on her desire to "save" him because she had been unable to save her own family and the patriarchal representation in him of her own father. "He was so learned, wise as my father." At the time of their marriage, Jacob was preoccupied with the losses, withdrawn, tense, and depressed. He was drawn toward marriage in an attempt to establish some continuity in his life by "bringing back his lost family." His religious beliefs had taught him "a man shouldn't stay alone."

Soon after their marriage, Jacob and Eva came to the United States and began their family. Jacob insisted on giving their first child, Hilda, the same name as one of his dead children.

Upon entering treatment, Eva expressed feelings of guilt and anxiety in relation to her two children. She felt that she "really could not be a good mother" to her children. She described her husband as being "very ill" and requiring her support. He, however, was dissatisfied with this support and felt that neither she nor anyone else was helping him.

Jacob B. was unable to relate to his children positively, remembering always "the wonderful children who belonged to the lost world." He was often openly hostile to his actual children, screaming at them and throwing temper tantrums when they disappointed him. Even Eva found him a "difficult person to live with." His dependence on her and his behavior toward the children awakened in her a great deal of preconscious hostility. She resented the role of "eternal savior," which he had assigned to her, but at the same time, her guilt over her own lost family compelled her to try and save him.

Hilda and her brother, Adam, had little respect for them. They felt themselves to be inadequate. Hilda, who acted out sexually, found no pleasure in this or any other activities. She always felt that she would never be loved as much as the dead children and that no matter what she did, her achievements would always fall short.

The guilt Eva felt in relation to her children resulted in a double-bind message to them. Her concern with trying to save her dead family by saving her husband left her emotionally depleted and unable to involve herself with them. At the same time, she would become overly concerned and protective of them and unduly involved in Hilda's and David's social lives. The father, who idealized the qualities of his dead children, used it as a measure of the present children's accomplishments, and as a result, he did not really know who his children were.

There were profound feelings of hopelessness within this family and its relation to the outside world. The parents, for different reasons, were unable to relinquish the past and live in the present. The children felt the burden of having to make up for the loss of dead brothers and sisters by giving up their own identities in exchange for those of the dead children.

Mr. and Mrs. Meir met and married several years after the Holocaust. Mr. Meir's first wife, who was seven months pregnant at the time, was sent to the gas chambers in Treblinka. He too was interned in Treblinka, but when they were separated, he became confused. He remembered her screaming "Save me!" as they were deported to different parts of the camp; not knowing what this meant, however, he did nothing to save her when she cried out but stood by and watched her be taken away. After years of working in labor camps, he developed a "muscle man" style of relating to the outside word.

Mrs. M., whose parents were killed by the Nazis during the war, succeeded in escaping to Russia. She was sent to a Siberian camp where she spent many years. The loss of the parents at an early age was significant for her difficulty in forming lasting object relations and her inability to trust others. A previous marriage to Mr. M. had ended in divorce even though she had two children from this marriage.

Mrs. M. was over thirty at the time of her marriage to Mr. M., but he made many demands on her to bear him a child. He fantasized about his lost, unborn son and looked forward to the birth of a child as a means of reconstituting his life and rescuing him from loneliness. His need for *Kadish* was—as it appeared in treatment—a trial connected with reverse fantasies and restitution needs to bring back the lost child and do "reparation" work.

Mrs. M. had many difficulties in attempting to give birth. Several pregnancies ended in miscarriages. She saw many doctors in her heroic attempts to become pregnant and was finally able to carry a child and give birth to their son.

Mrs. M.'s childhood deprivations led her to be overly concerned with the nourishment of her child. Later it was discovered that the son had diabetes. Mr. M. felt that his son's illness was God's punishment for not rescuing his first wife from the gas chamber. He continued to feel guilty through the years, and his son's illness was a reminder of his unresolved guilt.

Mr. and Mrs. Y. met in the labor camp at Dachau. While interned, he had aided in her physical survival by sharing the bread he got while working outside the camp. She felt her only chance for survival was to marry a strong man who could support and protect her. In the therapy with the family, Mrs. Y. revealed, "As a man, I despise my husband." During her first months in the camp, she had dreamed of the strong, handsome man she hoped to marry. She decided to marry Mr. Y. nevertheless because she thought they would never leave the camp alive. In addition, she had felt gratitude to him for having saved her from starvation and deprivation in difficult times.

Six months after they were married, the Y.'s were separated and deported to different camps. Four years later, after the end of the war, they were, by chance, reunited. The marriage continued, but their relationship was problematic, with sexual and financial difficulties.

Mrs. Y. was never able to erase the picture she had of her husband as a "slave, doing whatever they asked of him." Mr. Y. was himself deeply ashamed of the fact that he had "accepted the role of slave" in the labor camp and was deeply wounded by his wife's image of him and coldness toward him. He resented the fact that she would not "accept him as a man."

Because of his wife's distance, Mr. Y. turned to their daughter, Frieda, for the warmth and affection he did not receive from the wife. This was a source of much irritation to Mrs. Y., who was very jealous of their relationship. The daughter became the "wife" and confidante of her father that the mother refused to be.

The Importance of the Birth of Children

The birth of survivors' children must be understood in the context of their parents' self-image and self-representation. The survivors' bodies had been abused and emaciated to the point of exhaustion. Many women had doubts about their reproductive capacity, thinking that something "bad" was in them. Some women had ceased to menstruate in the concentration camps or were sexually exploited. Although the women fought against it, as a result of this defilement of their body image, many women accepted the self-image that the Nazis had created for them, that of "damaged, witch-like creatures who either could not produce, or, in doing so, would create monsters." Nevertheless, the survivors, both men and women, had an intense need for children to lessen their loneliness, restore their humanity, and replace relatives who had died.

The Schmidt and Berkowitz families illustrate the intense ambivalence that preceded the birth of the first child. In both families, one spouse wants to have a child immediately while the other desires to postpone having children until the partners have had time to adjust to new surroundings or, as with the Berkowitz family, the spouse must take physical risks in order to have a child.

The desire on the part of survivor families to replace lost family members is very complex. Associated with this desire is the need on the part of the survivor to restore his or her lost "self." What handicaps these survivors is their belief that their concept of self-sameness was disrupted by the Holocaust. They are unable to accept the continuity of their identity prior to the war, during the war, and following the war. They are, therefore, compelled to "restore" the self-image that was lost during the Holocaust.

The successful re-integration of Rachel and Daniel into their family and their community life was a function of their belief that "We are the same." They did not reject the image of themselves as victims of Nazi persecution but rather integrated this image into their ever-evolving self and family ego identity.

The traumatized ego identity that parents brought to their marriages helped to define the resulting family ego identity. We can now turn to the dominant themes in the family ego identity of survivors.

Over-protectiveness

During their pregnancies, mothers began to slowly recover their body and self-representations that had once been "damaged." One mother said, "Now I am looking beautiful, but my spirit is rotten. When I felt my child in me I began to feel hope that the badness was leaving me. I began to feel whole again." Through the mother-and-child relationship, survivor mothers began to experience a return to their former body image. Severe problems resulted, however, from their over-investment of libidinal and aggressive feelings toward the child without enough self-control, neutralization, and sublimation. Many mothers felt threatened when the child showed the first steps of autonomy because they were unable to differentiate between themselves and their child during the critical separation-individuation phase (Mahler, 1975).

As in the case of Sonia and Abraham K., Joseph heard his mother say again and again, "Be careful," awakening in him fears and suspicions about life. They used projective identification to avoid hostility toward the child, which awakened in them so much anxiety. This often led mothers to try to protect their children from an indifferent or hostile world.

The mothers adapted certain coping mechanisms that they had

learned in the camps to their parenting roles. They "over-protected" their children from their own worst experiences. For example, it was not uncommon for survivors to overfeed their children in order to make reparation for the hunger that they had experienced during the Holocaust. The expression "*ess' mein Kind*" (eat, my child) did not depend on the child's needs but rather on the mother's anxiety that her child should not suffer physical and emotional deprivation as she had done in the past. The M. family illustrated such behavior. The tragedy in this family, however, is that Mrs. M.'s concern with her child's nourishment is connected with the child's diabetes. Though probably not a direct cause, the mother's desire to protect her child has debilitating consequences, reinforcing the "bad" mother image she has of herself.

Compulsive Behavior

Some survivor mothers were preoccupied with obsessive-compulsive cleaning of their children. Appearance was the factor that had saved many mothers from being sent to the gas chambers and therefore appearance continued to be very important in their lives. They constantly bathed their babies, and as the children grew, their mothers were very demanding and critical regarding their appearance. This compulsive cleanliness had the symbolic effect of cleansing the mothers' souls from all the traumas they had experienced.

Many mothers who had repetitive persecutory nightmares would wake up to look at and touch their sleeping babies. The pattern of intense nonverbal communication was expressed not only in the early symbiotic phase of the relationship between mother and child but also later in the Oedipal and post-Oedipal developmental stages. The relationship was based on intuition and stressed the connection between the mother's and child's appearance and survival—"How do you look today?" Physical fitness and good looks were seen as indicators not only of bodily well-being but emotional well-being as well.

Obsession with Health

The survivor couples produced children whose mental health ranged from the very well-adjusted child to the child with behavioral problems and the child hospitalized and diagnosed as schizophrenic. In terms of physical health, there was also a wide range in these families. However, there seemed to be an overabundance of physical illness, both among the parental generation and the children.

Many Holocaust survivors suffered physical abuse, starvation, disease, and illness, which they continued to experience in their post-liberation lives. It is not surprising, therefore, that survivor parents should have exaggerated fears and are anxiety prone about the illness of their offspring.

Within the context of the ghetto or camp, any sickness could result in "selection for death," a state from which it was impossible to recover. Niederland (1968b) has pointed out that "somatization is a major defence among survivors and their families," a finding which is confirmed by my own clinical studies (Klein, 1971, 1973). The dynamics of somatization are always multi-determined, but in this population, they are related specifically to the Holocaust experience of their parents. Somatization serves as a continuation of the victim's survival-oriented hypercathexis of the body (Krystal and Niederland, 1968).

In the concentration camps and the ghetto, victims were unable to overcome the physical deficiencies connected with hunger, starvation, and lack of libidinal investment in their bodies. Most of the women survivors complained, "I couldn't care for my face, hair, lacerated legs, breasts, and wounded body." As a result, these people exhibited a preoccupation with health and illness that is a reaction formation against the limitations of their ability to care for themselves during the Holocaust. Evidence of such preoccupations can be seen in all the case histories presented previously.

Another reason for the obsession with illness and physical health was to anticipate and strategically avoid death by concretizing it. In relation to their children, the survivors tended to exaggerate their response and restoration needs when faced with any injury or disease from which the child suffered. This parental response motivated the child to remain in the sick role and thus incapacitated him from living fully.

Some mothers developed anxieties about the health of their babies as a way of negating their ambivalent and sometimes aggressive feelings. This manifested itself in frequent visits to medical and paramedical facilities. When a child became ill, mothers reported that it evoked in them feelings of being "damaged" themselves and re-awakened fears from their pregnancy that the child would be a monster or cripple. They were obsessed with the memories of the death and the destruction of the Holocaust. They feared that their contact with death had "infected" them and that they, in turn, could transmit this "disease" to their children. Hence, they felt guilty of being the "source" of their child's illness.

These mothers felt that they were "bad" and perceived their children's sickness as their own weakness or illness. Some children of survivor parents who are now themselves parents are concerned that they will repeat the same pattern of over-concern and preoccupation with their children's health. Some of these second-generation survivors feel "damaged" because their parents are survivors and hence are afraid to produce a third generation (Fogelman, 1978). In these families, the sickness was a symbol of the concentration camp experience, a reminder that the parent had once been helpless and would always need help to survive. Illness played an important role in establishing the "family myth" that consists of a series of fairly well-integrated beliefs shared by all the family members concerning each other and their mutual position in the family life, beliefs that go unchallenged by everyone involved in spite of the reality distortions that they may conspicuously imply. Although the family myth is part of the family image, it often differs from the "front" or the social façade that the family as a group attempts to present to outsiders.

The life "philosophy" of the concentration camp family did not include the concepts of health and autonomy. Instead, it posited two kinds of individuals in this world, the strong and the weak, the helper and the helped, and the savior and the victim. Each member of such a pair needs the other in order to exist; relationships are symbiotically interdependent. Survivor families used illness as a means of getting close to one another. If a family member became ill and the others could rally around and care for him or her, then intimacy which was otherwise avoided could be achieved. One eighteen-year-old child of survivors commented in therapy, "When my father is sick, it is usually the only occasion that we come closer together. I really feel sorry for him." The rule in these families was that if one wanted to get closer to another member, one must become weak or make the other weak.

Myth of Illness

In addition to the appearance of actual physical illness, in the majority of cases studied, another related factor was apparent. The myth of illness also operates even when the family has no real physical symptoms or when they are not connected to the real, present illness. This myth is used to manipulate relationships between the family and the outside world.

For example, in some families, the aches and the pains of the parents were invoked whenever they wished to hide their financial limitations or their need for self-punishment. They always said, "Were it not for our 'conditions,' we would enjoy life and allow ourselves to go to the theatre." In the Berkowitz family, there was another pattern, that of "protective wall building" around the identified patient. Mother "protects" Father from interacting with his environment by building a protective wall around him, helping him to sustain his "ill" role. By maximizing the significance of the aftereffects of a pseudo heart attack and by resorting to statements about his "general poor health," she maintained the distance between the children and their father.

The "epilepsy" of the son in the Schmidt family is a good example of the myth of illness. Joseph S. was perceived as "crippled" in the eyes of his mother but appeared "normal" when among his peers. By incapacitating the child, Sonia S. was able to "save" him and thereby ameliorate the guilt she felt at being unable to save her own family. She was compelled to protect her child, even from himself.

Because of the high incidence of alexithymia (the inability to express emotions) among survivor parents, the body language associated with somatization was often used to avoid the anxiety connected with separation, autonomy, and confrontation. In these families, it was not unusual to hear comments such as "Father is weak—let's not make him any weaker" or "I am so sick—leave me alone" instead of "I am afraid to confront . . ." The children frequently had an unrealistic image of the survivor parent's health and emotional condition because it was often represented as exaggeratedly strong (as evidenced in the parents having survived) or was represented as exaggeratedly impaired (as a result of the persecution suffered). Both conflicting views were sometimes apparent: "My father is a hero but is also very weak."

Illness, whether real or mythical, maintains the relationships among the family members and between the family and the outside world. Anthony and Koupernik (1973) found that the extra-familial effects of illness led to withdrawal of the family from active contact with their social world so that friendships and affiliations were gradually discarded as the family became increasingly absorbed in their "trouble" and disconnected from the environment (p. 131).

It must be emphasized that the illnesses of the survivor families are not only mythical; in many cases, they were very real. Frequently, however, they were invoked to maintain the family's homeostasis and its relation to the outside world in its accepted role of victim.

It is also interesting to note that those survivor offspring who have been diagnosed as schizophrenic display gross body-image distortions. One son of survivor parents thought he was pregnant. Another was obsessed about having widening hips. A third had an imaginary skin disease. The hypochondrias which was functional in some families was exaggerated in these three cases until it resulted in an incapacitating fascination with an extraordinary body image. This confirms Anthony's concept that the illness in the family provokes a general constriction manifested in rigidity, lack of spontaneity of feelings, narrowness of thinking, and refusal to take chances. They create "wide margins of safety" and avoid all hazards. They behave with extreme caution as if any unusual act on their part might release a Holocaust (p. 154). Guardedness regarding family illness protects each member from potential disaster and the return of persecution. The illness reminds them of the helplessness that they must defend against and binds them together against possible horrors in the future.

These families reaffirm the frequent finding that physical and psychiatric illness cluster not only in individuals but also in families. Bowlby and Parks (1970) discovered that "the health record is a good index of how a person is coping with the emotional problems of bereavement" (p. 197). The marriages of survivors and the births of their children were often connected with a desire to avoid the mourning process, and it is little wonder that such a high degree of real and fantasized illness appears in these families.

High Expectations

Many survivor parents put undue pressure on their children to achieve in school and in social situations to insure against the loss of the parents' newly acquired self-esteem. Survivors often said, "We only live through our children." Mothers, in particular, lacked patience with their sons if they were passive and incapable of mastering adversity in their peer relationships. With their daughters, they felt rivalry regarding their achieved womanhood and sometimes about their femininity.

In certain cases, the struggle between parents and children took the form of projective identification. A vivid example of this is evident in the following interaction between mother and daughter in the Young family.

Mrs. Young became very angry with her daughter when she started using makeup. She said to her, "What are you doing with such a goyish face?" During therapy, it became evident that this reaction to Frieda's use of makeup was a product of her own guilt feelings. Mrs. Young's entire family had perished in the Holocaust, but she had survived by disguising herself as an Aryan, using makeup.

Among all immigrant families, success is equated with material achievement and with ensuring that the children surpass their parents educationally and professionally. Among survivor families, obsessive rescue fantasies are linked to their children's success in life. For them, the normal desire for improved circumstances for their children is adumbrated by fears that lack of achievement will result in their annihilation.

While parents depend on their children's success, they also envy them for having opportunities that they had missed. This leads to confusion on the children's part as to what the real expectations are.

In some families where excessive demands were made and the children were high achievers, no success was good enough. One such incident occurred in a family where the son had just received his B.A. degree. The father's response to his son's accomplishment was "So what's the joy in that?" This father compared the achievement of his son to that of another son of survivor parents who had just received his M.D. This same phenomenon occurred in the Berkowitz family, where the father, who still mourned for his lost children, was unable to recognize the real-life accomplishments of his living children.

Separation Anxieties

On the surface, an outsider notices much warmth and intimacy in survivor families. A closer look, however, conveys unevenness in the "love" of the so-called "close-knit family" that cannot tolerate separation. Survivors fear their own aggression and hostility toward their children because it awakens in them a sense of inevitable destruction. Many are therefore quick to express love and warmth by touching and verbalizing in order to offset anger with their young. This interaction with the child exemplifies a polarity in object relations that is different from the "double bind" that is described in schizophrenic families.

Issues related to separation anxiety were present in most survivor families from the early years of their children's lives. The result was that many survivor parents "clung" to their children for emotional support, and there was confusion regarding the separate identities of the parents and the children. In a family such as the Youngs, the father turned to the daughter for the emotional support and warmth that the mother was unwilling to provide. Such a relationship between father and daughter often led to incest themes and taboos that came up in the treatment of survivor families.

The survivor parents' inability to allow their children to differentiate often led to a confusion of roles within the family. This was true not only of the individual roles within the family but also of the roles between generations. Children were forced, at times, to accept prematurely the role of parents while the adults lived out the lost childhood or adolescence that they had missed.

Separation anxieties were markedly apparent in those survivor parents who were never able to integrate themselves into their new communities. These survivor parents generally relied on their children for all contact with the outside world. Many had never overcome language barriers. They were unable to use the new language for emotional communication with their children or with their new environment. This was especially true in families where the survivor parents, during their pre-Holocaust years, had expressed great ambivalence toward their Jewish psycho-historical identity. They were unable to recover their "mother language," Yiddish, and found it very difficult to accept and master the language of their new homeland.

Separation anxieties often resulted in survivor parents being unable to discipline their children in a consistent manner. In families where a lack of boundaries between parents and children as well as an exchange of roles between them existed, the parents were often exaggeratedly lax in controlling their children. On the other hand, some parents employed a very rigid control system. Parents who were lax tended to gratify all their children's oral and anal wishes immediately. As for those who were strict, they controlled their children with angry outbursts when the children did not fulfill their parents' own needs.

Previous researchers have found a higher incidence of parental difficulty in controlling their children and reported more sibling rivalry among survivor families than in the non-survivor population. They attributed this rivalry to the parents' preoccupation with unresolved mourning, which made them less available for their children's needs.

When children reached late adolescence, the inevitable separation awakened anxiety in the survivors about themselves and the child who was leaving. For the parents, it was reminiscent of past losses and of being abandoned and helpless, and it aroused in them aggressive feelings toward the child about to leave.

In survivor families, a family crisis occurs during their children's adolescence in which the whole family unites against the trials of separation in order to avoid mourning and bereavement. In such a situation, the marital partners who married in order to survive and raise a family had to confront each other for the first time since marriage and reinvest their libidinal energies in each other. Although there was a revival of their Oedipal sexual needs, which had been suppressed for so long, they had doubts about the possibility of being able to satisfy one another since the children had been the basis for the marriage for so many years. In spite of their conscious wishes for their children to fulfill what they could not, the parents were envious of them and depressed about their own circumstances.

Victims versus Fighters

Survivor families often seemed to fall into two major categories. On the one hand, there are the fragile, helpless, and martyred victims who are more often to be found in homes of former concentration camp survivors. On the other hand, there are the superhumanly strong and capable ones, heroic fighters, generally found in homes of former partisans and resistance fighters. This distinction had crucial consequences with regard to the home atmosphere, attitudes, and behavioral rules governing interpersonal relationships within the family as well as between the family and the outside world. It was also of special significance in establishing the identity and self-image of the children (Danieli, 1980, 1981; Barocas et al., 1979, 1980; Des Pres, 1976).

This distinction, though helpful in characterizing certain family constellations, does not provide an accurate description of individual family member personality types. Whether or not a survivor came through the Holocaust as a victim or fighter was more often a matter of luck than of a conscious choice on the part of the survivor. Many factors outside the survivor's control were instrumental in determining where he spent the war years and under what circumstances.

Whether or not a Holocaust survivor was sent to a concentration camp or to a labor camp depended on the individual's sex, physical strength, or age. The professional training or number of languages an individual spoke determined the kind of work that was assigned to him and thereby the chances for survival. Survivors from Eastern European countries closer to the Russian border (or those from Eastern and Southern Poland) had a better chance of escaping and joining partisan or resistance groups. Many such groups in Western and Central Poland were decidedly anti-Semitic and often aided the Germans in the persecution and annihilation of Jews. The availability of and ability to use Aryan papers was a factor in determining the circumstances of survival as well.

The use of the word *fighter* to denote the dominant identity of a group of survivors is highly misleading. It describes the identity these survivors chose to convey because of (1) their version of the role, physical or spiritual, which they played during the Holocaust, or (2) the posture they adopted after the war to counteract the role of the victimized Jew. Many of those who chose fighter as their dominant identity lived through the war as partisans, resistance fighters, and members of the underground or skillfully hid from or fled Nazi persecution. Others actively struggled in the ghetto or the concentration camps.

When one speaks of surviving the Holocaust, it is of utmost importance to remember that active fighting alone did not save those who survived the fate of their six million fellow Jews. Most survivors would agree that luck was a crucial factor. Also it would be misleading to assume that because a survivor lived through the war as a fighter, he or she maintained that identity in postwar life. Tragically, many war fighters lived as victims after liberation, and this incongruous transformation created bewilderment in the development of a cohesive self-image for the offspring of such survivors.

The Role of Religion and Israel in the Life of Survivor Families

The typical generational conflict that one sees in immigrant families is apparent in survivor families as well. In some of them, this conflict develops around cultural and religious patterns. Among Holocaust survivors, we generally find an active ambivalence regarding the belief in God. One mother said, "I either hate God and deny His existence because He let me go through such horrifying experiences or I trust in Him because He performed a miracle in allowing me to survive."

This personal love-hate relationship with God often confuses the offspring of survivors as they struggle to understand what it means to be Jewish. Confounding the problem, many parents become enraged at their children for not identifying with the positive side of the ambivalence. In one family, when their twelve-year-old son decided that he did not want to attend *Yeshiva*, the father physically forced him to attend. The father would lose his temper over his inability to change his son's mind about quitting the *Yeshiva* and his disbelief in God. The father had spent a great deal of energy to financially enable his son to attend a private school and was in conflict with his wife about how to deal with the situation. Although the mother was more religious, she sided with her son. The mother thought that Israel would be the only place where they would find help for their problems.

For many survivors, despite their disbelief, orthodoxy became a defense against the past and a way of adjusting to a new society. For the parents, orthodoxy was a means of conforming, while the children experienced it as a burden and tried to assimilate into the American or Israeli Jewish way of life. Religiousness became a weapon through which the parents demanded that their children conform. In the S. family, the daughter was angry because of her parents' hypocrisy concerning religion. They sent her to a very orthodox *Yeshiva* despite the fact that their zeal had diminished since their concentration camp experiences.

Even in families where religious involvement was moderate, it was important for the parents to give their children some Jewish education. Many did not want their children to befriend non-Jews and marrying out of the faith was certainly not acceptable. In one family, the mother's brother married a non-Jew, and it was kept a secret from the children. In a few families, religious belief had many superstitious overtones. As an example, one family believed that their son's illness was a punishment from God.

Several children of Holocaust survivors were subjected to anti-Semitism, which no doubt brought to mind flashes of their parents' past. In one case, a fifteen-year-old schizophrenic boy had a severe reaction to this experience. After being called a "dirty Jew bastard" and being beaten up, he could not fight back. He then attempted suicide by drinking iodine.

An additional aspect of being Jewish after the Holocaust can be seen in the meaning that Israel had for many survivors. One mother regretted not being younger and stronger so that she could produce children who would serve in the Israeli army. One family that had lived in Israel prior to coming to the United States felt guilty about leaving Israel and rationalized their presence in the United States.

Contact with the Outside World

Survivor parents had limited contact with the outside world and continued to feel like strangers even after living in the United States for more than twenty-five years. Their relations with the external world were limited to the necessities of work and education. They even ended by limiting meetings with extended kin.

The theme presented itself in the M. family. Mrs. M. was hostile to "American women" because she was jealous of their lack of anxiety and guilt. Mr. M. feared that the persecution would return and his family would be taken away and killed like his first wife and child. These hostilities and fears were translated into modes of controlling the children. They were told that their mother would go away and the dreaded neighbor would come to replace her if they did not behave.

For many survivors, contact with the outside world brought back fears of persecution. They tended to teach their children to perceive the world as hostile and unsafe. At times, they would go through extreme measures to avoid contact with American society.

Adam B. recalled how his father would never attend parents' night of the Boy Scouts. He always used the same excuse that he was "old and tired," which was clearly a myth. The "old-age myth" and the "sickness myth" were used to maintain their isolation and the strength of the family bond. Hence, the children felt more isolated and alienated in their environment.

In many families where multiple problems blatantly existed, the parents felt it necessary, despite their hostile and suspicious attitude toward the environment, to maintain a "happy family myth" when face-to-face with the outside world. These families struggled to maintain their double mythology. They contended, first, that their members were sick and helpless and, second, that everything was fine and there was no conflict. The first mythology expressed their inner image; the second was a family portrait presented to outsiders. Both were distortions.

Much energy was invested in "keeping up a good front."

For the B. Family, it encompassed maintaining face in an ultra-Orthodox neighborhood despite the daughter's sexual candor, while for others it consisted of a proud display of neat, well-dressed children, despite their obvious emotional difficulties. This striving for maintaining appearances resulted in family solidarity against outsiders. This, however, was not the positive product of resolutions of internal conflicts but represented a false solidarity built on the fear of facing their problems.

The enormous stake these families had in presenting themselves to the world as socially acceptable and as being healthy on the outside while in fact sick on the inside is a phenomenon we have called "family dualism." Family dualism frequently made it difficult for the therapist to perceive the severe problems that lay behind the façade of a model family.

Holocaust survivors, like other new immigrant groups in the United States, concentrated a great deal of effort on materialistic gains, a type of trial at mastery and reactivation of socialized oral needs acceptable in American society. By achieving something that was lost during the Holocaust, an individual restored his damaged self-esteem and felt autonomous, vital, and in control of his life. However, along with these needs, there were also ambivalent emotions connected with changes of dependence, passivity, and over-protectiveness from society.

Many survivors became financially successful and devoted much of their energy to work. Families like those who sought out community mental health agencies for their children were from low socio-economic groups. This was a major cause for conflict within the family.

The concentration camp experience left many men as walking corpses who lacked any energy or drive, while the others invested all their energies in work as a means of survival. In some families, there were periods of time during which the mother supported the families or helped to contribute to the family's financial support when necessary. This meant that mothers as well as fathers were unavailable to their children because of their preoccupation with financial difficulties. The problems in the Schmidt family are representative of adolescent crises in financially overburdened survivor families.

In the S. Family, the mother often worked until late at night. Mr. S. was often sick and in bed at home. Unfortunately, though at home, he was unavailable to his children. Sara, the daughter, became a parent-child and took care of her younger brother from an early age onward. She resented this responsibility because she could not have her own infantile and dependency needs met. Sara was angry with her mother for forcing her to take care of her brother and for not allowing her much time for herself. The mother also wanted her to work in the family business and to share the family *tsurros* (problems). Mrs. S. was very strict with her daughter, stricter than she was with Sara's older brother.

Mrs. S.'s mothering ability was affected not only by her depressed and ill husband, a man who never recovered from his Holocaust experiences. There were other factors as well. She unconsciously envied her daughter's opportunity for a psychosocial moratorium and her ability to enjoy sexual feelings. Mrs. S., because of the war, never had an adolescence. She considered Sara promiscuous when she socialized with other teenagers, and there were ongoing daily battles between them when Mrs. S. returned home from work after a fifteen-hour day.

Another phenomenon that has been observed is that a survivor's education is often interrupted by the war and is never resumed. However, when discussing occupational circumstances, few survivors feel any possibility for change. Some choose to remain in jobs and roles similar to those they had performed in the labor camps, while others seek independence as an ideal goal. Those survivors who became factory workers tended to take these positions because they required no responsibility. At the same time, however, these jobs recreated the familiar frightening situation of being watched by a superior authority. Survivors re-experienced dehumanization and anonymity, causing fears of self-destruction which they felt during the Holocaust. When these men came home from work, they had a need for psychological as well as physical nurturing. They also tended to have a need for cohesiveness and so had to deny and avoid conflict within the family. If the children became too demanding, they retreated to their passive role as fathers who needed peace and quiet because they were ill. Traumatization of the fathers also enabled the women to take over the family in a domineering and controlling manner.

Among those survivors who lost promising careers and educational opportunities due to the war, there were reactions either of anger or total complacency. They tended to place the burden of achieving what they had not done onto their offspring. Survivors lived with an exaggerated hope that they would be able to live through their children's success in life. As a result, they expressed a great deal of anger and blame toward those children who did not fulfill their expectations.

Conclusion

Survivor families most often are made up of only the nuclear family. The emotional interdependence in such families is much stronger because there is no extended family to which to turn for support and the children have no object for identification other than their parents. It lacks the continuity of three generations, an extended family system and a stable system of values and a mythology of life.

Since survivors tended to intermarry, the impact of two such traumatized individuals coming together in marriage and raising a family often resulted in intense emotional conflicts. These conflicts were connected with the lack of a support system in the extended family or in the community. Preoccupations with survival emerged as the overriding concern in these families.

Through my work with survivors, I came to appreciate the survival mechanisms and the pervasive influence such mechanism, once triggered and in force for an extended period of time, can have years after their usefulness has disappeared.

Survivors often complained about the lack of friendship and warmth they encountered immediately following liberation. This was expressed in their lament: "Why did they give me money when I asked for warmth and friendship?" Survivors did not see their further survival psychologically but rather as a search to rediscover the spirit of their destroyed communities.

These families taught us humility and a need for modification in our approach. What they each encountered could have brought them to a regression of psychotic dimensions, yet they found strength to cope in spite of the temporary psychopathological structural change that may have taken place in their personality.

Chapter 10: Families of Holocaust Survivors in Israeli Cities and Kibbutzim

This chapter will discuss the re-adaptation and re-integration of non-clinical populations of survivor families in Israeli cities and kibbutzim. This particular group of survivors experienced a relatively normal childhood and then underwent extreme persecution and loss of their families during adolescence. They immigrated to Israel as young adults at the time of the creation of the state and established families on kibbutzim, which they helped to develop. Some of the families left the kibbutzim often in the first three years of adaptation, and some came to the cities where they had close friends or family members from their youth. They re-interpreted their Holocaust experiences in a context of meaningfulness; they had fought for their lives and survived for a purpose. Thus, the Holocaust had become the organizing principle in their lives and the lives of their families.

My own work, which has been confirmed by other research, indicates that in many cases, the survivors' functions as parents and mates are affected by the persecution and the massive losses they experienced. On the other hand, we had the opportunity to study survivors' families who have nevertheless shown adequate adjustment and considerable achievement in their psychological and occupational lives in a group of families living mostly in the cities and the kibbutzim of Israel.

This approach allowed us to investigate the modes of adaptation and the general coping mechanisms of the family and the possible transmission of psychopathology and social pathology within the family.

The following specific aspects will be considered:

1. The internal and external factors that determined survival and the various modes of dealing with experiences from the time of the liberation to the present.
2. The socialization process of severely traumatized people in the specific social form of community life of the kibbutz and the factors and modes of existence that have been helpful in the survivors' present adjustment,

for example the possibility of institutionalization of aggression within the kibbutz.
3. The relationships within the family—transference of attitudes from parents to offspring affecting their relations with the external world such as acting out and counterphobic mechanisms.
4. The correlation of disturbances of parents with those of their children. The defense and coping mechanisms mobilized in the survivors. The effect of the persecution in dealing with one's aggression (e.g., turning the aggression against one's self, depressive problems, and reactive aggression).
5. The specific psychodynamic significance of the symptoms of parents and children.

Throughout our study, we were impressed by the extent to which the specific social framework of the kibbutz and the general psychosocial atmosphere in the country could shape the adaptive processes and allow for growth of the individual person and his family as a whole.

Some of the survivors gathered to build kibbutzim in which all the members shared similar experiences and memories. Conscious unification around the Holocaust theme demonstrates their acceptance of their suffering and their need to reaffirm their unique self-image as "courageous fighters against tyranny."

The Holocaust-derived identity was augmented by a new group identity as builders of the kibbutz. The socially homogeneous kibbutz composition and their feelings of being valuable "outsiders" counteracted their self-image as blighted, displaced persons. Their collective bonds were forged on both the positive and negative aspects of their common experiences; the horror of witnessing the destruction of their own families, the hope awakened during liberation, and the joy of realizing their ideals in the kibbutz. The newcomers to what they called their homeland invested all their emotional and physical energies in the kibbutz and demanded from each other fierce loyalty to their abstract ideology and physical community. These young adults epitomize Erikson's concept of fidelity: "the vital strength which [youth] needs to have an opportunity to develop, to employ, to evoke—and to die for."

This study is based on research with families of survivors living on kibbutzim which included many survivors of Nazi persecution and was conducted from 1967 to 1969 (Klein, 1971, 1972a). Several families left the kibbutz and are living in cities where I was able to continue my longitudinal contact with them.

The kibbutz communities were engaged in agriculture as well as in cottage industry. Some of the members of the kibbutzim had been leaders of the Warsaw Ghetto uprising. All the families interviewed originated from the same country, Poland, and most had members who had belonged to Zionist youth organizations before the war. They had been adolescents at the time of the Holocaust. At least one partner in each marriage had been with the partisans or had escaped to Soviet-controlled areas. The families had a common social background. They came from the middle social class and seemed to be of above-average intelligence. The couples had married from two to seven years after the liberation, and all the families had one to three children. The oldest child in each of the families was born four to eight years after the liberation and had been reared and educated in the kibbutz.

A different kind of fantasy grew around feelings of entitlement to compensation for the suffering incurred during the years of oppression. This thought is connected with the survivors' feelings of having been a scapegoat for "the sins of mankind." In their frequent reference to the parable of "The Capture of Isaac," they tended to identify with the Isaac whom Abraham (mankind) was prepared to willingly sacrifice. They also expressed their anger at the injustice of God and their loss of belief in his beneficence. They felt that mankind, in general, must atone and compensate them for their suffering. The manifest expression of this "reward fantasy" was their expectation of special treatment from authority figures, such as prolonged vacations, special occupational arrangements, and assistance from social and professional organizations.

After the liberation, there was a general tendency to deny the fact that the family was dead. There were fantasies that one of the parents or siblings had survived, was somewhere in another part of the world, and would be magically found. Niederland described the same phenomenon in 1961 with regard to survivors in the United States.

The infantile wishes for omnipotence, to receive the dead and consequently become "whole" again, represented a denial of death as well as the denial of the feeling of fragmentation and emptiness.

The population interviewed expressed clearly the temporary feeling of loss of continuity in their lives and a subjective experience—which they felt in the first years after the liberation—of a temporary loss of their own body image and self-image. The feeling of world destruction was experienced here by a real break and destruction of the world. At this stage, there were overt expressions of hate and aggression toward the Germans through which the survivors attempted to restore their own self-image and rectify their hurt pride. This anger and these aggressive feelings are not regarded as acting out as such—although in most cases there was a displacement to the representations of the aggressor or to the world at large that "stood idly by"—but as a healthy expression of the self in a sort of "delayed fight" response, a catharsis of long-suppressed feelings of aggression. This is in contrast to many other survivors of concentration camps who denied their feelings of hatred and directed the hatred inward in chronic reactive expressions, or they could not express them at all.

After the liberation, there was an active search for the lost relatives. When these attempts to find relatives failed, there was a pairing need that served as an object substitution. Many friendships developed during the first months after liberation, especially in the *Hachshara* (kibbutz training camp) and, soon after, in the immigration to Israel.

Immigration Phase

During the early post-immigration period, they felt disappointed. In their vivid fantasies, Israel represented an infant's mother image, a mother who would make up to them for their suffering. The harsh reality of life in Israel at the beginning was very disappointing.

Their exaggerated hopes connected with Israel stemmed from identifying the country from which they had come as the "bad mother" and Israel as the "good one." They were greatly disappointed when the fantasy that Israel would compensate them for all of their suffering was destroyed by the reality of their new environment.

The survivors were gradually able to give up the fantasies that had enabled them to bear their existence up to this point: that their lost families would be found. The passing of time had brought overwhelming evidence of the death of their families and relatives, and the "restoration fantasy" that had made their existence bearable had to be abandoned. The dissolution of these two fantasies of hope—compensation and restoration—painfully forced the survivors to confront reality.

When the survivors first arrived in Israel, they displayed diminished libidinal investment in others. Their behavior was characterized by apprehension and a general lack of trust. They avoided intense interpersonal contacts and directed their energies instead into reorganizing their external reality. This tendency was manifested especially in their attempt to conquer their natural surroundings.

The survivors related to the general population with a mixture of disappointment, suspicion, and hostility. The legitimate coping mechanisms that had served them during the Holocaust period included suspiciousness, the binding of instinctual energy to the outside world as a constant source of danger (culminating in "identification with the aggressor"), the hyper-cathexis of the body (in the form of hypochondriasis and complaining) and of the body image and self-image, and clinging and oral strivings connected with physical and emotional deprivation. These defense mechanisms became progressively unnecessary as feelings of security developed. These mechanisms were not adequate in their new surroundings and invited the hostility of the non-survivors. The non-survivors were themselves afraid of the new immigrants whose experiences aroused guilt feelings in them and re-awakened their own insecurities. Some non-survivors fantasized the arrival of the survivors as the "ghosts of their people" coming for revenge. The aggressive expression of the survivors' fantasies for reward and libidinal gratification led to an aggressive reaction on the part of the non-survivors because of the latter's feelings of guilt and fears of revenge from their own lost families. This mutual suspicion along with the disappointment of their fantasies made the survivors feel "rejected."

The mistrust and suspicion was gradually mitigated by positive experiences in everyday life and work and the achievement of material and ideological goals. Despite their own fears, the older settlers accepted the new immigrants without recriminations. They were welcomed into their communal settlements, and some became members of the established kibbutzim. Others were given land and an opportunity to build a kibbutz and an equal chance for self-realization.

Before entering the kibbutz, the survivors spent time in a training camp (*Hachshara*). There they were able to develop ties so that they could go into the kibbutz with people they already knew.

Kibbutz Ideology

By definition, the kibbutz community elicits labor and voluntary commitment from its members in return for material and emotional support. Since these rights and responsibilities are an integral part of the ideology, the survivor families do not have to appeal to the community as survivors in order to receive support. Instead, the generally supportive atmosphere and economic assistance is automatically provided for all members and not only to individuals because of their unique deprivation. This egalitarianism has helped the survivors develop positive self-images and self-ideals as individuals and families who do not need pity. This is in keeping with living in a social environment that is unwilling to pity them but is willing to share. The children who insist that their parents not be pitied have incorporated this attitude: "They are saved and they are here, healthy and happy! Those who died are to be pitied."

The valued time perspective of the kibbutz ideology is to the future; the valued lifestyle is leadership and intense activity. This activity provides an antidote to the enforced passivity that was an especially oppressive feature of the persecution. The perversion and meaninglessness of activity and the suppression of aggression toward the persecutors had a destructive impact on the self-esteem of all survivors but more so on the males who were struggling to create a sense of masculine identity as part of their adolescent phase. The high value accorded to meaningful activity in the kibbutz and the reduction of guilt through fulfilling individual and community ideals probably accounts for the lower percentage of chronic depressive states among the survivors in the kibbutz than among survivor populations in other social settings. The opportunity to exercise initiative and to undertake personally meaningful, productive work was denied or prevented during the Holocaust. Its continued absence in the lives of survivors outside the kibbutz is conspicuously problematic.

Kibbutz ideology demands that members invest their whole selves in actual situations and the fulfillment of future goals. It provides members with a self-ideal as *chalutzim* (pioneers) which is highly valued and compensates for guilt feelings about the past. Survivors in the kibbutz derive satisfaction from its value system, which emphasized present and future contributions rather than yesterday's failures and guilt and provides them with feelings of acceptance and security. This collective ideology answers personal needs; it is not considered alien.

The ideology translated into daily life allows the survivor to stop struggling as an individual and to abandon certain regressive survival mechanisms of the concentration camps that are no longer adaptive. The re-acculturation and re-socialization processes of the survivor families have provided them with a means of adaptation that concurs with the demands of the social and ideological structure of the kibbutz.

The kibbutz environment provides the survivor families with an opportunity to incorporate the values of the social system into a personal ego-syntonic coping mechanism in the service of maintaining a sense of order and purpose. The social structure allows the survivor himself to mobilize anxiety and aggression as part of a group rather than as a lonely, struggling individual. The humanistic, democratic, goal-oriented, structured, and predictable quality of daily life, contrasted with the former chaotic world that he experienced, evokes in the survivor on the kibbutz the lost feelings of basic trust and security in his environment and allows him to take a positive and active responsibility for his fellow members and to structure his life according to a living social model.

Beginning New Lives

The first attempts to cope with the acknowledgment of the death of family members were to establish love relationships. While this could be perceived as an attempt to avoid mourning, it in fact represented a positive reaffirmation of life. Survivors tended to marry each other because they felt a close bond with those who shared the same experiences. A marriage bond also provided the opportunity to mourn together and not feel abandoned by mankind.

Sometimes a crisis situation occurred immediately after the marriage or after the birth of the first child. In the concentration camp, there had been no possibility of ritualized mourning. The emotional crises, as expressed here in depression and guilt feelings, were connected with a late mourning reaction, as there had not been any possibility of emotional catharsis during the period of persecution.

In general, those survivors who had been in the Soviet Union had a higher level of formal (secondary) education than those who had been under the Nazi rule who had had no such opportunities. In spite of the educational differences, at the present time, all the families have similar systems of values and expectations for their children regarding intellectual and social achievement. There is a definite wish that their children should be socially active and be capable of mastering adversity. There seems to be a definite pattern of relationships between parents and children. The families of survivors tend to spend more time together within their own homes with their children than do the other families in the kibbutz.

They see in their children a source of security and gratification. There is a tendency to see in their children the lost parents or siblings or to experience them as replacements for the lost ones. For instance, they are given names of deceased fathers or brothers or names that symbolize survival.

The dominant motif in the family seems to be the restoration of the lost family and the undoing of the destruction. This has consciously motivated most of the marriages immediately after the liberation. During the early mother-child relationship, the mothers had fantasies of themselves, their children, or both as being damaged; some of the mothers had obsessions during pregnancy that the children would be monsters. The fear of transmission of the damage and the stigmatization by the encounter with death is frequently stated: "We have such good children despite all the persecutions we have suffered."

The source of these fantasies, as opposed to neurotic mothers with unresolved Oedipal conflicts, was found in these cases in real experiences in the ghettos and the concentration camps, during which they lived with the daily fear of death. In some cases, these fantasies were acted out by women remaining sterile for many years, suffering miscarriages and amenorrhea, or on occasion, all these conditions.

There is an over-protectiveness and identification of the first-born children with the lost members of their original family. This has resulted in inappropriate emotional and physical responses to those children during their first months of life. The parents have lived in fear that something terrible would happen to the children, especially during infancy; this continued for many years.

The parents may have many fears about their children, derived from their fear of the return of persecutions. There is a fear of separation that is shared by the children. This fear becomes conspicuous in situations of danger (such as the war in June 1967) or when the children become ill. At such times, the parents show compulsive ritual behavior, for example, frequent nighttime inspections of the children. The parents suffer from repetitive persecutory dreams. These are almost unmodified memories of Nazi persecutions, dreams that involve having their children with them in concentration camps in which they are trapped without escape.

The survivors talk about their experiences during the Holocaust with their children. The children in the kibbutzim do not identify fully with their parents as victims; they view the traumatic past somehow as a lost battle, compensated for by more recent victorious ones leading to the rebirth of Israel. Interviews reveal that these children of the survivors are able to find continuity, responsibility, and the capacity to deal with authority both in terms of accepting it and exercising it. They develop social skills as well as responsibility, with positive experiences in leadership and in the spheres of sexuality and their own competence.

Illustrations

Case A

In my capacity as a psychiatric consultant to a kibbutz, I became acquainted with one of its founding fathers and current leaders.

This thirty-five-year-old man, married and father of two children (aged five and eight), had spent five years between the ages of ten and fifteen in a ghetto and later in a concentration camp. The Germans, leaving him as a sole survivor, annihilated his parents and his seven-year-old sister. He immigrated to Israel in 1946 at the age of sixteen, soon after his liberation. He contributed vitally to the development of his kibbutz, specializing in a specific branch of agriculture and eventually became the secretary of the kibbutz. He was involved in the underground *Palmach* movement and participated in the 1956 and 1967 wars.

This rather well-adapted man gradually recounted to me his recurrent preoccupations with the traumatic events of the past. He told me, with tears in his eyes, about the repetitive thoughts that occurred to him whenever he held a child on his lap—young children being hurled against the walls, being murdered by the German soldiers. His immediate response to this fantasy was to shout to himself, "I shall not let them. I shall kill them."

Gradually he began to talk angrily of the helplessness of his parents who were unable to protect him. He discussed his preoccupation with his own feelings of guilt associated with his inability to fight for and save his sister. Such experiences, it might be added, do not, as far as is known, exist in the realm of childhood fantasy. In this context, a recurring theme developed in his therapy. It was the parable of the sacrifice of Isaac by Abraham and his own experiences during the Holocaust. He perceived himself as the one who had sacrificed his own family so that he might survive but also as the one who was abandoned.

A vivid illustration of his struggle with current conflicts rooted in the experience of the Holocaust—and at the same time of his newly acquired achievements and hard-won new identity—was his account of the encounter with the first German he had met since the liberation.

Upon being confronted unexpectedly with a German volunteer in a field one day, his immediate reaction was one of rage and utter bewilderment. He had fantasies of killing and destroying the "anonymous German." However, he gained control of his rage and expressed his feelings by the symbolic act of giving the young man grapes he himself had cultivated. This gift was accompanied by the words "Your father gave my father Cyclone B. I am giving you the first fruit of the land of Israel." They both cried and, as a result of this mutual catharsis, were able to relate on a man-to-man basis rather than on an aggressor-victim basis.

By virtue of this act of forgiveness, his rage toward the aggressor could be relinquished and he could deal with his own aggression in the spirit of his newly achieved self-image. It seemed to me that by this act, he had managed to liberate himself from the negative identity that the Germans tried so hard to impose on their victims.

If we consider his whole life cycle in Erikson's terms, his new society, the *kibbutz*, which functioned as a new extended family, freed him from feelings of shame. It also provided him with tools he could use in the mastery of his conflicts. It engendered a new system of values and contributed vitally to feelings of self-sameness and personal continuity. He felt that there he was the host, the man of the earth, no longer a displaced, uprooted wanderer craving revenge. Through participation in the struggle with the desert and through his continuous effort of building his own community, he finally regained a sense of belonging.

Case B

Joseph and his wife were in Poland during the Holocaust; she was in a ghetto and a concentration camp, and he, born in 1927, was similarly in a ghetto for a time and then in a concentration camp. He finally ran away and lived as a so-called Aryan. They have two children, a girl of thirteen years and a boy of nine. This is a family of intellectuals. The father is leader of the kibbutz and is very active in the political movement. He was an adolescent during the years of the Holocaust. His family had four members; the Germans killed both his parents and his older brother. When speaking about his memories and his associations to the Holocaust, he tries to be very intellectual, rationalizing his feelings and describing his own experiences as if he was speaking about a part of history. He stresses that his own feelings are not involved in it. When talking about his experiences, he always uses the plural form "we": "we" experienced it, and "we" had the same kind of experience. Sometimes he talks of himself in the third person. It is obvious that this man's whole life is centered on the theme of the Holocaust. He tries to rationalize his own experiences in the broad concept of the "continuity of Jewish existence."

During the Holocaust, the most difficult experience for him was to hear of the death of his older brother, whom he idealized. He was in a forced labor camp at the time when he found out that the Germans had killed his brother. He cried for the first and only time at this news. Immediately thereafter, he escaped from the labor camp. In a different area, he lived as an Aryan to avoid detection. It seems that those years of fearful watchfulness left a permanent stamp on the way he views and experiences life, for example feeling that he is watched and that he should not disclose any real emotions since such an outburst might cause his arrest and death. It seems that until we met, his position toward the world had been that of an intellectual and "an example for others," but somehow I felt that he was hiding something. It was obvious that he was experiencing himself as a kind of symbol and felt that he had to live up to the expectations of others.

While hiding on false papers, he was in constant danger of being discovered and having his true identity revealed. Therefore, he felt it necessary to maintain a cold and detached attitude. Actually he was stressing the need he felt for continuity. He did not have feelings of hatred or revenge. He dedicated himself to a constructive solution of his own needs for warmth, family, and continuity of Jewish existence. He had a definite purpose when he ran away from the labor camp. He would build his home in his own homeland and thus fulfill the ideal of his older brother who was a Zionist movement leader.

The greatest experience for him was the War of Independence. He said, "Here I found myself and my brother. Here I felt that I was fulfilling something which was his ideal." Joseph relished his image as a hero, able to master difficult situations. During the 1967 War, his older daughter was very ill, having been made an invalid through a traffic accident that resulted in osteomyelitis. Even while the child was in a critical condition, he was able to fight on the front. After returning from the war, he sat at the child's bed, day and night, with warmth and calmness, unflustered by the rapid, emotionally charged events. He stressed that the Holocaust gave him strength to overcome every dangerous situation. His identification with his brother and introjections of his representation are like a reaction formation. He has to be a hero, fulfilling the ideal of his brother.

His life is so dominated by these needs and fantasies that he gives the impression of being detached and cool. His use of the plural first (or third) person pronoun instead of referring directly to himself may be a kind of defense against the possibility of any emotions occurring, or it may be symptomatic of the incomplete introjection of his brother, suggesting that he and his brother were the "we" during the persecutions.

His wife comes from a more religious background and now works as a nurse in the kibbutz. She is also the sole survivor of her family of seven. She was the fourth child. She seems to be a very warm person in her relationship with her husband. She does speak about her own experiences. She allows herself feelings and emotions, obviously not denying her own experiences. In contrast to her husband, she adopts a more historical viewpoint, with a need for intellectualization and generalization. She speaks warmly about her Chassidic father and the Sabbath celebrations of her youth to her children. I met the whole family on a Friday evening. They observed the Sabbath evening ceremony despite the parents' irreligiousness. The mother described the Friday evenings in her parents' home. One of the children said, "You are telling us this story so vividly that I can imagine my grandfather. I can imagine the house in which you lived." This point was the highlight in the interview, stressing the continuity of their existence.

We could observe that the mother is a source of warm emotion; the father, through the intellectualization of his reactions to the persecution, is giving the children a dispassionate account of the experiences that he has had. Thus, they can speak without anxiety about their parents and view their father as a kind of hero. When the mother spoke about her own experiences, of how she taught children during the time she spent in the ghetto, one of the children, the one that was very ill, said to her mother, "How could you be so warm, so nice to the children during those terrible times?" The children themselves talked about the forthcoming "feast" of the Holocaust, referring to the day of remembrance of the Holocaust observed annually in the kibbutz.

For the children, the day of remembrance is a sort of "convention" when thousands of people from the entire country come to the kibbutz and its museum. It is a holiday comparable to *Passover*, a religious holiday with historic meaning—not a day of mourning but of pride and joy. The members of the kibbutz symbolize the Holocaust with the burning of a yellow Jewish symbol, a sign of the slavery. They speak about the transition from slavery to independence. This phenomenon could be seen as a denial in its specific form or a full reaction formation.

During the Eichmann trial, the husband and wife began to write their own memoirs. This was a very emotional experience for them. The recollections brought back not just sad memories, anger, and hate, but also feelings of pride about their friends, their families, and themselves. They took pride that despite the extraordinary persecution, they continued to relate to each other as human beings. The husband was able to entertain a Polish friend with whom he had lived during the Holocaust and was able to express his feelings of gratitude. He felt secure enough to relate to his friend without bitterness and anger. He found himself capable of expressing friendship.

The children themselves speak of running away and escaping from the Arabs. They speak about the war with anger and anxiety, but in their relationships to other children, there is warmth and a feeling of security and belonging. Their ability to experience and express aggression seemed adequate. The injured girl seemed to have recovered quite well from her own traumatic experience of the automobile accident. Although she is unable to walk, she is active in the group at school and in other social activities. Neither child shows neurotic symptoms and unlike many other children in the kibbutzim, they do not suffer from pavor nocturnus, enuresis, or other symptoms.

Case C

Eva comes from a middle-class religious family, of which she is the sole survivor. At first she speaks reluctantly about herself and about her family, but soon she becomes flooded with affect. In both interviews, she seemed to be under pressure to express intense feelings. She is aware that she has emotional problems stemming from the persecution. She has tried very hard to run away from her Jewish identity. After the liberation, she became a Communist in liberated Poland but she could not "make it."

In her childhood, she felt very strong ties to her father, who was a member of a Chassidic sect but also a very tolerant man. Her mother was much more of a fanatic, and Eva felt that she was a strong, obstinate woman. During the Holocaust, she experienced her mother more positively and felt her to be a strong heroic woman. Her feelings toward her father changed when she saw his clinging to life and his fear of death, which she experienced as cowardice; he did not live up to her expectations. These experiences shook her image of the father whom she had usually felt to be strong and a good man, especially when he tried to run away and hide, leaving his family alone when the Nazis came for him. In contrast, her mother went to the Gestapo, trying to save him. She has obsessions about the question of why he was so afraid and why he did not try to save the family instead. As a result, she identifies much more now with her mother's position toward life and now tries, as her mother used to, to suppress her emotions. During the Holocaust, she was in the ghetto as well as in a concentration camp. She ran away from a transport to Theresienstadt and lived as a Polish girl on Aryan papers. She sees herself as a woman of initiative who in her childhood (at the age of twelve) was already involved in Communist activities, stressing that it was not a protest against her parents but an identification with the poor people—trying to save them from their suffering.

Even before the war, she suffered from anti-Semitism in Poland. After the liberation, she saw something in the Communist ideology that would save mankind from anti-Semitism as well as from slavery. She married a non-Jewish man who was a member of the Communist party. However, after one and a half years of marriage, she decided that her place was among Jews. During this time, she was working in the secret police in Poland, where she could express her hatred and need for revenge. She took the revenge into her own hands. She felt that this hatred gave her strength during the concentration camp experience and allowed her to survive. After a year and a half, she felt she could no longer be a Polish girl. She felt she was running away from her identity and betraying her parents. She went to Israel, learned the language, and remarried. Her second marriage is quite successful. Her first marriage to the Polish man gave her satisfaction in the sexual sphere. The second marriage was motivated by the need for security as well as the need to return to her Jewish identity. She married a man fifteen years her senior, a father figure who himself is a strong man. This man was not imprisoned in a concentration camp. He ran away to Russia, where he had very difficult times but was able to save his family and identity.

Eva has some neurotic symptoms in the form of her anxieties, mainly about her children. She also suffers from depressions. Her anxiety is expressed in restlessness, connected with her feeling of a lack of sexual fulfillment in her marriage. She feels that the kibbutz gave her a feeling of security that she could not find in Poland or anywhere else than the kibbutz. She thinks that her child is much stronger than she because her child has been influenced by other parental figures in the kibbutz. She likes to hear stories about the Holocaust and cannot at all deny her own suffering. It seems that with the death of her father, the Oedipal conflicts became colored with tragedy, which influenced the future course of her life. Her attempt to live as a non-Jew in Poland, by marrying a non-Jew, was a neurotic solution. Here in Israel, in the kibbutz, she achieved a feeling of fulfillment from the point of view of finding social justice as well as finding a security that she could not find elsewhere.

In spite of all her neurotic conflicts and symptoms, she is quite well adjusted in her role as a teacher. With her very strong superego, she is able to give her children and her pupils a system of values. However, she is well aware that she cannot transmit to them the kind of zeal for justice that dominated her childhood. Summarizing her own feelings about the past and her present life, she said, "Sometimes I feel I need to run away from the closeness of the kibbutz but the experience of the kibbutz is so strong that it gives me strength. I couldn't live in any other surroundings."

Yael, Eva's fourteen-and-a-half-year-old daughter, described her own feelings about the 1967 war and the problem of aggression. On the first day of the war, she and the other youngsters thought that it would be another kind of Holocaust, that the Arabs would possibly come to the kibbutz, and that everyone would be destroyed. She dreamed a lot about the war and said, "At one time, I didn't think that I would fight them—I thought only that we would run away and hide." Never having seen her parents cry makes her afraid to cry. However, early in the war, when her teacher was killed, she as well as the other children cried. The morale was very low, and she said, "We wrote a lot of poems about this teacher." He was a kind of symbol of strength and love of life for them. She thinks that the older people in the kibbutz could not express their feelings; they did not cry because they had so many dead people to mourn. She stressed that separation is difficult for her. When she thinks about the family and friends of people killed in war, she thinks it is not important for them to have been heroes. What matters is that they are no longer living; it is not important how they died. She loves to read stories about the Holocaust and heroic acts of Jews. When she speaks about anger between the children, she stresses that she and her friends in the kibbutz cannot be angry at each other; they feel that anger is dangerous. When she thinks about the "new" children of the immigrants from Argentina who are in her classes, she says that they are much more able to express their anger and indifference.

I have the impression that this is a child who is very intelligent and also very sensitive. The defense mechanism of the denial of aggression toward the parents and her peers is very conspicuous. We can also observe the doubts about the strength of her own people to defend her against man-made disasters and her dependence on her peer group as a defense against her anxieties and helplessness in a situation of danger. She does not think that the adults could protect her against dangerous situations. She feels there are strengths in the kibbutz that are lacking in her own parents. She is aware of the sadness in her mother and sometimes in her father about their past.

She says, "I can understand mother because she lost everyone in her own family." In this way, she is trying to defend herself against the ambivalent feelings toward her mother. As for her mother's depression, she blames outsiders, the aggressors—not the mother herself.

Case D

Deborah is a woman born in Poland in 1924. Her husband was also born in Poland in 1918. They have two children, a son of fourteen and a daughter of twelve and a half. She works as a teacher and does not feel any discontinuity in her life. In her childhood, she had many friends and was active in Zionist organizations. During the war, she worked in the underground and was very close to all the leaders of the uprising in the Warsaw Ghetto. She sees herself as an ambitious woman who has always had a need for a purposeful life.

During the war, when she was active in the resistance, she was one of the most important members of the Jewish underground in the Warsaw Ghetto. She was purchasing weapons for the resistance movement as well as remaining outside the ghetto as the contact with the Polish underground. At considerable risk to her life, she entered and left the ghetto repeatedly in the service of the resistance. Eventually she was caught and sent to Auschwitz and later to Ravensbrück. Even at that time she was not alone; she had friends in the concentration camps. She was quite ill (she had typhus) but gave help whenever it was needed. When I asked her what gave her the strength to live through the concentration camps, she said that all she thought of at the time was that her two brothers were alive. Also her feelings of hatred toward the Germans were so intense that it gave her the strength to live through the two years in the concentration camps. She now reproaches her mother, who survived, that she did not help them to survive. After the war, she had a kind of shock reaction. She was sent to Sweden for rehabilitation and learned that her brothers had been killed. Upon hearing this, she attempted suicide, feeling she had "nothing" to love.

Deborah's aimless drifting after her suicide attempt was interpreted as an expression of her hopelessness and her feelings of being unloved and devoid of emotional ties. With the dissolution of her whole world, she repeatedly experienced a previously suppressed feeling of destruction. She then had a period of sexual activity with different men. In joining the Zionist movement, she was trying to retrieve the self-ideal of her pre-traumatic adolescence and maintain the continuity of her identity. When she came to Israel, she became one of the organizers of the kibbutz in which she now lives.

Of her relationship with her children, she says that she cannot free herself of the fears that something terrible will happen to them. She is driven to return hurriedly to the kibbutz from the different school activities in which she takes part. In the concentration camp, after every "action" (selection and mass murder), she would wash herself "to make her feel as a human being again." She did not marry for love but because of the need for her own home. She sees her husband as a father figure who "does everything for her."

She sees the kibbutz as an extended family. She experiences especially those people who shared the fight in the ghetto, with whom she had been in the resistance and who are now leaders of the kibbutz, as relatives. She has a very strong relationship with them and has developed deep feelings of dependence and interdependence. There is also a need to maintain the myth of glory, and she feels that she is one part of it and has to live up to the expectations of the other people in the kibbutz. During the founding of the kibbutz, she felt that there was quite a difference and disharmony between the concentration camp survivors and the group of leaders of the resistance movement of the Warsaw Ghetto. The concentration camp survivors were trying to forget about the Holocaust. The people of the resistance movement were forced to bring the past back to the survivors who were trying by suppression, regression, and denial to be "normal people."

However, in the course of the years, the differences have diminished, and there is now a kind of feeling of pride in the leaders and a feeling that "we are in a kibbutz and that is the pinnacle of our lives." The source of identity has shifted from the Holocaust experience to the kibbutz itself, the consensus being, "In the kibbutz, we find the realization of our ideals of the past and the resolution of our problems of the present." Deborah and her family share these ideas and agree that the kibbutz has given them security and fulfillment. No longer is there a need to suppress and deny their Holocaust experiences.

Deborah's son, who is fourteen years old, is quite introverted and had a difficult time between the ages of seven and eight when he was quite aggressive, sensitive, and did not make friends. The family pays attention to the development of the intelligence of their children, and they are proud of their intellectual achievements. The children like to visit home. The parents very often speak of their past in the ghettos and especially about the resistance movement.

The father tries to be "both father and mother" to the family. He speaks with pride about the activities and the achievements of his wife during the war. He views the concentration camp and ghetto experiences as part of his own and Jewish history. By the defense mechanisms of intellectualization and identification with the kibbutz and the new generation, he is able to overcome some of the effects of his traumatic experiences and sees in the development of the kibbutz and the state the fulfillment of his aspirations and emotional needs. Also, in his children, he sees the fulfillment of his own needs and wishes.

Their daughter is very proud of her mother also, although she does not say so quite openly. On the surface, she is quite aggressive toward her. She does not have the same inhibitions that her older brother had. She says that her mother taught her a great deal about the Holocaust and about her activities during the war. The personal suffering of her mother is denied. Her reaction to the death of her teacher may have been a displacement. Early in the Six-Day War she feared it might turn into an "Arab Holocaust" and thought the best solution would be to be together and not alone. Expressions of anger and hostility against the Arabs were absent. She says that there are no reasons to be angry with them. Between the children, there is also no expression of anger. They are trying much more "to educate one another." It seems that the daughter has special anxieties about separation and about death, but she denies every expression of aggression because of her own anxieties.

She tries to intellectualize and rationalize in order to defend herself against expressions of anxiety. Only from her did I learn that her mother is suffering from high blood pressure, which she developed after the war. In retrospect, I think that the high blood pressure is connected with Deborah's suppression of anger, hostility, and aggression during the time spent in the concentration camp after her heroic struggle in the resistance movement. The hopes and the emotional needs of a woman who tries in her behavior to be active and "to save others" are manifestations of her self-ideal. She ran away from her image of her passive parents who "gave themselves up to slaughter," as she put it. There is some kind of reaction formation in her exaggerated activity in regard to her own needs for passive gratification despite being loved and secure. She is always the one who gives. In the kibbutz, the whole family received and developed a feeling of pride and fulfillment and especially security. They feel that they could not live in any other place because here they have found an acceptable substitute for the lost relatives.

Kibbutz Children of Survivors

All the families except one had firstborn girls. However, the family whose oldest child was a son brought their daughter, second born, to the interview also. None of the children showed any conspicuous disturbance in their behavior. Still, ten of the twenty-five children had symptoms such as nail biting, enuresis, and thumb sucking, and in one case, there was a history of frequent crying and withdrawal from others when feeling hurt or insulted. The child and her mother shared this last reaction pattern.

All the children were brought up in the kibbutz. At school, all of them showed application and success above the average level. They showed very high intelligence and good verbal ability. The following common problems were noticed during the interviews and psychological testing:

1. The youngsters show an unconscious denial of conflict situations with the world of the surrounding adults—parents, teachers, and homeroom teachers—and avoidance of overt expressions of anger or aggression toward parents. In their TAT responses, there is a marked tendency to change frightening situations into pleasant ones and to invent happy and positive endings. Denial is prominent where aggression-provoking situations are represented, especially when they are confronted with separation or death.
2. When confronted with open aggression (from children and adults as well) or with the danger of war, the children's tendency is to react passively, to escape, to hide, to cry, to stick to the group of children, and not to respond by active aggression. When they observe children fighting, they try to persuade them to stop or ask for adult help.
3. All children tend to stay as much as possible with their parents. They dislike any kind of separation, even for a short trip outside their home. There is severe anxiety aroused by separation from family members, educators, or even friends, and a great deal of emotional energy is mobilized in the avoidance of separation or denial of it.
4. There is a wish to protect the parent who survived the Holocaust—to take special care of him and to avoid asking any questions that might hurt him. As to the questions concerning the Holocaust and the parents' part in it, the children tend to emphasize the heroism of the parents. They are proud of the active part their parents took during the persecutions and even today as defenders, saviors, or representatives of the persecuted. There is no reference to suffering or any traumatic situation that occurred to the parents. It seems that there is a common

> denial by the children and the parents who never speak about the suffering and the torture they went through in the ghetto or the concentration camp. They handle this memory like a common secret; they negate and deny. The girls give verbal expressions of pride by statements such as this: "My father is going to Germany in order to testify against a Nazi," or "My father is a member of the 'Association of Holocaust Survivors.'" The girls affirm that their parents are not to be pitied: "They were saved and they are here, healthy, and happy. Those who died are to be pitied!" They agree that they are sorry for the parents who have no brothers and sisters.

During the interviews, the subjects showed a very low tolerance for traumatic memories of the past. It appeared that the ghetto especially was a source of deep conflict because at the time the families were still together, but the feelings of helplessness were overwhelming. The physical struggle for survival in the ghetto created a deep feeling of shame and guilt since the basic trust and security of the family group was destroyed. They tried very hard to forget and suppress this experience while they were all equal in the concentration camp, fighting for physical survival, and each prisoner in an isolated, solitary state. Parents avoid telling their children about these traumatic experiences, which might lower their self-image and provoke feelings of helplessness. This suggests that survivor guilt, anger with parents who have "abandoned them," and residues of humiliating, degrading experiences are active and have to be hidden.

We understand the establishment of kibbutzim, in which most of the members are Holocaust survivors, as the transformation of the model of communal living from that of a passive, coercive experience in the concentration camps to an image that is positive, active, and voluntary. The survivors correlate the past with helplessness, dependence, and death in contrast to the animation of the present in which they see themselves as the energetic, resourceful masters of their own lives and the lives of their families and community. For them, the kibbutz is a symbol of life, a reaction to the destruction of their former world. The vitality of the survivors' new environment is founded on accepting the importance of their persecution and transforming it from a negative into a positive symbol.

These individuals attribute their survival to the existence of tightly knit supportive groups during the Holocaust. Survival is intimately linked with the community. This principle motivated their establishment of a kibbutz and informs their continuous emotional investment in it. The kibbutz is invested with the meaning of life, survival, and the importance of the "group." It is also a link with and continuation of their former, pre-Holocaust existence in small east European towns (*shtetls*). Both *shtetl* and the kibbutz have similarities with closed social systems in which daily life and relationships are stable and where interpersonal ties are strengthened by feelings of distance toward "outsiders" and all sources of gratification are defined as contained within the boundaries of the community. After the liberation, the survivors needed a strong, cohesive in-group that would help them rebuild their shattered identities.

The kibbutz is also a symbol of the stable, supportive, warm environment formerly provided by their extensive family networks. It not only replaces the family structure that was methodically destroyed by the Nazis but represents all those admired individuals who perished. The survivors consciously elaborate some of these interpretations; for example, they refer to the kibbutz as their family. Other symbols are maintained on the level of fantasy; for example, they dream of the kibbutz as a resurrected extinct family or community or a bridge over a gap or an all-encompassing shelter. The kibbutz embodies both basic elements of the family: the father image (activity, protection from the outside world, and provision of physical needs) and the mother image (emotional nurturance and unconditional acceptance). The unification of these two universal representations in the image of the kibbutz underlies the survivor's ability to utilize it as a replacement of the lost family constellation.

They also needed to regain at least a part of their lost sense of trust in themselves and in their community, arising from the feelings of helplessness and ineffectiveness that resulted from their being scapegoats of external aggression. Most of the survivors who joined kibbutzim had been members of socialist Zionist youth organizations during their adolescence. Their ideological fervor and binding ties of interdependence that characterized the "movement" of their younger years are continued as elements of their present-day environments. In this way, the kibbutz symbolized for them their ability to create links with their childhood (family and *shtetl*), their adolescence (vitality, fidelity, and the ideology of youth movements), and their common trauma (bravery, loss recovery, and common fate).

Parent-Child Relationships

The families of survivors have been observed to deal with each other in a highly emotional manner, as if suppressed affects re-emerged and were invested in new love objects. The difference between the style of family life of survivors of persecution and that of other Israelis was evident not only during periods of crisis but also in their general modes of living.

The survivors' families often described the early years of growth and development of their own children in a similar manner. Inhibition of affectivity or emotional ability for nurturing in the mothers was not observed. However, the activities of the firstborn children were often closely scrutinized, with phobic concern and compulsive questioning of the safety of the child, constantly projecting danger to the outside world.

The unique child-rearing system in the kibbutz with its separate sleeping quarters for children and specially trained *metaplot* (house mothers) to care for the children in groups intensifies separation anxieties among survivor families but reduces the mothers' fears that their own mothering would harm their children. The intervention of the *metaplot* and other substitute mother figures provides relief to the survivor mother. As the children grow, the mother's sense of security develops parallel to that of the child. Throughout these years, the survivors recount to their children stories of their experiences during the Holocaust. They defend themselves against identifying with the "victim in their parents" by transforming them into heroes who performed miracles. The children perceive the memories of their parents through a "happy ending" perspective, interpreting all of their parents' experiences as occurring for the sake of the re-establishment of Israel and the birth of the children.

The adolescence of the firstborn presents unique problems to the survivor family because the parents suffered the persecution during their own adolescence. In a previous article, we suggested that the achievement of a relatively normal level of adaptation after massive traumatization is most likely to occur when the victims undergo external trauma during their adolescence. The unique qualities of adolescence are intimately related to the ability to survive and re-adapt. Adolescence is a period in which one is old enough to have developed the necessary strengths and skills to survive and young enough to begin life again if given a chance. Although traumatization during adolescence possesses certain compensatory features as compared to the impact of other stages of psychosocial development, it also creates certain stage-specific difficulties. The moratorium on responsibility, the opportunity to experiment with various roles, and the satisfaction of sexual curiosity and longings were denied these survivors because of the abnormal circumstance of their adolescence.

When their own children reach adolescence in the supportive environment of the kibbutz or later in the cities, they strive for independence and libidinal freedom. The kibbutz ideology predefines the adolescent role as one of intense activity, burgeoning responsibility, and increasing independence. This ideology makes it possible for the children to compensate for their parents' bypassed adolescence by engaging in role experimentation and expressing libidinal strivings. The conflictual feelings awakened in the parents who observe their children fulfilling what had been impossible during their own youth are mitigated when the parents allow themselves to remember some of the joy that they experienced even during the persecution.

Family Themes

The major theme dominating the survivors' present lives in Israel is that of personal, family, and community rebirth. In the establishment of the Jewish state, they feel their own revival. Even after the overwhelming crisis they had undergone in the physical, psychological, and interpersonal spheres, they implicitly felt that it was possible to begin again. This belief was accompanied by openness to acculturation and internalization of values from the new environment. The physical and social environments of the kibbutz, which they had specifically chosen and accepted, provided a framework within which to develop new libidinal ties. The survivors' "rebirth" fantasies expressed their internal reality, as they provided a rationale for surviving the Holocaust and a new image of self-realization as pioneers and builders of a new society. In fact, the major changes that the survivors underwent from the period of symbolic death in the camps to their present life in the Israeli kibbutz can, without exaggeration, be compared to a "rebirth."

The restoration motif underlies the naming of the children and the meaning that each parent invests in his child. Most children are given names that symbolize life, rebirth, hope, or names of those who perished (a Jewish custom). The firstborns are more likely to be identified with the victims of the Holocaust than are the later-born children, but all of them are seen as substitutes for those who did not survive. Parents frequently interpret the very existence of their children as compensation or restitution. Many of the feelings that parents retain of their Holocaust experiences are displaced onto their children (guilt and anxiety). Despite these distortions, the parents also perceive their children as a source of security and gratification. They sometimes remark with real surprise that they have wonderful children despite the fact that their parents suffered so greatly.

Our observations lead us to an appreciation of the nature of such collective instances of mourning occurring in larger communities, even on a national and international level. The identification of the group with the individual mourners has reciprocal qualities. The group projects its own feelings, mourns its own losses, consoling itself and the mourners. The recognition of the deeds and the horrors of the past enable a group to experience a sense of historic continuity and to mobilize group empathy as a positive force.

The survivors of the concentration camps and ghettos of the Holocaust were unable to mourn during or immediately after the war. It was in the kibbutz, in the secure environment provided by the other members and by their own families, that they were gradually able to work through their grief. The children's healthy ability to mourn their own losses are continuations of their parents' successful attempt to work through these feelings. The children fulfill the function of continuing the mourning of the past while simultaneously representing the hope for the future.

Survivors and Non-survivors

In the mixed kibbutzim, it was not only that the survivors shared in the common identity with the non-survivor members, but the reverse as well. On the day of the commemoration of the Holocaust, for example, the entire community mourns together in a collective spirit. The rituals that they have created, for example, burning six candles before every home to symbolize the six million who perished, or displaying flowers and fruit to symbolize the hope and vitality of the present and the future, become a bond that enables the individuals to express together their grief and feelings of rebirth. The non-survivors utilize the occasion of mourning to express the grief about their own lost relatives and to acknowledge that, although their histories were different from those of the survivors, they too experienced a rebirth in the kibbutz.

In the kibbutz, there is a definite community pressure on the survivor families to deny the Holocaust experience as a negative symbol and to accept it as a positive force. Although there is some denial of the affective quality of the Holocaust experiences and an attempt to suppress feelings of guilt, there is no general suppression of the memory of the past as such. Other members (non-survivors) are able to express empathy with the survivors without merging with them into a depression. Mourning, although in some ways incomplete on an individual level, is accepted as a collective spirit and is participated in together. The ability to share pain makes the kibbutz members' ability to share rebirth even more meaningfully.

The ability of the non-survivors to express empathy with their fellow kibbutz members' experiences without merging with them in a collective depression serves as a model for the survivors in dealing with their painful memories. The non-survivors' behavior and attitudes represent alternative models of handling the traumatic past as well as providing a possibility of a dialogue about the most basic experiences in the survivors' lives.

For many years after immigration to Israel, the survivors maintained coping mechanisms that had been in the service of their survival during the Holocaust—suspiciousness and rejection vis-à-vis the outside world. With the gradual subsequent satisfaction of their extensive need for security, support, and compensation, these defenses subsided in the kibbutz. Nevertheless, the Holocaust survivors looked upon those who had not shared their experience with a certain measure of wariness and hostility. These attitudes reinforced their self-image as "not understood" and "different from normal people" and tended to isolate them as an exclusive group.

The Eichmann trial had a decisive impact on destroying the mutual isolation of the survivors from the non-survivors outside the kibbutz by clarifying many myths and emphasizing the collective fate of the Jewish people. In contrast to the analysis of Hannah Arendt, who stressed the helplessness of the Holocaust victims and the cowardliness of their leaders, we found that the Eichmann trial brought to public awareness the positive experience of solidarity, *camaraderie*, and the strength of the life forces in the ghetto in the face of death. The trial provided an opportunity for a national emotional catharsis. In the sharing of grief and anger, those who had not personally known the horrors of the Holocaust became aware of the historical facts and were no longer clinging to the stereotypes of survivors as "sheep," "devils," "heroes," or "holy men." The process of consciously dealing with this traumatic material served to weaken the needs for denial and distortion. Today an Israeli national memorial "Day of the Holocaust" has been established through the pressure of the survivors. This day provides links between survivors throughout the country with all other citizens for the symbolic re-experience of death, rebirth, liberation, and the re-establishment of families and communities.

Conclusion

Although the survivors in the group we interviewed achieved a satisfactory adaptation to their new life circumstances, the Holocaust remains with them in their conscious and unconscious life in dreams, memories, discussions, and writings. The intense effect of their traumatic experiences is not continuously re-experienced, however, because the survivors have developed coping mechanisms of ritualization, intellectualization, and various forms of sublimation and idealization of the "family." The children of these survivors identify with their parents' attitudes toward the Holocaust as a basic experience of their own lives and deal with it by adopting similar coping mechanisms. These families demonstrate that both healthy patterns of adaptation to massive traumatic experiences are relived even one generation after the Holocaust.

The concentration camp survivors in our study were able to retain a crucial sense of fidelity to the past because of its ultimate connection with having experienced "average good mothering" (as described by Winnicott). Their pre-traumatic childhood experiences were good enough to come back to for a sense of historic ego continuity. In addition, they were not estranged from their former experiences because their surroundings were essentially ego-syntonic with their past realities of the *shtetl* and intense Jewish community life. We wish to emphasize the historic continuity with the past that these survivors developed and maintained, in contrast to those investigators who have stressed the revolutionary uniqueness of the kibbutz and its disruption of tradition. The tradition of work was a mere substitution for the tradition of learning in the ideological framework that defined life's meaningfulness for these survivor kibbutz members.

With the passing of time, the survivors' personal and collective ego ideal was recovered from erratic, chaotic experiences of the past into an organized ego-identity by way of the general process of adapting to the country. In their efforts to revive their lost families by creating new ones, we see a revitalization of a whole range of ego strengths.

On the kibbutz, the post-traumatic psychic stress for survivors is minimized by collective identification and expression of loss, mourning, and aggression toward the past tormentors. Their common experience of suffering at the hands of the Nazis is expressed in many forms of group mourning, stressing always that they suffered as part of a group and not only as individuals. Similarly, it was as part of a group that they survived the past and were spared the massive denial with which most of the modern world reacts to the Holocaust. The lifestyle of the survivors and their families on the kibbutz provides an alternative to denial without approaching the extreme of obsession or victimization. We suggest that the relatively healthy adaptation of these families is related to the solidarity and values of their kibbutz communities, the meaningfulness of their work, and their ability to express their suppressed aggression in socially legitimate forms. These factors counteract the meaninglessness and helplessness experienced during the Holocaust.

We have also been impressed with the impact of the survivor and his family on the external environment. With the passing of time, non-survivors in the kibbutz and in the rest of Israeli society have approached a resolution of their conflictual feelings of guilt and anxiety vis-à-vis the survivors. At this moment, there is a process of mutual identification between the survivors and the larger society, a process that was catalyzed by the Eichmann trial. The unique characteristics of the kibbutz and the ability of Israelis to empathize with these survivors have allowed them to consider themselves merely "different" rather than "abnormal and helpless."

PART IV

The Psychotherapeutic Treatment of Survivors and Their Families

Chapter 11:
Delayed Affects and Aftereffects of Severe Traumatization

From my previous clinical and psychotherapeutic work with survivors of the Holocaust, the question to be answered was the following: if and how the vicissitudes of mental functioning during and after the traumatization can be understood in the framework of psychoanalytic theory. In this section, I propose to take up some questions that emerged from my previous clinical research with survivors and deal with them from an analytical, theoretical point of view. I will concentrate on clarifying my point of view on (a) the concept of trauma and stimulus barrier and the adaptation processes during the traumatization period of the Holocaust, and (b) the aftereffects and delayed affects of the traumatization.

This section of the chapter on the psychotherapy of survivors and their children presents a trial analysis of the psychological aspects of the ego-adaptive processes of a group of Holocaust survivors from the time of the beginning of the war through the present stage of their life cycle. An examination is made of the meaning for them of previous traumatic experiences at various stages in their intra-psychic and interpersonal reorganization and of the defense mechanisms that they developed to handle their traumatic past. Emphasis is placed on the issues of death, mourning, and grief in the continuity of life experiences.

Qualitative Aspects of Traumatic Events and Trials of Adaptation During Traumatization

Among the survivors whom we studied and treated, no evidence of manifest severe individual or family psychopathology was discovered in the early childhood experiences during the Holocaust. The fact that they reached the period of the Holocaust in their adolescence, after having experienced the previous developmental phases in a relatively warm, supportive family atmosphere is perhaps one of the determinants of the survival in this group. They seemed to possess good internal object representations as resources for fantasy formation. During the Holocaust, their adequate self-object allowed them to use the specific supportive dyadic or triadic small groups as a source for life and hope.

During the Holocaust, they were forced to become the passive witnesses of the massive destruction of their families and communities. Common features in their responses to the persecution appeared in their personal histories. The first reaction to oppression was an attempt to master whatever could be manipulated and rescued in their external environment, an increased libidinal cathexis of family members and other group formations, and a diminished level of interpersonal conflicts. Intrapsychic conflicts of childhood origin were also characteristically diminished in the face of real danger and the pressure of having to decide existential questions with life-or-death consequences for the self and the family. Aggression was diverted against the external hostile environment through the projection of anger and bad internal objects onto actual oppressors. Trials of externalization of aggression toward the hostile world were made, and at the same time, supportive groups were formed in the ghetto and at school by getting food for the extended family, which was an *eo ipso* act of rebellion against the aggressor. Let us review and conceptualize some of the factors involved in effective protection against traumatization of the ego, especially the functions of perception and affect.

All the survivors suffered physical impairment as a result of continuous extreme hunger, with an intake of 800 calories a day. They also suffered extreme emotional deprivation with consequent doubts about their own body image and self-image as men and women. As long as conditions in the ghetto permitted, the survivors maintained a relatively active personal and social life. However, they had little opportunity for role experimentation or libidinal object choice. They also could not enjoy a moratorium from adult responsibilities. When the oppression became so pervasive that active resistance was not feasible, they became, in most cases, helpless and passive and, of necessity, suppressed the massive feelings of aggression against their tormentors. This caused only a temporary state of paralysis of action and temporary "psychological" numbness of feeling in them that occurred as a characteristic temporary ego reaction. The persecution period consisted of several phases of psychosocial responses, including trials of active mastery of the libidinal ties and finally passive compliance with the aggressor. These could be seen as trials of adaptation and development of specific coping mechanisms for the strains and the dangers inherent during the Holocaust period.

The question that arises is what happens to the individual in the psychological sense when the external reality is more fantastic and phantasmagorical than his own sadomasochistic fantasies? It is well known that such fantasies occur even in situations of adequate mothering (Winnicott) and in an average expectable benign environment (Hartmann) in the pre-Oedipal phase. As survivors of "inborn developmental conflicts," the individual carries "normal" (psychological) scars with him throughout his life cycle. For the Holocaust survivors, the unlimited cruelty inherent in the reality situation of the Holocaust abolished all notions of causality, resulting in an inner world of chaos and the development of a false self, as Winnicott postulated it.

Only the briefest review of the concept of psychic trauma pertaining to the stimulus barrier is possible. Most authors define trauma by its economic nature, a disturbance of the usual distribution of psychic energy, the temporary overriding of the pleasure principle and regression to an archaic fantasy level (Freud, 1893a; A. Freud, 1951; Furst, 1967; Winnik, 1969.) The traumatic situation initiates the traumatic process which is a chain of unconscious events and reactions, resulting in certain immediate symptoms and long-term symptomatic aftereffects (Freud, 1939a; Rangell, 1967). As we know, what differentiates trauma from other pathogenic situations is the "abrupt overwhelming of the ego" and its regression to "primitive pre-ego mechanisms which are, in and of themselves, pathogenic." Thus, the relation of trauma to pathology is given; it is implicit in the traumatic event itself (Furst, 1967). Which of these definitions is applicable to the traumatic events of the Holocaust? I have tried to describe and redefine here the main characteristics in the following way: "Whereas in traumatic neurosis there is typically a sudden single traumatic experience which destroys the defences against excitation (*Reizschutzdurchbruch*), the oppression of the Holocaust is a long series of traumatic experiences aimed not only against the life and physical integrity of the individual but also likely to impair most essential and fundamental psychological, biological and social functions. They are thus likely to shake the emotional basis of the individual's existence" (Klein et al., 1963, p. 341). It may well be that in these cases, the organism develops a raised barrier without which the individual could not continue to exist. It is my hypothesis that under continuous cumulative traumatization, changes of this kind could become permanent acquisitions of the personality in some of the survivors after the return of peacetime conditions.

"This progressively increased stimulus barrier (*Reizschutz*) is likely to form a barrier which the individual is unable to break even under considerably changed life conditions" (ibid., p. 342). We can compare this with Lifton's concept of "psychic numbing."

Of course, trauma in these cases is also determined by:

1. The pre-traumatic psychic reality of the individual involved in it.
2. The quantitative and qualitative stimuli overwhelming the stimulus barrier.
3. The resulting dynamic changes and disarrangements connected with the constellation in the internal world with which the ego finds itself unable to cope rather than by any external situation.

However, the Holocaust itself, because of its nature, structure, and prolonged duration, was potentially traumatic to any person exposed to it. Perhaps Freud had such a cataclysm in mind when he suggested that such a situation as this was a realistic danger of destruction that would mobilize fears of death as well as castration anxiety. He also stated that in such dangerous situations, the ego reacts as if in a state of being deserted by the protecting superego—by the powers of destiny—which puts an end to security against every danger. In all our previous clinical observations, it was stressed that the Holocaust experiences were potentially traumatic in each of the possible ways elaborated by Fenichel (1945), such as the following:

1. The overwhelming of the ego by external and internal stimuli.
2. The enforcing of longitudinal partial regressive changes in the ego's perceptual and cognitive functions and regression of the instinctual drives. The enforced psychic passivity and lack of the full possibility of reality testing has long-term effects or enforces the blocking of ego functions.
3. The repetition of the traumatic events in the service of mastery (dreams) which, however, had to be postponed till many years after the liberation since, at the time, it endan-

gered physical and psychic survival.
4. The upsetting of the entire economy of mental energy and of the equilibrium between repressed impulses and repressing forces.

Following on from the thoughts of Fenichel, one can add that this longitudinal partial regression of the ego and of the instincts was an adaptive mechanism for the survivors of the Holocaust in the service of psychological and physical survival. However, after liberation, this mechanism was not only no longer adaptive but actually blocked psychic functioning and recovery, particularly in survivors who were fixated in their style of repression without being involved in a supportive group system.

Fantasy Formation as a Defense Mechanism

In such a traumatic situation, it seems to me, fantasizing and remembering the past, as a special kind of thought activity, had a defensive function that was to serve as a tool to disconnect part of the chaotic, overstimulated world and to bring back the internalized world of the past when causality was still functioning. As a patient mentioned, a poem about hope and love of mankind remembered during extermination action enabled him to save his self-image. In normal situations, when the ego needs to pursue the reality principle for external reasons, it renounces temporarily or permanently some of the objects and aims of its desires for pleasure. In the cruel reality of the Holocaust, this would have been very hard to endure, and the domination of the pleasure principle was partially replaced in daily living by the strengthening of the safety principle (Sandler, 1960) through the above-mentioned regression of ego-activity in which fantasy, as a special kind of mental activity (Krystal, 1968), enabled the ego to return to relinquished sources of pleasure. Here they were free from the demands of cruel reality and from experiencing the reality of the ghetto and the concentration camp. As we know, in fantasy, every longing and dwelling upon a wish fulfillment brings satisfaction, even though the knowledge that it is not reality remains intact. This realm of fantasy acted like a reservation of humanity that had been reclaimed from the phantasmagoric reality of the ghettos and the concentration camps. Freud, in *Civilization and Its Discontents* (1930a), refers to this when he speaks of the intention to "make oneself independent of the external world by seeking satisfaction in internal psychic processes." In turning to such internal processes, the connections with the unsatisfactory external reality are still further loosened. Satisfaction is obtained from illusions from the recollection of idealized memories. These are recognized for what they are, without the discrepancy between them and the reality being allowed to interfere with the feeling of security and the diminishing of unpleasure. At the time when the development of the sense of reality emerges, the fantasy imagination is expressly exempted from the demands of reality testing for the purpose of fulfilling wishes that are difficult to carry out. As we know, of course, Freud links the emergence of fantasy in the child with the development of *object love* and the sense of reality. This specifically exempts such phenomena as hallucinatory gratification of the infant from the domain of fantasy. Here the fantasizing may be seen as one of the hallmarks of a still existing ego functioning. It enables the person to differentiate the inner world of fantasies, where causality and reality exist in recollections and daydreams about the past, from the external chaotic world of aggression.

In the group of survivors studied, the specific component parts of these fantasies were memories of youthful love, derivatives of childhood memories, and transformations that had an element of current compensation about them. I use the term *memories* in Freud's sense when he refers to fantasies as a product of compromise in the struggle between what is repressed and what is dominant in the present. Fantasy formation as a defense is not stereotyped but fits into the subject's shifting impressions and oscillations of life that changes with every change in his life. It seems that fantasy formation allowed the survivors to create a different psychological situation related to the memory of early satisfying experiences and to the fantasies of the future that differed from the actual traumatic situation and represented a fulfillment of the wish for security and pleasure. Of course, these daydreams drew upon elements of recent and present experiences as well as on past repressed memories. Denial as a defense mechanism was used to modify and elaborate the actual current impressions by the screening of semirepressed memories of the good object representations that still should not be too far removed from reality (Krystal, 1968).

I am referring here to that group of fantasies that show the influence of the working of the subject's preconscious; that is, they have been subjected to modifications of self-ideal experiences in the pre-Holocaust, to parental messages, and to the secondary process. They are receiving the attention of consciousness only in times of extreme danger or catastrophe. They seem to be influenced by family and present group relations and experiences as well as the identification with sacrifice and the sanctification of life, *Kiddush HaShem*, as a meaning for their choice of life and as a defense against death wishes. I am suggesting that the capacity to survive and to recover psychologically following liberation was dependent on their pre-Holocaust personality organization in the life phase during the Holocaust, the time spent in various ghettos and concentration camps, the physical conditions of those camps, and their ability to establish a supportive psychosocial group. It depended as well on the frequency with which the survivor was removed from these supportive groups he had established. We could differentiate between the psychology of adaptation to the Holocaust and the psychology of recovery. In all of the patients we have studied, we have seen the importance of the mutual aid and protectiveness of these small social groups. These groups consisted of intense dyadic or triadic attachments similar to a small family relationship, such as mother/daughter and father/son. These attachments and group formations occurred spontaneously in the ghettos and the concentration camps and helped them overcome the previous disruption of social and community bonds. Erikson, Davidson, and Krystal stress the importance of the disruption of social and community bonds in all forms of catastrophic situations. Therefore, it would be important to recognize the significance of such pairing and group formation in such a catastrophic situation as existed in the Holocaust. They had not only psychological and sociological significance but deep psychological significance as well. As one survivor in therapy related,

> One friend in particular who came to our camp from the horrible concentration camp Maidanek where he was serving in the dead body disposal squad, a fellow they called Katzetnik, became very attached to me. He was older than I was and probably thanks to him I survived the war . . . I can say that he taught me a lot about life in the camps and how to survive. Because of him I matured quite a bit and I am glad I didn't lose humanity. He was a good fellow to me and because of him I think I helped

> several other people to survive. In S., when several of my friends got ill and were taken to the prisoner's hospital where no food was given to the prisoners, I shared my meager ration with them. I know of one fellow who definitely survived because of me.

The small groups that had spontaneously established themselves in the ghettos and the camps provided a setting in which the everyday interpersonal relations and experiences, human feelings of caring, ambivalence, hostility, and jealousy could be expressed again and again (Carmel, 1969). These experiences included extreme commitment to friendship, sharing, and sacrifice and were similar in intensity to those experienced in the previous pre-Holocaust life. One survivor, an adolescent during the Holocaust, remembered in therapy her anger toward an old lady who had been very kind and protective when she arrived at the new camp.

> I became angry with her because her friendship and kindness kept me from running away and leaving her. She reminded me so much of my mother from whom I was separated and could not save. So I stayed to take care of her, and she of me, until the liberation.

Such experiences helped the survivor in maintaining self-cohesion as well as the self-object matrix within which he could retain and reinforce his self-esteem and self-continuity.

The Phase of Recovery from Traumatization: Aftereffects and Delayed Affects

With physical recuperation after liberation, a period of acting out of aggressive and sexual fantasies ensued. In some cases, the previously suppressed rage was expressed at this stage by actual revenge and fantasized revenge against the tormentors. During this phase, the survivors expressed compensation and restoration, especially in such concrete forms as food and dependency needs as manifested in fantasies about the resurrection of their lost families. When subsequently confronted with the reality of the irreversible destruction, the survivors underwent emotional crises with depressive features, suicidal thoughts, and psychosomatic symptoms.

The short-lived crisis period was replaced by a process of renewed interest in forming relationships and in social, cultural, and political activities. It was at this stage that the survivors, in groups or as individuals, began to emigrate mostly to Israel and the United States. The conscious and unconscious motivations for immigration were related to needs for the rebirth of lost families and communities, contact with relatives who already lived in Israel, and fidelity to the ideological ideals of their adolescence. The move to Israel was the first step in the revival of diffused identifications and identities.

The need of the survivors to deny the destruction of their families led to the searching activities characteristic of mourners; they not only tried to trace missing members in a reality-oriented way but also scanned crowds in unfamiliar environments in order to discover a face from the past. This "urge to search for and to recover the lost figures" (Bowlby and Parkes, 1973) stems from a rebirth fantasy connected with regression to magical thinking. Scanning the environment for signs of the departed persisted despite the certain knowledge of their death. Conscious expressions of grief were, however, delayed until after the initial phase of re-adaptation in Israel. The fantasies of the restoration of murdered families, which had sustained many survivors during the persecution, were only gradually and partially abandoned as the evidence of their death became indisputable.

With physical recuperation, the gradual satisfaction of their powerful oral needs in their new environment, and the growth of a community with common interests, the survivors began to re-establish libidinal ties in intense friendships and marriages. These relationships were motivated by the attempts to escape from feelings of loss and grief and restore the lost family. The attempts to establish love relationships frequently resulted in postmarital crises characterized by depression and guilt feelings. In some cases, this crisis period was an important transition which served as a "trial period" for the spouses to attempt to relate to each other without fearful clinging and projections of their lost objects.

The theme of personal, family, and community rebirth was central to the survivors' lives in Israel or the United States and coincided with the theme of the re-establishment of the Jewish homeland. This implicit belief that even after the overwhelming suffering they had undergone, it was possible to begin again was manifest in openness to acculturation in their new environment. The rebirth motif also provided the survivors with a rationale for their escape from extinction as well as a positive self-image as pioneers and builders of a new society. A residue of chronic apprehension was expressed in dreams whose themes were running away from the Nazis, indicating fears of a return of the extermination of the self and the family. Despite the conscious efforts of survivors to rationalize their anxiety, they displayed a very low tolerance for dealing with painful memories and survival guilt. They were people marked by changes of personality in the form of character neurosis. This expressed itself in difficulties with intrapsychic and interpersonal conflicts, irrational fears of the future, survival guilt toward murdered members of the family, and subjective feelings of loneliness. From my experience, it was obvious that *survival guilt* was a way of working through late mourning and bereavement for the loss of beloved ones and of the restitution of lost human values and the restoration of their own human image. It is interesting to note that the guilt feelings of the survivors of the Holocaust were:

1. A means of identification with the lost world.
2. A possible way of restoring the feelings of justice and security in the world.
3. A protective symptom against overwhelming anxiety and animosity.
4. A kind of defense mechanism for living in a chaotic world where all objects of love have been lost and where there are no people to cry and share the grief. This is in complete contrast to the denial and rejection of any kind of guilt by the mass murderers of any age.

It is also possible to observe patients with mixed neurotic features, usually hysterical and depressive symptoms. In psychotherapeutic work with a group of survivors, I found that they shared similar problems of feelings of discontinuity in their personality, of changes of values, and of a lack of basic trust. Their interpersonal relationships where characterized by aggressive tendencies. Their ego structure was characterized by an active mastering of their interpersonal and intrapsychic conflicts. During the period of stress in concentration camps and after liberation, they had succeeded in living with people who offered empathy and support. For all these patients, the everyday confrontation with problems of the Holocaust made suppression and denial of their traumatic past very difficult. They were confronted with these problems through the different media of communication—newspaper and radio—which brought detailed news about trials of war criminals and of political discussions and decisions about relations with Germany. Moreover, living together with so many people with the same tragic experiences and the annual recurrence of Remembrance Day of every destroyed community complicated attempts at suppression. However, from another point of view, the inner reality of the patient in treatment was also influenced by the specific reality of the country, its politics, and physical threats to existence. It provided the possibilities for active mastery and legitimate expression of long-repressed hostile feelings toward the aggressors of the past and toward actual enemies, be they outside the country or within it.

It is my hypothesis that in the period of the long traumatization of the Holocaust, fantasy formation functioned by itself as a defense against traumatic overstimulation—as an attempt to get distance from the "fantasy-like" world of aggression and hopelessness. Briefly, in the fantasies of survivors in the short, relatively traumatic-free intervals during the Holocaust, hope was an essential resource in the tolerance of pain and painful affects. This hope for a better life in the future had its foundation in religious or other ideological motivation (socialistic, Zionistic, etc.). It was based on feelings derived from positive self-evaluation—the feeling that life was deserved—from the presence of benign introjects, and from an effectively functioning time sense of past and future. These functions all seemed to be derived from satisfactory nurturing experiences in the past and constituted an important part of the ego-organization in withstanding active hopeless feelings in these painful states (Krystal, 1968). For example, a female survivor who had not succumbed to the sexual pressures of a Nazi in the concentration camp later said with pride in therapy that the knowledge that "there would be a future in which she would tell her daughter about herself" helped her to remain pure. This enabled her to hold to her self-ideal and was her means of self-preservation. However, the countercathexis against these hopeless feelings in some of the survivors impoverished the ego, so that the later feeling of ego depletion in the post-traumatic period seemed to be connected with this lack of internal and external resources of containment during the period of and after the Holocaust.

The repetitive nightmares were like trials to find a better solution to situations that had not been successfully mastered. Could it not be that the hopelessness and fantasy-like phantasmagorias of the concentration camp period in actual recurring dreamlike states of nightmares of survivors are a repetitive, compulsive counter-balance of the ego that learned to react with fantasy formation at times of threat, be this a threat of external or internal source? The environment and the human resources available would also determine the stimulus barrier at the time of the traumatization.

Briefly, in the tolerance of painful traumatic experiences and painful affects of the Holocaust, certain ego functions were involved, notably the recognition of affects as states of the self and the feeling of confidence in their inability to overwhelm or destroy the ego. Self-awareness and insight were not only possible but also again a continuous need during the traumatization period and in the initial phase after the liberation when the massive traumatization resulted first in general avoidance of intense affect. The fear and anger of having painful affects caused them to "snowball." The painful affects represented a threat of retroactive traumatization. They had anxiety about being totally overwhelmed by their feared affects of vengeance and aggression, leading later to alexithymia. The resulting dread, therefore, was of affects and the drives they represented, especially the aggressive ones. The massive traumatization resulted in instinctual diffusion, which became a secondary contributor to the delayed effects of trauma.

Our experiences with the survivors of the Nazi persecutions indicated that indeed a progression from a state of excited anxiety to a state of passive surrender and, in many cases, catatonic reactions (*muselman* stage) did take place during the phase of unavoidable life-threatening danger (Klein, 1963; Krystal, 1968). Many years after the liberation, these survivors of the Holocaust showed a tendency toward overactivity, anxiety, and somatization (Klein, 1963; Krystal, Niederland, 1968). Thus, an overwhelming of the defensive and expressive functions of anxiety to the point of inhibition, with surrender to destruction, is traumatic in itself. It causes a disturbance both in affect handling and affect tolerance similar to that described in deprived children by Greenacre (1952). I have to interpolate here that the traumatic feeling of impending shock and death awakened automatic anxiety. The question arises:

was it the intensity of the anxiety felt during the ghetto period, or were there specific effects of the continual state of brushing with death in concentration camps that caused this? In the later (delayed) stage, when painful affects re-emerged after many years of "affective silence" and when the survivor was exposed to commonly occurring failures of nurturing and unfulfilled needs, he responds with rage, fear, and the re-somatization of affects. They "rebound" (Krystal, 1968) with spectacular intensity, notably in states of separation. These states mobilize so much painful affect that they can be considered the forerunners of the *Todesangst*—mortal dread—not a fear of dying but an enormous overwhelming anxiety linked with feelings of helplessness and worthlessness. This is considered to be the reason for the overwhelming nature of automatic anxiety (Stern, 1959; Krystal, 1968). Stern interpreted adult mortal dread, together with the feeling of impending annihilation, as the re-experiencing of the infant's panic and total stress situation resulting from the absence of the indispensable mother.

The delayed appearance of painful affects of mourning, depression, and separation anxiety can also be seen as signs of an ability to tolerate painful affects at a time when the ego organization of the survivors is strengthened. This awakened ability to tolerate painful affects could be an essential aspect of the prevention of retroactive traumatization. Krystal pointed out that small amounts of painful affect are released (e.g., as signal anxiety—but other affects can also function as signals), and they mobilize defenses to ward off the flooding of the ego by great quantities of these affects. After the earlier phase of the survivor syndrome, with its somatization of anxiety, we can see that affects utilizable as signals must have undergone a process of de-somatization and a separation from common precursors of specific events. Schur (1955) has pointed out that de-somatization and verbalization, as witnessed in the course of psychotherapy, becomes a means of controlling and avoiding more intense stressful somatic responses. While in adults the physiological aspects of depression and anxiety seem to be antithetical, in survivors the precursor of these resemble anxiety-depression. These undifferentiated precursors of affects (primary affects) remind us of what Engel calls the "primary affects of displeasure," which cannot be utilized as signals. They are mostly somatic, vague, and uncontrollable (i.e., they continue to be the all-or-nothing response).

In other cases, survivors resumed their lives with a relatively intact self, immediately expressing their intense need to find ideals and objects of love. In some, the feelings of revenge and the need to forgive their tormentors began immediately after liberation. The preservation of their own identity and intact self made it possible for them to engage in a very long and intense mourning process and to seek out new objects in the postwar ruins of Europe and to recover forgotten self-representations. The following recollection of a survivor illustrates the capacity to maintain dignity and continuity and recuperate the self and the previous system of values of the superego in spite of extreme changes in the physical surroundings and his emaciated body. He had the capacity to preserve the connection with the self-experience of the humanistic adolescent before the war, his close to *muselman* "walking corpse" existence as a victim of persecution, and his feelings of freedom after the war.

> I was liberated at the age of eighteen near the Elbe. The angry, hungry and emaciated survivors looked at the German prisoners of war under the Russian guards who beat them, took off their shoes and spat in their faces. Immediately the feeling arose in me that we shouldn't be as they were—the beasts of yesterday. I called to the group "Let us not be as they were yesterday." I could take their anger but could not take their behaviour.

The second vignette:

> On the same day, weakened by typhus exactimaticus, I came to a home left by the Germans—a beautiful house filled with furniture, objects of art, silver, with the exquisite tastes of another world of beauty—so different from where I had come from . . . . I went to the library of the house and discovered the book by Heine, *Das Buch der Lieder*. When I read the poem "Im schönen Monat Mai"—and it was the eighth of May, my liberation day—it was the first time I began to cry.

These two experiences were possible because the ideals of the nuclear self had been maintained within the camp, despite the ego depletion connected with the emaciation of the body and long periods of hunger.

I view the maintenance and sameness of the self as an important goal of the psychotherapeutic situation and the survivor guilt as an attempt to achieve self-esteem, self-cohesion, and re-individuation. We will see in the symptoms of pathological mourning and pathological survivor guilt a compromise formation to maintain self-continuity and self-cohesion. In some of my ideas, I come close to the views of Kohut and Orenstein, with their concept of the polarity of the self. In *The Analysis of the Self*, Kohut stresses the need and the capacity to "maintain sameness and continuity despite the changes in our body and mind, in our personality make-up and in the surroundings in which we live" (Kohut, 1971, p. 177).

The first problem in the psychotherapeutic treatment of survivors of the Holocaust seemed to be the problem of motivation for treatment. The unique experiences of the ghetto and concentration camps evoked two basic phenomena:

> 1. Fear of losing the uniqueness of these experiences and of being changed from one who was saved from catastrophe and who has conquered death to one who is mentally ill. These experiences actually don't lend themselves to expression—hence, the paradox of the therapeutic situation.
> 2. Desires of infantile omnipotence on the one hand and a feeling of irretrievable loss on the other due to the experience of a prolonged struggle with death at the time of the Holocaust. As a consequence, two transference tendencies toward the therapist manifest themselves:
>   a. to see him as a potential aggressor and representative of a cruel superego (this tendency finds its expression in direct questions such as, "What do you want from me?" and "Why are you blaming me?");
>   b. to see him as a redeeming figure, one who gives and excuses without end.

Characteristic was the fact that the adaptation to the problems of death and abandonment and to the cataclysm of the destruction of a world known since childhood expressed itself on different levels and at different stages in the treatment. At the first level, the patient expressed his disappointment toward his environment and his suspicion toward the therapist whom he accused of coldness and lack of understanding of the patient's problems. It seemed that most patients hadn't actually accepted the loss of their parents as a fact and weren't able to face up to it for many years. Only at a later stage of the treatment could the patient grapple with the very fact of the death of his parents by mourning and expressing guilt feelings.

Still, it could be observed that the largely verbalized and de-somatized feelings of anxiety, depression, grief, and shame appear during therapy when the patient-survivor discovers ego resources for tolerating pain and painful affects connected with the self-representation. If this self-representation includes modes of behavior acquired by introjections and identifications with benign object representations, he is able to use his defenses and actions as a protection against becoming overwhelmed by painful affects. On the other hand, too rigid a separation of the self-representation from the idealized dead love object representations seems to be a source of the disturbance in the handling of aggression and guilt toward the lost love objects and actual persons. The violent destructive impulses are repressed or denied, resulting in the rigid walling-off of object representations from the self-representation. These repressed and denied impulses return and are experienced as depression in those survivors who could not retain their self-respect and self-cohesion.

To summarize, I have attempted to trace the occurrence of traumatization, the adaptive processes that take place during the traumatization, and the use of fantasy formation in trials of mastery as they occurred during the different phases of psychotherapy with survivors in their memories, thoughts, and fantasies. The relative maintenance of psychological survival and the specific defense mechanisms employed may be used as a bridge toward confrontation and integration of actual psychic reality against the background of previous traumatic experiences during the Holocaust. We view the goal of therapy of the survivor as providing experiences of self-sameness and continuity, satisfying the need for mutuality and the working through of the survivor guilt as a re-individuation process and the recovery of his old nuclear self by relating to his own personal myth of survival. This is accomplished by respecting his capacity to create new life in his family and by helping him to recover the chain of connections between his previous self-ideal, his family representations, and his present life cycle.

Chapter 12:
Problems of Countertransference in the Psychotherapy of Holocaust Survivors and Their Children

It seems that there exists a continuum of transference and countertransference issues that compel our attention in different phases of therapy, regardless of whether the patient is a survivor or a survivor's child. We as therapists who are themselves survivors have a common experience: we have all survived the most excessive of all traumas, the individual and collective death of the Holocaust. But in our lives, the issues of loss and death are prominent—we are living in the shadow of the Holocaust and are reliving the survivors' experiences in treatment. When confronted during therapy with the cruel phantasmagoric memories of the Holocaust, we ourselves are overwhelmed by our empathic identification with the victim and the aggressor in us—overwhelmed that human beings can endure these experiences. And then, in the countertransference, there occur (1) detachment tactics, (2) the need for general conceptualization, (3) over-identification, (4) anger, (5) helplessness, (6) the guilt of survival, and (7) doubts about one's own capacity as a therapist and doubts about one's own profession.

Being bombarded by repetitive recollections of and encounters with death, the therapist should differentiate between various transference modes of the patient. Sometimes the repeated memories of his humiliation and helplessness are invitations by the survivor for salvation by the therapist. Survivors often repeat in the transference the theme of Abraham's binding of Isaac, trying to mobilize the benign parental representation of the therapist as a savior. Very often, the therapist tries to live up to this image in his countertransference and then feels disappointed by his patient's emotional vicissitudes. The therapist is rather required to show empathy, consistency, and compassion without being overwhelmed by his own feelings of guilt. He should be consistently attentive to his countertransference problems. The initial doubts that we can help survivors who went through such extensive experiences are universal and found in therapists in many countries. These doubts are connected with their own guilt feelings, which may lead to their own basic problems of living in their generation of repetitious man-made disasters, the main genocide of our century, unfortunately called the Holocaust. I would rather refer to it as "Human Trembling" in association to Kierkegaard's concept of Abraham's trembling when he was commanded to sacrifice Isaac.

The preoccupation of many therapists with the need for therapeutic distance with survivors is understandable but nevertheless problematic. In 1967, Anna Freud expressed her personal doubts about the possibility of therapy with survivors because of the impossibility of maintaining an "optimal analytic distance." It seems to me that when I am thinking of my experiences with therapists in different countries, such as Israel, Germany, and the United States, the difficulty lies in the universal guilt that besets us—the therapists as human beings. Having been preoccupied with our professional identity as therapists and our self-sameness as human beings, we unfortunately employed important theoretical concepts, such as trauma, without allowing ourselves to question whether they were relevant to understanding the survivor and healing his wounds. In this way, we only rescued ourselves—an expression of the narcissism of our generation. In my opinion, the fact of overemphasizing "survivor guilt" in the therapy of survivors was misrepresented as a pathological feature, part of the "survivor syndrome" (Krystal, 1968). In my earlier paper (1968a), I saw the survivor guilt as an attempt at reintegration of the self—as an attempt of the re-individuation of the survivor after a period of anonymity during the Holocaust. I would add today that this attempt is a restitutive process of the benign inner representation of the parental images—an attempt of the restoration of the self. In the children of survivors, we can also observe the reappearing leitmotif of the preoccupation with the lost representations of members of the family in different phases of the therapy as an attempt of delayed mourning, the *Trauerarbeit*, which the parents could not themselves achieve. This continuing process of mourning is itself a restitution of family representations that have been forgotten, fragmented, and avoided and that now, in their vividness and vitality, become part of the self-representation of the child who allows himself to mourn what his parents failed to do. This is only possible when the therapist allows himself to experience and participate in this mourning process not as a detached participant-observer but as one who experiences and re-integrates his own losses and mourning. It reminds us of Freud's discovery of his own survivor guilt about his brother's death in his self-analysis and its influence on his creativity (1985c).

One of the positive steps occurring in the therapy with children of survivors is the phase when the therapist allows his patient to deal in an un-accusing way with his parents' Holocaust experiences. In such a way, he encourages the patient to ask questions about his parents' experiences without a bombardment of accusations toward them that because they were survivors, they are responsible for his unresolved problems. These accusations are unfortunately often strengthened by the countertransference of the therapist who views the survivor with such stereotypes as the "Pawnbroker," "Capo," "Untouchable," "Field Prostitute," "*Nebich*," and "Holy (*kadosh*) Victim." The therapist must allow the child to deal with his parents in such a way that allows them to share with their child their need for parenthood as an expression of courage and revitalization of their lives. In such a way, the child is better able to differentiate between the reality and his fantasies about his parents. The difficulty in differentiating between internal and external reality is prominent in the child's object relationships. They feel that their aggressive impulses could destroy their parents because the parents themselves, in their self-accusing attitude during the Holocaust, did not always differentiate between fantasy and reality when telling the child about their own pathological guilt feelings. At this point, a common mourning process takes place in which all participate: the child, his therapist, and the parent survivors, which allows the acceptance of achieving restitution of trust between the parents and the child. Then we can observe in the child a re-integration of the self and a stabilization of his ego boundaries, when instead of sadistic and masochistic fantasies about his parents' past, the child is confronted with their guilt of not having been able to save, in a superhuman way, their family and friends. The child no longer has the need to act out the fantasy of being a victim or a savior. The historical reality of the parents helps him to replace the sadomasochistic fantasies about them with the integration of benign representations of their lost world.

In the therapy, Miriam, a twenty-two-year-old whose mother is a survivor, complained of being repetitively accused by her mother, "By not marrying, you are making me sick" or "By marrying that goy, you are destroying me." The mother was unconsciously reliving the return of the aggressor by projecting it onto her daughter. The daughter accepted the projected identification with the aggressor. The all-too-often heard complaint between survivor parents, "You are a Hitler for me," is a kind of bind between fantasy, verbalization, and magical realization occurring in the mind of the child. The goal of this therapy would be a stabilization of the ego boundaries of the children by expansion of the family ego through knowledge of their family background, going back to the previous generation. Instead of the obsessive suicidal and homicidal fantasying connected with the perpetrators who destroyed the family and the acting out behavior of punishing the parents, the patient came in touch with the real parents and not the fantasized murderers, capos, and field prostitutes as she had seen them. The family's historical reality replaced the fantasy world of their wasteland.

The therapist who faces suffering and life experiences of such magnitude is liable to have impulses to act out his own guilt feelings because he himself did not suffer or did not do enough during the Holocaust to fight the evil. He may have to deal with mounting impulses to turn into an omnipotent "good mother"—one who gives and receives, without being able to relate to the problems of ambivalence, aggression, and guilt feelings in his patient or in himself. A frequent reaction to such countertransference feelings as anger, boredom, and guilt is often covered by the use of isolation of affect, intellectualization, or the excessive use of psychoanalytic conceptualizations or clichés and generalizations taken from another patient-survivor's material. These defensive reactions are the result of the anxiety of the therapist caused by the imagined danger of his own traumatization, stimulated in him by his patient's life vicissitudes. This is often a response to the patient's projecting his anger, hostility, and helplessness onto the therapist in the transference situation.

In the fifties, we asked ourselves in our therapies and studies what is happening to the children of our parent-survivors? The central theme of the complaints and the preoccupations of survivor parents was "What are we doing to our children?" As a mother of a five-year-old son in a DP camp repeatedly asked, "Why am I always afraid that something will happen to my son? I am scolding him and at the same time trembling for his life." At the beginning, the child was a bridge to life, with expectations of the restoration of his own family and the restoration of the mother's narcissism or of her obsessive fears about her inability to give birth. Still in the pre-verbal mother-child relationship, as experienced in the therapy, the mother was not able to express a flexible empathy for the anaclitic needs of her child. The lack of the "defensive shield" function of the mother against the overflow of aggressive memories in the symbiotic and individuation phases of the child awakened in the child the feeling of its own helplessness and lack of basic trust. Themes of her own traumatic experiences and coping mechanisms were often transmitted to the child. For example, the mother's continuous hunger during the Holocaust was connected with fears of death. She acted out her fight against the danger of annihilation in the oral phase of her son by compulsive over-feeding associated with a continuous preoccupation with the child's oral needs. The son developed diabetes and hyperglycemia as a defense against his mother's intrusions.

We should also be aware that the specific psychosocial structure of the particular country where the survivor was living shaped and helped in the achievement of different personalities and identities of the children of survivors. Awareness groups for children of survivors in the United States are very popular, in contrast to Israel, where the need and indication for such groups are doubtful. The children of survivors in Israel have no need for homogeneous awareness groups, not feeling alienated and different from other young adults in their country.

The treatment of survivors implies a general problem of empathy and countertransference among psychotherapists who are struggling to relate adequately to the unique suffering of these patients. Frequently the therapists report that the survivor's history evoked guilt, frustration, over-protectiveness, or anger in them, and they defended themselves against these feelings by denying, minimizing, or excessively stressing the importance of their patients' past in the immediate therapeutic relationship.

During supervision, most of the therapists revealed feelings of defensiveness and guilt for not having shared the survivor patient's past. Like many children of the survivors, the therapists themselves could not help but wonder whether they would have fared as well in such an inferno. As one therapist said, "They had managed to live through hell and yet find hope and ego strength, whereas the most traumatic experience I have had could not compare with this."

One of the therapists fantasized about the survival of her patient and these fantasies blocked communication between them. The following excerpt from her supervision is not only a striking example of the conspiracy of silence that developed but also of the therapist's rationalization of her inability to engage the patient in the therapeutic process:

> In the process of interviewing the K. family, I learned that Mr. K. survived the concentration camp experience and Mrs. K. had been in a series of labour camps in Germany. She tended to gloss over this experience, seeing it as a positive one. I find it extremely difficult to believe that life was as rosy in the camps as she would indicate and that made me angry and suspicious.

In the supervision, the therapist questioned whether this was the patient's defense against wanting to discuss it or whether, indeed, her experiences in the camps as a young girl had been bearable only because of her internalized representational world—her always thinking about her Chassidic grandparents and her fantasized magic rescue. The therapist did not feel that it was relevant to get involved in this discussion of her patient's survival because of mixed feelings about her own sadomasochistic fantasies when confronted with her greed, which she projected onto her patient.

Another instance of a therapist's inability to deal with the frightening, humiliating awareness of the Holocaust occurred when the psychotic son of a survivor couple was hospitalized. The information about his Holocaust background was isolated and was not linked to the son's illness for fear of injuring the parents. The information never became part of the therapeutic process. It seems impossible to do meaningful therapeutic work with the offspring of Holocaust survivors without incorporating representations of their parents' real and fantasized experiences. This rigid stereotyped representational world of fathers as murderous capos and mothers as prostitute-victims needs to be changed into a realistic image of the parents as human beings with rich and varied experiences who succeeded in spite of their phantasmagoric experiences "to save the image of God in themselves."

In several instances, therapists responded in an equally inappropriate manner with a specific countertransference of guilt and became fascinated with details of Holocaust persecution to the exclusion of all other material about the previous personality, actual problems of living, the transference situation (which could shed light on pre-Holocaust problems), and problems of guilt and unresolved mourning of the murdered families.

Both the therapeutic treatment and the scientific research in the field of Holocaust survivors and their families are extraordinarily difficult and delicate tasks. The survivor-patient contributes to the mutual distortion by his rejection of the need for personal help, his intense suspicion of anyone he feels is "investigating" or "examining" him, and his denial of his personal traumatic experiences.

As we have observed, the variety of professional responses to a survivor family ranges from denial to over-identification. The fear of being overwhelmed by pity, depression, and guilt often drives a wedge between the therapist and the patient and blocks the understanding of their struggles and strengths. A therapist who attempts to deny the Holocaust experiences of his clients in their manifold complexity or who stresses them excessively implicitly encourages the survivor to persist in his own denial and helplessness. However, a more helpful approach would be for the therapist to confirm the survivor's self-concept as a person who succeeded in surviving in spite of his experiences and who tried to give meaning to his own life and the life of others.

Conclusion

The knowledge of the complexity of the complementary factors relating to Holocaust traumatization and its late effects has a specific interplay with the pre-Holocaust personality, the specific psychodynamics, the life phase during the Holocaust, and the knowledge of the patient's family background, structure, and roots. Re-experiencing emotional elements of the original pre-Holocaust family as well as the existential situation of the family during the Holocaust makes it possible to break down these stereotypes.

Many psychoanalysts and therapists share the opinion of Anna Freud, who said during the psychoanalytic congress in 1967 that it was impossible to analyze survivor patients because the therapist cannot maintain an optimal analytic distance. This extreme approach is based on real problems with the countertransference, which seems to be formidable in the continuum of emotions that I could observe in my own work and in my function as a supervisor. The range of issues in the countertransference is manifold: from over-identification with the victim to distancing through isolation in denial mechanisms and extreme emotional outbursts of the therapist by projective identification with the aggressor and returning to the original aggressor-victim bind.

These are difficulties that face us all the time, without any differences between "survivor therapist" and "non-survivor therapist." Here the problem is that our excessive sympathy (in German, *Mitleid*—to suffer together) extends not only to the survivors themselves but also to ourselves as potential survivors of extermination. "It could happen to me is subconsciously all the time on my mind," as one therapist said when he described why he became angry and detached when confronted with the vivid horror of the death of a sister of a patient, which was the recurrent theme of survival guilt of his patient. As if many therapists are confronted in a psychotic realization of phantasmagoric unresolved problems of their own childhood, we, the empathic listeners, must know and accept these feelings in ourselves from our own lives, and there is no escape from common mourning and bereavement that enables the patient to leave the frozen isolated position of victim, to leave the fixated position of psychic numbing—or psychic acting out of sadistic fantasies—derivatives of the Holocaust.

In many patients who are suffering manifestly from impairments in recognition and utilization of emotions as "signals to themselves" (alexithymia) (Hoppe, 1968; Krystal, 1968; Sifneos, 1967), we could identify a deep unresolved mourning as another basic deep-rooted emotion that is masked by vagueness and a confusion of feelings. These "alexithymic" patients are only able to verbalize their emotions and share them in respect to affective responses of the therapist.

When we listen to these children, we might get lost in our fantasies about their parents' experiences as well as about our own children and our own involvement with that period. We might do so to a greater degree than we are usually inclined to do when listening to our "usual" patients. Herein lies the danger: that our fantasies might override our attention to the specific interpretations and fantasies that the children of survivors have about their parents' experiences.

This specific example leads us to a major countertransference problem in these cases. The children's fantasies about their parents' fate, their fears, and the horrors that they had lived through are inevitably bound to components of sexual derivatives, connected with the assimilative traumatization in their childhood by parental memories and attitudes. As empathic listeners, we must know these feelings in ourselves as well—we, as psychotherapists and psychoanalysts, must not banish such feelings and ideas from our consciousness.

Here, too, belong our resistances to accepting the assignment in the transference situation of the role of "victim" or "perpetrator" in tune with the shifting role identifications of the patients.

I would like to hint at another of the problems in treating children of survivors. They feel themselves as exceptions, as being "special," and I think this is becoming more so at this time when it has become easier to talk about the Holocaust.

However, as in all other instances of the analysis of the "exception," to analyze this "privileged status" means taking something away. There again we may encounter a countertransference obstacle; we may unconsciously say to ourselves, "Do we have a right to inflict such pain on top of that which their parents have gone through?" This in instances where we might have to ask, moreover, "Are there perhaps other actual psychological and sociological events, events that are very poignant for their own generation and which the children of survivors may be avoiding by their concentration on their parental fates?"

The same issue of being able to arouse pain arises in relation to the breaking of the taboo of speaking to their parents about the latter's persecution experiences. Can we allow ourselves to be "cruel" enough to make them talk of their sadistic fantasies about these experiences so that they eventually might find a way of approaching their parents on these matters? Otherwise, it seems that very often the therapist "takes sides with one party"—over-identifying himself with the parental representative fantasized by the children of survivors as "capos" or "prostitutes," without confrontation or clarification.

In my experience, it seems that the child of survivors is ready to ask questions—and the parents to answer them in real dialogue—when the therapist is ready to be involved, if he is allowing himself to hear.

In consideration of these countertransference problems, we have to raise the question each time: for whose sake are we tempted to introduce "parameters" in the treatment of these patients, theirs or ours?

Another matter is drawn to our attention by one of vignettes about the person who quit treatment and invited the analyst to join him in following a guru. As in many other similar clinical instances, particularly during adolescence, only action seems to suffice for some patients. They must live something through in actuality in order to work over what has *actually* happened.

Chapter 13: Mourning and Survivor Guilt

When we speak of survival, we are referring to death or to the threat of death that is not normally anticipated during the life span of the individual. We can differentiate between two categories of survival. One type has to do with the single situation of danger experienced by an individual alone, such as a natural catastrophe or accident. The second category has to do with the extended experience of danger by a group of people in which some people survive, while others who are significant to the survivors do not. This latter case, common during wars when people outlive their families, friends, and colleagues, has been a common theme in literature throughout history, especially in the writings of Dos Passos and Hemingway, following the First World War. A recurrent theme in the mythologies of many cultures depicts the survivor who has confronted death returning to a society that warns him not to return to the experience, not to look back. This theme is present in the Judeo-Christian tradition (in the myth of Sodom and Gomorrah) and in the Greek tradition (in the myth of Orpheus).

In a singular confrontation with death, it is not uncommon for the individual to review the course of his life in a condensed way. We know from studies of such individuals that they become preoccupied with the people who have been significant in their lives as a kind of bidding farewell in regard to them. After such an experience, there is no guilt but rather feelings of gratitude to Fate or to God that they were able to stay alive. Afterward there is no need for a repetition of the experience except in a limited number of cases in which the experience becomes the nucleus for a traumatic neurosis.

In the situation in which others died while one survived, there is always the question of "Why did I stay alive while the others died?" I have heard this question asked repeatedly by the survivors of the wars in Israel, especially when close friends toward whom one experienced some ambivalence perished. Often the theme that accompanies the question of one's own survival is "I did not do enough to save him." It seems to me that this experience of guilt is connected with the experience of death wishes toward significant people in childhood when the magical omnipotence of thought leads the child to attribute the actual death of a love object to his own wishes.

This guilt also seems to be associated with the archaic strata of the unconscious in the feeling that someone must be sacrificed in order that we may continue to live. The ritual expression of this need to sacrifice, observed in many cultures, is also connected with magical thinking. This is not to say that at times in the history of some societies, sacrifice did not have some adaptive, reality-oriented component to it, when with limited resources, the survival of part of a group may have been dependent on the sacrifice of some of its members. Sacrifice can also serve as a displacement of guilt. The victim or animal is sacrificed so that others may continue to live. In religion, the sacrifice for purification has been a strong element in enabling people to deal with death wishes and murderous fantasies. These feelings and wishes related to sacrifice have their roots in the collective unconscious that is transmitted from one generation to the next.

Survivor guilt is familiar to us in individual experiences of mourning, as in the case of the widow who asks, "Why did I have to stay alive when you died?" Part of the process of mourning is the expression of anger and hostility toward the lost one: "You left me, and now you have it better than me." Thus, in every situation of mourning, there are elements of survivor guilt: the envy of the one who stayed alive toward the one who died and the question of why one stayed alive when others who were better did not.

Both of these elements of survivor guilt can be heard in the expressions of the survivors of the Holocaust. They often ask whether it would not have been better if they had gone to their death with their siblings and parents, feeling that in death they have it better—they have become holy. The question why one survived when others who were better than oneself did not often leads the Holocaust survivor to search for some rationale or particular meaning for his survival. The rationale for many survivors was that one would be a witness to others of the terrible atrocities of the Holocaust.

Survivor Guilt and Neurotic Guilt

One clinical case, that of Isaac, a survivor of several ghettos, labor, and concentration camps represents the complexity and interconnection between many aspects of survivor guilt, personal "mythos," present-life traumas, and Holocaust experiences.

Isaac was born in 1923 in the Jewish quarter of a major Polish city, the only son of orthodox, upper-class Jewish parents. He is married to a survivor partisan and is the father of one daughter. He came to psychotherapy in 1958 after having suffered for years from severe depressions, accompanied by psychotic decompensations.

Isaac's most tormenting preoccupation was his unrelenting guilt feelings and his fears that he could not live up to his remarkable intelligence and natural talents. Although he had graduated as the top student in his high school, he did not pursue an academic career and the position he eventually obtained and worked in, although involving a great deal of responsibility, was far below his capacities and was of relatively low professional status. He lived in a continuous dread of "making mistakes" at work that would jeopardize his own life and that of others. He was especially afraid of destroying his wife and daughter by his "actions" or inaction. His guilt feelings and suicidal tendencies reached their peak when he witnessed the burial of the ashes of the martyrs of his own town, which had been brought to Israel from Poland in the early 1970s.

There was a prompt change in his behavior—he stopped eating, washing, and shaving, and refused to leave his bed. His demeanor resembled that of a *muselman*—a walking corpse—and he ceased communication with his family and friends. When he did speak, it was only to repeatedly and relentlessly question himself why he had remained alive when all the "righteous people" (*Zadikkim*) of his town had been killed by the Nazis.

The most cogent question that arose again and again in Isaac's psychotherapy was whether one could sufficiently understand his clinical picture, the intensity of his guilt feelings, and his extreme transference feelings toward his therapist as his "savior" in the framework of the accepted psychoanalytic therapy of guilt as related to his genetic development and his ambivalence toward objects.

When parents and children were killed during the Holocaust, some survivors vaguely felt that their unconscious and preconscious wishes had come true. The obsessive preoccupation with the destruction of their world and the deaths of family members in the Holocaust contains the fear of the realization of such expectations. The phantasmagoric reality of the ghettos and concentration camps became mixed with the internal drama of their own lives, and in this respect, the Holocaust brought about the fulfillment of unconscious death wishes occurring normally in childhood during earlier phases of life.

From a genetic point of view, the feeling of guilt is connected with the emergence of the infant from the symbiotic unit. This process reaches its culmination during the second year of life. Prior to this, there is an omnipotent fusion with the mother's representation (Mahler et al., 1975). To the infant, even a brief absence of the mother is the prototype of separation and leads to feelings of loss, confusion, and guilt feelings about separation: "I am guilty for having been left."

In his investigations of emotional deprivation, anaclitic depression, and hospitalism in infants, Spitz (1965) found that in extreme circumstances, children became unable to direct libido and aggression outward. Instead they turn their two diffused drives against their own person with destructive effects. The absence of the mother evokes a feeling of helplessness, emptiness, and depression.

The actual loss of the mother, even when it does not bring about an anaclitic depression or marasmus, leaves a child with permanent imprints and deep-seated unresolved conflicts, or, in Kleinian terms, aggressive tendencies that are related to the "bad breast"—the representation of the archaic mother who could not satisfy the infant's wishes for total love and total security (M. Klein, 1959).

It is usually only very late in the treatment of survivors that they are confronted with their death wishes toward a love object. It took one patient many hours to face the screen memory of the fantasy of having cannibalistically destroyed his mother when he was seven years old, many years before she was killed in the Holocaust. As a child, he had felt abandoned and humiliated by her and, as a consequence, had had murderous fantasies toward her. Having articulated these fantasies, he was able to work through, at least partially, his symptomatic, identificatory, death-like seclusion in which he had erected a barrier between himself and other living people out of an unconscious distrust of everyone.

Freud himself experienced a minor paradigm of object loss in the middle of his second year, in the death of his brother Julius. He acknowledged a "germ of guilt" (Schur, 1972, p. 119) and probably sensed the finality and irreversibility of death even at that tender age, although he was incapable of comprehending it. He later saw in his patients regressive instances of identification with lost objects, object cathexis being replaced by identification, not only in melancholy and mourning but also as a general basis for character formation (Freud, 1917e). He stated that "Identification with an object which is renounced or lost, as a substitute for that object . . . is often limited and borrows a single trait" (pp. 107–109). In the case of the aforementioned patient, the mother's *death* in the Holocaust was the overwhelming focus of his identification. A network of associations disconnected from the Holocaust as well as experiences related to her in early childhood only secondarily covered this. The fantasy of wish-fulfillment turns one's own death into a means of recapturing the lost object, regaining thereby its full presence and compensating for the deprivation and frustration experienced through its loss. Identification in turn affects activity, as Schafer (1976, p. 161) writes: identification means "a change in the way one conceives oneself and perhaps in the way one behaves publicly."

The developmental phase of separation-individuation, which is accompanied by increasing autonomy, furnishes the primary death instinct with a specific content: separation identified with death becomes a real possibility. One child of survivors, a twenty-four-year-old student, could not leave Germany for many years because of the anxiety that his parents would die after his departure. He repeated the theme of separation identified with death, a theme especially strong in his family.

Prior to the establishment of a punitive superego, there is pre-Oedipal guilt. Freud (1930a), modifying his earlier view, wrote that "as to a sense of guilt, we must admit that it is in existence before the superego . . . . the direct result of the conflict between the need for the authority's love and the urge towards instinctual satisfaction" (p. 136). Thus, the threat of the loss of love precedes the formation of conscience.

Melanie Klein and her followers confirmed the existence of early guilt and believed that depressive anxiety appeared as early as the fourth month of life due to the fantasy of destroying the mother and thereby losing her. They expounded upon the rapprochement of the "good" and "bad" breast of the mother, intense ambivalence, and sadistic-destructive urges projected onto the parent and re-introduced into the personality later to form the early superego.

Modell (1971) reviewed the origins of some forms of pre-Oedipal guilt, including those with a cast of oral envy and greed and those in which there is the fantasy of causing the mother's death by one's own growth and maturation—the "separation guilt." Even a narcissistic withdrawal or other disruption of the object relationship may lead to a deep sense of guilt.

Many analysts have challenged the Kleinian hypothesis that these processes unfold during the first half-year of life; however, it is outside the present scope to participate in this debate. The principle itself, disregarding temporal considerations, remains consensually valid. In psychoanalytic thinking, the two types of guilt, Oedipal and pre-Oedipal, represent different degrees of object *representations* in addition to different object relationships. One is reminded of Blatt's (1974) distinction between anaclitic and introjective depression according to epigenetic stages of object representations—from the sensori-motor level through the perceptual, iconic, and finally, conceptual levels. He found actual, apparent, or fantasized object loss to be a major precipitant of depression. The abstract and symbolic object representations are still fragmented and contradictory in introjective depression, and they possess ambivalent, hostile, and aggressive features, whereas guilt indicates for Blatt a somewhat higher level of object representations. Schafer (1976, p. 350) enlarged upon the bearing of depression on resulting behavior: depression—and, in fact, any other affect—is action; "actions" include conditional and would-be actions (p. 366). This leads us to look again for actions against the self in the survivor but also to the striving for positive growth and individuation connected with the re-establishment of the self and the lost self-representation.

Survivor Guilt and Personal Mythos

Holocaust history is an essential part of the survivor's self-representational world. It becomes a treasured possession to which the survivor is attached with peculiar, intense devotion. Ernst Kris's expression "personal myth" comes to mind, which, like all living myth, extends from the past into the present. Some aspects of the survivor's patterns of living can be viewed as a re-enactment of past, suppressed fantasies and experiences of the Holocaust. The survivor, as a kind of protective screen, uses autobiographical memories. This screen as a whole is carefully constructed over the years after the Holocaust and is built from some isolated memories that include distinct, vivid imagery of the self in contrast to others, with firm outlines, intense coloring, richness of detail (*hypermnesis*—the psychiatric term for detailed memory of past traumatic experiences that cannot be repressed) intended to cover what may be significant omissions and distortions and which stress the *self-ideal of humaneness* that must not be forgotten.

This does not fashion a total history of the Holocaust but only more or less well-defined isolated stretches of personal experience that have been worked up as a screen. The question arises as to which dynamic and developmental conditions favor the choice of this method of defense and working through. The dynamic function of these memories can be seen in the transference situation—in the survivor's reactions ranging from regressive repetition to controlled re-experiencing in thought and fantasy since fantasy was an important defense against the psychotic realization-like and de-realization-like states occurring during the Holocaust.

Which dynamic and developmental conditions favor the choice of this method of defense and working through? We must look at the interaction of the following factors: (a) the nature of the persecution experiences, (b) their sequence in time, (c) the historical period of the Holocaust, (d) whether the survivor was alone or part of a group during traumatization, (e) the character of such a group and its connection with life prior to the Holocaust, (f) the predisposition of the person, and (g) the developmental stage at the time of the personal myth. The style of the personal myth is specific to different groups of survivors. It has a special quality and gives a secret core to the different styles of recalling.

The stories of Lot's wife and of Orpheus, neither of whom could refrain from looking back, portray the human inability to invest fully in here-and-now relationships as well as a lack of perspective for the future on account of a longing for the past love object. The survivor's remorse that he did not live up to his ego ideal and the fact that he is caught between guilt rooted in the superego structure in conflict with primitive aggressive urges that become real because of the Holocaust means that he lives in an insoluble dilemma. He is perpetually looking back.

One survivor recalled his experience:

> My name is XY. I am a survivor of the Holocaust. I was born in 1921 in Poland and during the war, I was incarcerated since 1943. I spent three years in various concentration camps, first in Poland and then in Germany. I was liberated on the last day of the war in Theresienstadt, on May 8, 1945.
>
> What did I feel? Helpless. We weren't receiving any help from the outside world or the local population, and

we were just counting the days until we would eventually be exterminated. I remember the first days of the German occupation, how they marched into the town. I stayed in the town. As a matter of fact, I was wounded on the second day of the war—one bomb shrapnel injured me. So while some people escaped to the east, I stayed in town.

From the marketplace, we were taken on horse-driven wagons to another town which had a railroad site from which the transports were going to wherever they were going. We, together with other Jews from adjacent villages, stayed there three or four days, waiting to fill up the train—under horrible conditions, sleeping in the open air. There were no toilet facilities, no food. Finally, before the day when they started loading the transports, they took a group of the older Jews and loaded them up on the horse-driven wagons. They drove them uphill to face a firing squad. I had this picture before me of these old people, wearing their prayer shawls, going to die. This is a picture of *Kiddush HaShem* to me, slaying the people.

Then the selection. A group of officials from the German railroads with SS people came, having to fill a requirement of several hundred people for labor camps. So we lined up and they selected able-bodied people, teenagers and young people. The rest of them were led away. Of course, throughout this, they were making announcements that these people would be resettled in the eastern territories. But that is how I was separated from my family, and that is the last I saw of them. This was in September 1942.

Strangely enough, as I said before, I came from a fairly assimilated home, not religious, but in the camps I became religious. I believe that were it not for my belief in God, I wouldn't have survived in camp. I had the hope and I strongly believed in that and I still believe *that in the afterlife, I am going to see my family again.*

Back to my religion. I felt that there is God, despite the terrible things that happened to us. I couldn't deny

> the existence of him, ever. I remember after the war, when I was liberated in Theresienstadt, there was a big pile of religious articles, *tefilin* and prayer books, and I just thought, *Where are the people who had them?* But I didn't want the chain to be broken. I don't know, I couldn't picture the person who had them, I don't know. The book was falling apart; it must have been used many times. But I'm glad I'm using it now. It was a big pile, a mound, thousands.

For the survivor, death is not only a possibility but also a continuous reality for the self. The fantasy of wish fulfillment turns one's own death into a means of recapturing the lost object, thereby regaining its full presence and compensating for the frustration and deprivation experienced through its loss. So we see in many survivors the longing to die and to restore the beloved. They ask, "Was it worthwhile to invest so much for our survival?" Death, which was such a real possibility during the years of persecution, offered the "opportunity" to join the lost beloved ones. In the "hereafter," there is the thought of being with them once more, all "alive" again. Paradoxically, the wish to die and be reunited with the parents is often associated with the fear of separation from one's own children. This is often expressed in the survivors' parasitic clinging to their children—an expression of unresolved guilt in relation to the parents projected onto the children. Separation, known from earliest childhood on as a source of anxiety (and associated with death), can thus be assumed. This reunion in death also erases problems of the loss of love, the loss of love objects, and guilt.

The question arises whether the goal of psychotherapy with such people is to confront and clarify the two sources of guilt—the one that is directly related to having survived the Holocaust, and the other, which is the neurotic source, linked to unresolved childhood conflicts that contained aggressive, death-colored wishes predating the Holocaust. It is essential that we differentiate between the two prototypes of guilt derived from these two unrelated sources. The one reflects the survivor's anguish and existential disappointment in himself and the world and is connected with the Holocaust experience of total destruction. Phenomenologically, we are not dealing here with a feeling of guilt per se: no survivor feels guilty just for being alive, even if he chooses to express himself in that stereotyped fashion. What he does feel is rather a sense of contamination, of *having become part of* the experience of atrocity through which he had been forced to live and to which he cannot help but bear witness. He finds himself in a desolate no-man's-land, between the world he lost and the one that he cannot fully join, overcome by a sense of being too tainted to live in the present yet having irretrievably lost his treasured past. The other guilt, the neurotic one, is rooted in the cruel superego structure that comes into conflict with primitive aggressive urges toward parental representations that predate the Holocaust. These urges become dangerously close to being realized, through the brutal acts of persecution carried out on the parents, siblings, and friends by the perpetrators. The perpetrators, therefore, assumed demonic features in the survivor's mind as "angels of death" who executed their own most primitive and unacceptable fantasies, thus blurring the delicate boundary between fantasy and reality for the survivor.

It is this neurotic guilt that is connected with the inability of the injured ego of the survivor to alter his feelings of guilt toward his lost family, his present family, and current love objects. Moreover, the normal phenomena of life in which past guilt joins the present one and is acted upon in minor restitutional ways that do not constitute an obstacle to new human experiences and responsibilities are far less effective in the survivor. The motivation of choosing and relating to object representations with acute savior fantasies is different from restitutional processes, so important in the course of mourning and the acceptance of responsibility. The Holocaust survivor, weakened through the confrontation with death and without working through the survivor guilt as a part of his mourning, is unable to allow for the restitution of his old self and his full re-involvement in the stream of life.

Emerging from a chaotic collective world of destruction in which one was de-individualized by having no name, only a number, and being persecuted and killed not as an individual but as a member of a group of "vermin," one can rebuild one's own boundaries and recover a sense of one's self again, one's own individual history, and one's own family mythology only by means of a very intense psychological process of mourning, thereby leading to a recovery of family representations and re-individuation. The pain of loss, the specific pain of remorse and collective bereavement, and the process of individual mourning are elements that help to revive the individual survivor's consciousness and boundaries of himself.

By constantly recalling the image of the lost relatives, the survivor indicates that they have become part of his inner world. He has "incorporated" them—he is like them. It is not only a matter of conscience to think of them—they have become part of him, part of his self-sameness and continuity. By accepting guilt for being a survivor, a degree of "causality" is re-established, and by finding causality, the way for forgiveness is presented as well. The dead allow the living to pursue their lives and to strive for the pursuit of happiness. Thus, the survivor can turn to the future and is free to cope with the problems that may be offered in his contacts with new objects, particularly his children.

We see that the "permission" to live, to hope, and to embrace life is a part of the guilt in those survivors who received from the deceased during his/her life the message: "You should live when I die." In such cases, the life of the survivor becomes a testimony to the life of the deceased. The message of the deceased was not only frequently manifested during the Holocaust itself but was often transmitted continuously during earlier phases of the child's life when "good mothering" was present. Thus, in survivor guilt, we can discover traces of internalized transactions associated with separation and death in the family. During the Holocaust, these internalized dialogues that took place in the shadow of imminent death and meaninglessness were overshadowed by doubts, hopelessness, and confusion. However, every structured message carried over from the past contained within it the possibility of becoming a starting point around which a new structuring of life and meaning could emerge.

Forms of Pathological Survivor Guilt

The question arises as to whether the survivor's guilt, by functioning as a structuring process, can be conceived of as a defense against fragmentation, and if so, what agencies in the mental apparatus might be involved in it? The survivor guilt functions as a structuring process after the chaos and void left by the Holocaust. The psychic structures of ego and superego were changed considerably by this experience, not only in content but also in their interrelatedness—overwhelmed by instincts and panic. The recovery and rearrangement of the psychic structure are aided by the survivor guilt, when the survivor asks not only "what have they done to me" but also "what have I done or not done." In such a way, he changes from a passive victim of the past to one who accepts causality and to the possibility of taking responsibility for his present life and future.

Thus, we can see survivor guilt functioning as a structuring process that enables an adequate relationship between the concept of reality and the new emerging superego and ego. We can see the lack of survivor guilt in severe manic defenses as well as in character disturbances connected with the externalization of guilt and the projection onto others. This is related to the need for overcompensation, repetitive acting out of fantasies, and the inability to accept responsibility in the therapy. The clinical outcome related to the relative presence or absence of survivor guilt and its quality are as follows:

Presence of Survivor Guilt	*Clinical Outcome*
Absence	- Manic defenses, fragmentation, and massive denial
Severe	- Depression
Moderate	- Neurotic obsessive and paranoid coping
Mild	- Conflicts and problems related to various life phases (separation of children, mid-life crisis, empty-nest syndrome, anniversary reactions, death of close friends, and acceptance of responsibility toward society)

The absence of survivor guilt takes on different forms—it is expressed in characterological as well as manic and psychotic dimensions. It often manifests itself in the use of massive denial and reaction formations as in the statement, "I am not guilty but am accusing others for their guilt."

A fifty-year-old survivor, a tremendously active man, was unable to share feelings and emotions in his family. He married a few months after the war, unable to mourn or relate to the loss of a wife and a six-month-old child who were killed by the Nazis. He married a woman, also a survivor, a few months following the liberation, after meeting in one of the DP camps in Germany. His present lifestyle involved the use of hypomanic defenses and was marked by the presence of hoarding money and a kind of pseudo-muteness with all acquaintances. He would give huge parties for everyone he knew, again and again, hoping to find support systems outside of his family. He lived well above his means.

This survivor was always absent from his family, and his marriage eventually came to a stalemate. Once after a gathering of survivors in a kibbutz on the day of commemorating the Holocaust in Israel, as he was driving home with his wife, the car broke down, and he was unable to repair it. He became enraged by his own helplessness and cursed his wife. Also enraged, she accused him of being able to help everyone but his own family. The quarrel continued to the point that his wife called him Hitler. In a fit of rage, he hit and killed her.

In his therapy, it became apparent that this man had denied his guilt feelings, was unable to feel sadness, and only by constant activity and the hoarding of money did he feel that he could give and feel secure. The quarrel that precipitated the murder was connected with unresolved feelings of guilt and helplessness. The inability to repair the engine, "to do reparation," and the accusation of being a Hitler awakened in him his suppressed feelings of rage and helplessness and the murderous impulse to destroy—the symbol of his inability to mourn and have emotions.

In the absence of survivor guilt, we often observe the characterological disturbance of affective alexithymia—the inability to feel in individual terms. In such a case, the survivor is unable to relate personally to the history of the Holocaust. The relation to the Holocaust past resembles that of an objective historian, often with the repetition of the theme of the cruelty of the perpetrator and the helplessness of the victim. Very often, this stance is associated with the denial of isolation of affects, an obsessive preoccupation with action and achievement that creates in others a feeling of distance from the survivor. These patients usually come to our attention only when there is a breakdown of functioning in the form of physical exhaustion accompanied by somatic complaints.

Severe forms of survivor guilt are manifested in depression. This depression is very often expressed in a "walking corpse" appearance, the inability to enjoy life, and repeated attempts to awaken in others the need to punish them. The individual suffering from such severe survivor guilt experiences life as a punishment. His self-punitive tendencies become especially pronounced when there are chances for success and fulfillment and, at times, when there is the opportunity to share joyful experiences with his children. It is as if at these times, he must remind himself of his guilt for surviving.

A middle-aged man fell into a severe psychotic depression with a suicidal attempt after the marriage of his daughter. The daughter was named after his mother, who had died in the Holocaust. He expressed classical fears of impoverishment that he would not be able to live up to the needs of the newly wedded couple. In his therapy, he expressed severe guilt feelings for not having been able to save his mother. These feelings were evoked in him when he heard the words in the wedding ceremony, "We should bring the memory of Zion to the surface of our joy." This prayer, expressing the counterpoint between the joy of the wedding and the destruction of the temple, brought him in touch with his incomplete mourning and the guilt that his mother was not alive to witness the joy of his family. He felt remorse, worthlessness, and anger toward himself, asking himself why he was living when his dead family could not be there with him to enjoy the present occasion.

The patient mentioned previously, Isaac, suffered from major psychotic depressive breakdowns all of his adult life. The last psychotic breakdown was in 1978, after "Black Sabbath," when terrorists killed a large number of Jews on a bus near Tel Aviv. Isaac came from Tel Aviv to my office in Jerusalem with delusions of being persecuted by Dr. Mengele and the commandant of his camp, Goeth, who had killed the population of his town in Poland. In his delusion, he heard them speak in a combination of Arabic and Polish. They chased him, wishing to kill him and his therapist. When he arrived at the therapy session, he asked me not to be afraid of Mengele and Goeth, who were waiting outside in the garden. He assured me that since he was an officer in the army, he would not allow them to kill me. After the session ended, he did not want to leave my office, expressing the wish to stay with me and to fuse with me in order to save him from the persecutions he felt in his delusions.

In this phase of therapy with Isaac, it became more obvious that his suppressed guilt was connected with the fantasy of killing his father by leaving him during the selection, after his father had become a *muselman*. From the generality of guilt in the transference situation, we were able to relate to his ambivalence as a human experience. Through his survival guilt, he was able to reconnect himself to his father and to both his strengths and weaknesses, thereby changing the psychotic world of the camp. He accepted the responsibility for leaving his father, and his support and affection. He also accepted the responsibility for his present family, particularly his daughter, who for him had previously been an object of guilt and remorse.

In my countertransference, I felt his hostility and aggression by his trying to change me into the one who should be saved from the persecutors—"the *muselman* father"—and himself, the hero fulfilling a self-ideal that he had failed to live up to during the Holocaust. By refusing to leave my office and forcing me to cancel my later clients, he became the unique omnipotent survivor who gets my whole love. This attempt to fuse with me was an effort to overcome his ambivalence of love and hate.

The presence of mild survivor guilt can be seen in many survivors who are adapting themselves quite well in many aspects of their lives. It could be traced in the emotional overinvestment in their own families and in their society. In Israel, we can observe the survivor guilt in the survivor's over-identification with the issue of the survival of the state, their preoccupation with the need for security, and with the repetitive tendencies of "never again"—"I will not allow the destruction of my state and my community." In the intrapsychic life, the survivor guilt is seen in the repetitive dreams of one's own survival and in the preoccupation with the lost world of families and friends, with the wish to come back to one's own roots, to return to the places of childhood and destruction. It can also be seen in the tendency to idealize the beloved and in the acceptance of total responsibility for all the skepticism about one's own achievements. In line with Freud's paraphrase about changing the neurotic misery into the normal miseries of life, the working through of survival guilt in these persons during the analytic process helps them to change this source of survival guilt to a responsibility for their own life and to a source of hope, representing the lost world and transmitting the richness of the lost world and its system of values.

In the gatherings of survivors, we often see different elements of relating to the collective survivor guilt—from the deep mourning (collective and individual) for lost loved ones to the ritualistic forms of mourning to the joy of being alive with others, yet with some glimpse of survivor guilt in "why are we alive and not they"—often experienced in a stereotypical way. These gatherings are the expression of the solemn need to be witnesses as a motivation for staying alive, which is connected with the survivor guilt. They often carry the message, "I am living for them."

Another form of sublimation of survivor guilt is seen in the many survivors working as historians, writing their memoirs, remembering again and again those who were cherished and loved and who are now a part of their internal representational world.

The glamorous meetings of survivors are often portrayals of exhibitionism—of material achievements, of their own and their children's successes, as if to say, "I am whole, a success in spite of everything I went through." But as one survivor experienced in therapy, "being at the Waldorf Astoria with the other survivors was for me a *Purimspiel*—behind the masks of happy faces and pseudo togetherness, I saw in their faces my own face from Auschwitz. Maybe to be a hero and holy, you have to be young and die in the Holocaust." This patient was able to accept his survivor guilt as part of his identification with his lost world, to relate differently to his children, to come out of his depression, and to be creative in his own endeavors.

Survivor guilt is often a source of creativity. The working through of survivor guilt is evidenced in many writers, artists, and people during recent years, creating memorials of their own experience as a way of bringing rationality to the present and future generations. The feelings of vengeance toward the perpetrators that had been a source of motivation and excuse for living are worked through in the form of individual and not collective processes previously mentioned. The manifestations of this mild form of survivor guilt appear in different life stages.

From Guilt to Responsibility: The Constructive Working Through of Survivor Guilt

The question of turning survivor guilt into a sense of responsibility occurred to me many years ago in my own analysis as I tried to understand my own motivation in life. I left the hospital in 1945, after suffering from a variety of diseases including typhus exactimaticus, tuberculosis, and dysentery, and after having been in a prolonged state between death and life. I weighed as little as sixty pounds in Theresienstadt. After liberation, I was not immediately able to enjoy life like many others. I could have participated in the black market but did not. Something inhibited me from acting in a way that would have identified me with the aggressor.

I remembered that on the day of my liberation near the Elbe River, Russian soldiers brought hundreds of German soldiers they had taken as prisoners of war. My comrades from the concentration camp fell on them, taking their boots and watches. I remember a group of Hungarian women I called to, "You shouldn't do to them what they have done to you yesterday. Why do you do it?" And I cried from helplessness and anger, unable to believe that these young soldiers with their eyes turned toward the ground were the killers, as the others did. It was difficult for me to seek vengeance. It had to do with my guilt at having survived. As I could not save my family and friends, I could not confront myself with their deaths. I avoided their deaths. So, too, I could not take vengeance.

I returned to the DP camp to work with children as an educator, feeling that I had to do for the children what I was unable to do for them before. In front of me stood the daughter of my sister and the daughter of my friend, Gebirtig. It was a kind of self-realization that here I would build my own kibbutz, a fantasy from my days in the concentration camp when I dreamed of the utopian kibbutz I would build after the war that would help, accept, and save me. I taught the children Hebrew, Jewish history, *Torah*, and religion, giving them what had been important for me.

How was this connected with responsibility? Responsibility would come to mean for me the transformation from aggressive hostile feelings toward the disappointing world to the acceptance of one's own past as one's own and of one's own inactivity in that past. It is not a fixation to the past; that is, it does not involve splitting in which all of one's aggressive feelings are directed toward the perpetrator as the cause of destruction. But it is an acceptance of the human responsibility for one's inability to die as well as one's own ability to fight. To choose to actively die was in my mind to accept the doctrine of Hitler that the Jews must die. One could not accept this verdict that one was not worth living.

Responsibility involves having a realm of play, room for enacting not experienced as a must. Thus, it allows one to be in touch with one's id, ego, superego, and self, in touch with one's inner resources. The realm of play gives one the feeling of one's own growth and restoration of what was destroyed in the concentration camp—one's freedom to make decisions, to develop ideas of responsibility to one's self, and to one's family. It involves the restoration of those capacities that were diminished during the concentration camp by hunger and the threat of death.

Responsibility also involves the restoration of one's ego ideal. Ego depletion and constriction were characteristics in the traumatic neurosis, occurring intensely in the survivor. Responsibility is an act of creativity, one that enriches the self and the ego—a good feeling toward the self is restored as well as ego functions being enriched. It is a self-restoration process in which there is the pleasure of functioning and mastery. The restoration of the ego ideal and the perpetuation of responsibility also have an influence on object relationships in which the object is not just a "container" (M. Klein) but one who grows through oneself in transaction. Through responsibility, I also fill the object by myself. Through giving and sharing, there is an enlargement of the ego and the self-spheres, as we observe in people who take responsibility in their own societies. Arriving at responsibility allows one to come in touch with the nuclei of one's previous development when one shared the early reunion with the mother in symbiosis and rapprochement—"I am with you and you can leave." The person who takes responsibility acts toward the other person as if he was a part of himself, allowing him to playfully leave with the possibility of rapprochement and autonomy.

The inability to mourn in functional language is described as the countercathexis against the libidinal object. It is as if a foreign body resides in the self, which one must suppress and control. Consequently the person is unable to cathect new objects. In countercathexis, the object is particularly invested with aggressive feelings so that one cannot move toward another person; it is like sitting on dynamite. In the mourning process, there is the total over-involvement with the lost object. The labor of mourning allows one to slowly decathect the lost object—as in the ritual of Shiva where the lost object is remembered and spoken about in both their good and bad aspects as a way of gradually detaching oneself from them.

Thus, the notion of responsibility came to involve some of the following features. It is the coming together of doing and being according to one's own ego ideal and in one's own time. It involves the acceptance of one's mourning and bereavement without attempting to make it an alibi for an inability to move and relate to actual persons. It takes place on two vectors—in terms of the continuity to the past and the present, to the actual problems of one's own generation and of future generations. It implies the possibility to change roles and affects. The element of play enables one to move, to liberate oneself from the repetition compulsion, to relate to different elements in oneself, and to go from one role to another. Today, I can be the friend, tomorrow the father or the child.

There is a sequence of roles that allows for the object to go through corresponding roles. This capacity takes one out of the static rigid role of victim or survivor.

Responsibility involves the acceptance of death without the literal images of destruction. It involves the acceptance of the life phases of generativity and decline and the acceptance of the growth of others in which one can see one's own realization, transmitting values, experiences, and credos to youth; expressing the feelings and experiences that belong to another time; and attempting to make sense out of those experiences—the role as witness, the capacity of a man to think and to rebuild himself, the primitive but concretized images of death in the form of the death skull, the actualization of the inferno in the ghettos and concentration camps, and the symbols of the cry for transcendence in their complete metaphysical strength, as in the clinging to the religious song that says, "Our soul is waiting for God. He is our shield and our help."

Responsibility always involves symbolization or else it becomes a series of concretizations—you may have sexual relations, but you will not love or be a lover without symbols—so it is also with responsibility. And finally, responsibility involves awakening guilt in others, in one's society, people, children, and the Germans. There is the responsibility of taking them out of their anonymous void of guilt and mourning.

Chapter 14:
The Dilemma of the Survivor in Psychoanalytic Treatment

Just as modern man is beginning to deal with the Holocaust history, so the survivor is now beginning to express his way of dealing with his traumatic Holocaust past, reflecting on his experience in the form of diaries, meetings of survivor groups, and dialogues between themselves and non-survivors. Most prominent is the expression of his anger and anguish toward society for not coping adequately with the Holocaust, not having saved the survivors and their families, and relating to them afterward as refugees and not as their beloved brothers returning from the inferno. We find these expressions in many of the studies, papers, and oral history documentations related to the biographies of specific heroes of ghettos and concentration camps. The oral histories convey not only the cognitive aspects of their Holocaust experience but also the belated labor of mourning, which they were unable to engage in after the Holocaust due to ego-depletion and the necessity of coping and making a superficial adaptation to society. They were then unable to attack the neutral position of society in Israel and in the United States, where they were looked upon with suspicion and pity, with the fear that any identification with them might be contagious, and with the threat of being overwhelmed with mourning and depression. There was no common denominator of "we" but rather of "they," which characterized the masses in Palestine as well as in the United States. Instead of a real dialogue with the survivor, there was a philanthropic approach toward them that awakened ambivalence and doubts in both parties.

We now witness in the survivor's dealing with his traumatic past and present-life situation strong indications of his capacity for revival. His existential malaise as well as his ability to confront and master death during the Holocaust serves as a continuous reminder that it is not a closed chapter of history.

Ultimately, the survivor's problem is qualitatively different from the psychological difficulties with which we are more familiar. It is one of dealing with the Holocaust experience through the longitudinal process of mourning, a task more complex than the usual therapeutic relationship encompasses. It is an existential problem because it embodies not only his biological and psychological existence as an individual but also his symbolic existence as part of a nation and community that was seriously threatened by Nazi ideology. The survivors' search for a satisfying "theory of survival" has until now been belittled and undermined by interpreting it solely in the light of reactivated childhood conflicts and death wishes toward their families. Therapists who consider becoming involved with survivors and their children might empathize with, describe, and validate their inner experiences, but no reparation and undoing of the Holocaust is possible. The ethical, political, sociological, and psychological phenomena that compose the Holocaust can only be "worked through" by the survivor with the therapist, considering all the losses, communal as well as individual, over a long period of time. But it can neither be repaired nor undone. The survivor's recovery of feelings of hope within his memories of the Holocaust as well as in his life afterward is accomplished through the reconnection with his internalized family representations and system of values and with a choice for life.

Can we say that the values and attitudes of the therapist, even if they can be transmitted and accomplished in the therapy, can help the survivor to live with his past? The therapist cannot be expected to handle empathically any problem of the survivor as if it were outside the complexities of human experience, for if the therapist attempts to undo the reality of the Holocaust experience or to subject it to his own definition of relevance, he is engaging in fragmentation which is incompatible with the continuous humanizing dialogue of the therapy. On the other hand, is it unreasonable and unfair to demand that the enormity of the Holocaust be understood and made manageable by the therapist? He cannot hope to provide answers but must address himself to the questions that the survivor-patient is able to ask in the process of the therapy. These questions pertain to the survivor's role and responsibility in the Holocaust and are connected with reawakened survival guilt or the mourning of his children. Just as psychiatry does not provide immediate answers to the moral dilemmas posed by the continuously changing problems of human history, so a survivor of a part of this history is not, by definition, a psychiatric client automatically in need of those answers.

Since we have not yet found satisfying ways of coming to terms with the experience of the Holocaust, it would be naive to view the survivor who is attempting to cope with his Holocaust experiences in the context of a psychiatric conceptualization alone. During my work with survivors, I became aware of the importance of fitting together an understanding of the survivor's specific Holocaust experiences with his pre-Holocaust personality and his psychosocial stage of development during the traumatization.

It is understandable that even sensitive psychiatrists felt themselves constrained to adhere to the mode of professional expertise, emotional detachment, and a neutral stance in relation to Holocaust survivors. This kind of approach revealed a desire on the part of the therapist to remain untouched and unharmed by the real tragedy of the Holocaust. Perhaps therapists finding themselves in this situation feared that they would lose the capacity to maintain therapeutic neutrality or an alliance with their survivor patients. The therapist's concern that the survivor would experience him as helpless is a displacement of the real sense of helplessness that anyone must feel before the inexplicable. This hesitation mirrored society's inability to relate to the survivor without avoidance and denial.

Both the therapist and his patients, be they survivors or the children of survivors, must contend with the complex reality of the Holocaust. For the therapist to counter that reality (which is often foreign to him) is to be empathic and share the patient's feelings of frustration, humiliation, and powerlessness in the face of their real experiences in the Holocaust and requires him to recognize that these recounted experiences are not an expression of sadomasochistic fantasies. Through the patient, the therapist learns about his own capacities to experience anguish and sometimes helplessness and aggression, without losing his own empathic, therapeutic role or his boundaries. In this transaction, the patient re-experiences the inferno, the Holocaust, but now in a therapeutic framework where acceptance of both positive and negative transference give him hope and allow him to return to a new reality acceptable and accepted by both of them. Within the adequate therapeutic context, the survivor is able to express themes in the transference of longing for love and full acceptance as well as fears of abandonment, while the therapist in his countertransference expresses his anguish of identifying with the survivor's experiences. Moreover, the therapist learns to respect the survivor's struggles for renewal and to accept his fantasies of rebirth and revival.

If we agree that re-experiencing the traumatization within the therapeutic relationship makes it intelligible and meaningful and shared in some way, the question still occurs to some therapists whether the psychotherapeutic dialogue is the best context in which such an experience can come about. But in my own therapeutic encounters as an analyst, this re-experiencing is possible only when the stabilization of the transference processes occurs, when the survivor, in contrast to the original situation, is not alone in the inferno of the Holocaust. In the therapeutic alliance, which for the survivor patient is not only a container of reason and hope, the patient is allowed to confront himself with all the feelings that were previously avoided, diminishing his pathological guilt and feelings of loneliness and supporting his sense of an actual responsibility. Many therapists with different approaches have questioned the dangers inherent in psychotherapy with survivors. Niederland warned, "No physician should go to exploratory depths with these people without inviting catastrophe." Others were more optimistic. They stressed the importance for the patient to re-experience the Holocaust with the therapist. This would diminish the survivor's isolation and transform the incomprehensible diabolical experience of the Holocaust—in which the Nazis tried to project their own concretized dehumanized representations onto the survivor—into a humanized dimension in the present. In this dimension, concrete phantasmagoric imagery is changed by verbalization, using pre-Holocaust symbolic language to give meaning to the experience. This is the problem: how to give meaning to the experiences that were meaningless, out of reality. Freud probably had it in mind when he observed in *Civilization and Its Discontents*:

> No matter how much we may shrink with horror from certain situations—of a galley-slave in antiquity, of a peasant during the Thirty Years' War, of a victim of the Holy Inquisition, of a Jew awaiting a pogrom—it is nevertheless impossible for us to feel our way into such people—to divine the changes with original obtuseness of mind, a gradual stupefying process, the cessation of expectations, and cruder or more refined methods of narcotization have produced upon their receptivity to sensations of pleasure and unpleasure. Moreover, in the case of the most extreme possibility of suffering, special mental protective devices are brought into operation. (*SE*, Vol. XXI, p. 89)

Particularly empathy, a newly developed sense of causality and achieved reality orientation experienced during the therapy organized the changes in the first and second generations of survivors. They were able to develop real object ties rather than internalized fantasized images.

Is "coping with trauma" to forgive and forget and to remember and work through? These questions are raised by survivors in psychotherapeutic encounters, experiencing the therapist not only as a transference object but also as a container and source of reality and hope.

Some of the vignettes presented seem to demonstrate that the behavior of those survivors with whom psychiatrists came in contact appeared similar to those presented by patients suffering from other psychological disturbances. This is undoubtedly due to the fact that our human psychic apparatus has only a limited repertoire of reactive psychosomatic responses to overwhelming external stimuli when, flooding the ego, they break through the stimulus barrier. That the psyche cannot produce entirely new systematic responses even to the onslaught of such massive traumatizations as those experienced by survivors of the Holocaust lends theoretical support to the role of the traumatic causation of the behavior of any individual who is labeled "mentally ill" and further suggests that there are typical patterns of reaction to dehumanization connected with external persecution as a member of a hated minority or as a scapegoat within the nuclear or extended family.

Because the presenting symptomatology seemed identical to that commonly found among patients with neurotic disorders, some psychiatrists labeled their survivor-clients as "mental patients." Labels are significant only because of the consequences they evoke. The consequence of labeling survivors as mentally disturbed was, among others, the orienting and organizing principle of the therapist's judgment of them. With this label, the survivor became part of a large category of people who were considered to be in need of psychiatric therapy to relieve suffering and to facilitate a return to health. On the basis of pioneering psychiatric clinical studies often showing great depth and sensitivity, Krystal described specific types of psychological damage. In contrast to his clinically related studies, it is also possible to approach the life of the survivor from the standpoint of a meaningful life experience rather than from an approach of "psychological damage." We see the survivor as perpetually trying to come to terms with and overcome death in order to embrace life. If the survivor did not wish to accept the sick role in this relationship with the therapist, he was considered to be at fault, poorly motivated or self-deceptive.

A frequent question asked both by survivors and non-survivors in different countries is "Are survivors more disturbed than non-survivors?" For survivors who sought to find security in a world that had lost its equilibrium, there was an intense need to fight off the false identity projected onto them during the oppression by the Nazis and, later on, mostly unwittingly and unconsciously by society. Survivors need help to allow themselves to change their defensive life patterns to positive self-realization, to change from organizing their lives around the quest for security to conducting them according to the pleasure principle, as embodied in the Jewish tradition "*Im ein ani li, mi li?*" (If I am not for me, who will be for me?").

Even those survivors whose behavior and mental functioning were unremarkable were seen by some researchers as engaged in massive denial and repression of their "survival guilt." Thus, all survivors were defined as in some way suffering from a static survivor syndrome. The specific quality of the "survivor syndrome" and their families is not to be found in a particular diagnostic spectrum from character disturbances through borderline syndromes, depressions, and schizophrenia. Nor is it to be only found in the particular contents of fantasy or in dream life, as it is clear that Holocaust symbolism is found in the dreams or the literary expressions and fantasy life of non-victims, nor in metaphors, as Holocaust metaphors were absorbed in the poetic and dramatic expressions and fantasy life of non-survivors. Rather they are found more often as stable elements in the conscious and unconscious life of survivors and their offspring. In turn, they color the transference and countertransference and intensify the treatment. The therapist becomes a "member of the guilty society." There has been no recognition that this syndrome is a dynamic, changing entity with defensive and adaptive functions. It usually appeared in the initial phase after liberation and in the transitional phase after immigration, usually functioning as an adaptive measure up to the time when the survivors were ready to begin the process of revival.

The syndrome concept introduces a polemic that underlies many discussions. To classify an individual as suffering from the "survivor syndrome" is to abandon the classic diagnostic categories and substitute a psychosocial category. Some psychiatrists used this very example to demonstrate the theoretical advances of social psychiatry. Social psychiatry may offer partial solutions to the problems of diagnosis through the designation of categories of phenomena combining social and intrapsychic disorders. A dramatic illustration of such a contribution is the "survivor syndrome." In other words, the survivor of massive psychosocial traumatization, such as the Holocaust, presents a range of experiences and means of adapting to post-Holocaust life, which cannot be adequately subsumed within the existing psychiatric typologies but must be considered as an example of unique psychosocial consequence to a specific psychological trauma. Rigid diagnostic labeling can only obscure the survivor's experience. Furthermore, all diagnostic categories (including "syndrome") must be appreciated as psychosocial products that lose their applicability in changed space or time. A quick glance at the history of psychiatric terminology attests to the short life span of classification systems that at one time occupied the status of "scientific truth." We know their influence by the psychosocial pressures and needs within a given society, as for example, the vicissitudes of the diagnosis of homosexuality or the question of diagnosing and labeling Vietnam veterans' disturbances in American psychiatric nomenclature.

During treatment, when confronted by the question, "Why did they survive?" the survivors responded that it was only by magic, faith, or pure chance that they survived. The physical strength and initiative was not enough unless it was matched by the will to live as well as a strong sense of purpose. They could not conceive of their survival only as an expression of their will and organized reality-oriented actions. The phantasmagoric fantasy of the Nazis was concretized in the inferno of the concentration camps and not connected with reason, causality, and action as we try to develop it in ourselves and our children throughout the lifespan. Only during treatment can they accept that their survival was also an act of affirmation and purpose. Each survivor used different tactics to "transcend" the dehumanizing conditions in ghettos and camps. They believed that survival only had meaning insofar as it gave witness to life, values, and hopes of themselves and of their deceased families and friends. They knew that by surviving, they would demonstrate that the might of death was not absolute and the Nazi tyranny could not entirely destroy the human soul. This task expressed their resistance to evil. As one victim said, "I wish to survive one day after his defeat [meaning Hitler]. That would be enough."

The decision to choose life was paradoxically taken when the survivors were confronted with massive, collective, and senseless death as an expression of vengeance. This feeling of vengeance mobilized one survivor to choose life when, in the death train on her way to Auschwitz, as her ten-year-old brother died in her arms, she experienced a tremendous mobilization of vitality when she felt "I have to live for him to revenge his death. I have to continue my own war." When she imagined Hitler's image, she was roused to vengeance. Survivors used every symbol, idea, and concept to give meaning to their survival in the absurd, meaningless world of the camps. Despite the terrible reality of hunger, filth, chronic illnesses, tortures, chronic sleep deprivation, which resulted in ego depletion, the prisoners demonstrated that their spiritual and moral self could remain intact by the affirmation of their humanity in defiance of constant efforts of animalization.

Some prisoners communicated with nature, feeling special contact with the universe, sun, stars, moon, and forest in a kind of pantheistic embrace in order to alter the reality of filth and despair of their barracks. Others used humor and singing as a vehicle to regain vitality and a feeling of inner freedom. In some victims, changes in their ego-self occurred with an ad hoc development of a "false self" (boredom), a genesis different from Winnicott's (1960) description. These changes in the personality of victims expressed themselves especially in isolated victims in a kind of "robotization" and automatization of functioning, movements without any emotions as well as a lack of object relations (Niederland, 1968b; Meerloo, 1962). These regressive changes in ego functions, also described in the film *The Pawnbroker*, seem to me to be the result of the changes in the stimulus barrier of the ego. The longitudinal changes in the stimulus barrier in the form of "the armor of the ego," developing a shield of automatized ego functions, helped these victims to function and not to be flooded with anxiety-panic in spite of the permanent sadistic actions of the Nazi aggressors with their continuous connotations of death. Such permanent confrontation with aggression and collective death in normal ego conditions should, due to clinical experience (Freud's second anxiety theory, 1926d), result in anxiety-panic states and fragmentation of the ego that did not occur in the victims.

This powerful perception of the meaning of their survival in the treatment situation ran counter to the popular view of survivors as traumatized individuals requiring psychiatric treatment, as expressed in Bettelheim's controversial papers and books. We see the survivor as perpetually trying to come to terms with and overcoming death in order to embrace life. The survivors experienced themselves as unique in having "been saved" from destruction in the midst of a general catastrophe and in a way to have "conquered death." To enter treatment was to give up this special status and to view themselves as patients—not omnipotent but, on the contrary, damaged people. The injured narcissism reflected in this theme is not verbalized readily and creates one of the therapeutic paradoxes. For the survivor who sought the professional help of a psychotherapist, numerous difficulties arose. The survivor's inability even after many years to put his experience into words and his sensitivity to and suspicion of authority and examinations sometimes culminated in the transference in an identification of the therapist with the Nazis. Very often, in our theoretical conceptualizations, we unwittingly provide a basis for these suspicions. This happened at the Symposium on the Children of Survivors at the International Congress of Psychoanalysis (New York, 1979) when in a paper entitled "Children of Survivors and Children of Nazi Perpetrators," the existence of the old-fashioned victim-aggressor bind was assumed rather than the possibility that the children of the Nazi perpetrators would be required to find solutions to the problems of psychosocial identity quite separate and distinct from those required by the children of survivors.

From the symptomatic perspective, we find the same problems in relation to their perceptions of their parents. For both populations, the identification processes are disturbed. Devaluation of the parental representations also occurs in both groups as well as the problem of the avoided, suppressed shameful secret of the family. But as we observed elsewhere, for the Nazi aggressor and his children, there is no survival guilt or guilt connected with his crimes.

The survivor's shame in failing to fulfill his old ego ideals often led to muteness, memory distortions, glossing over, and psychic closing off in psychotherapeutic encounters. As for the survivor, paradoxically, survival guilt appears on the road to recovery and revival from the traumatization in the Holocaust. The countervailing muteness of the therapist in the face of the inexplicable, his own guilt, frustration, and anger often contributed to a conspiracy of silence between the patient and the doctor. As we have already noted, engaging a survivor in effective psychotherapy was seen by many authors as potentially traumatic both for the survivor and the therapist. These difficulties are reflected in the paucity of literature dealing with the "therapy of survivors" as compared to the abundance of references to the "psychopathology of survivors." The reason for this was the inadequate restitution requirements of the German government that demanded that we formulate a medical and legal basis of understanding the psychopathological damages due to the Nazi oppression. If categories describing essentially similar phenomena but derived from dissimilar periods lose their efficacy, how much more so the inapplicability of dated categories for wholly unprecedented conditions such as the Holocaust traumatization. And in case a conservative diagnostician would argue that "there is nothing new under the sun with which psychiatry has to grapple," he should simply think of Krystal's sentence: "Traumatization through the Holocaust is of a kind and intensity never before encountered for study by modern psychiatry." Lifton's and Niederland's contributions of highly original, descriptive concepts to delineate the "survivor syndrome" are especially useful in providing the groundwork for building a specific vocabulary to communicate about and with this unique group.

To move beyond the classic Kraepelinean definitions or the modern *DSM-III* with its diagnostic category "Post-traumatic Stress Disorders" to create new terms and correspondingly novel modes of relating to the experience of the individual allows one to step outside the rhetorical question, are the Holocaust survivors mentally disturbed?

There are several typical subgroups of survivors with different patterns of behavior and different self-concepts. Following the perspective of social psychiatry, mental illness is not considered to be something that is disease-like and inherent in an individual but rather refers to the quality of an individual's participation in a system such as a marital pair, the family, the community, or a larger society. If mental health and illness are transformed from a medical entity to a pattern of an individual's integration into a particular environment, then bizarre or even suspicious behavior can begin to look reasonable. It is only if we consider the nature and extent of the events of the past that we can abandon organic and constitutional determinants as etiological factors in the KZ syndrome and recognize that the survivor was reacting appropriately to a chaotic reality, a psychotic world, a world that showed a close affinity to the world destruction fantasies of psychotic individuals.

The general questions that come to mind in man-made disasters are complex and not easy to answer. What is the meaning of causality in psychiatry relating to massive psychic traumatization without antecedents in the survivors' own life and in previous generations? What is the difference between the trauma of childhood and that of later years? What situations are in essence traumatic and which become traumatic only when they are so defined by an individual? What is the nature of the ability and will to survive?

Our clinical and therapeutic work with people who have undergone traumatic experiences of catastrophic proportions has shown that the boundaries between destructive fantasies of one's internal reality and those experienced during the external realities of the Holocaust are not always clearly defined. Each of us needs to struggle with the "survivor" and the "aggressor" within himself. We are all survivors of various developmental crises during the course of our lives, and some of us carry scars within our egos which are ineradicable. Despite this, we possess within us a potential for development and growth at later stages, a fact that some psychiatrists with a tendency to concentrate on psychopathological processes sometimes forget.

This capacity lies not only in individuals but also in groups and nations in which trauma, by its very nature, mobilized emotional strength and the development of appropriate ego-adaptive mechanisms. It must also be said that the self is influenced by actual object relationships and transcendental experiences and by the intense emotional experiences of ego mastery during war and peace. The aggressive impulse is often not only an expression of destruction projected from ourselves to the external world or merely an expression of Thanatos; it can also be an expression of self-assertion in the service of the ego, a means of release from a situation of helplessness and hopelessness. When an element of hope and responsibility appears also within the psychotherapy itself, it is precisely at this point that we see a sublimated expression of aggression in the service of self-assertion and the building of the personal, group, or national boundaries. It is this sublimated aggression that facilitates the emergence from a state of helplessness and hopelessness.

In Israel, the aggression seemed to be in the service of the superego as well as the ego; it was integrated in the self and expressed in situations following war or massive trauma by massive criticism of the leaders, psychosocial structures, and ideologies that proved useless in solving current problems. Such criticism was expressed in psychoanalytic treatment during the phases of re-integration or in a psychosocial framework in crisis situations. It is also expressed in the psychosocial developmental phases of individuals, as in adolescence or in group processes in the history of mankind. Such expressions are legitimate early signs of renewal and expansion of the ego, both of the individual and the group. It is appropriate then to interpret the post-Holocaust search for ideologies and meanings more suited to the new reality as an assertive attempt to renew the individual and collective superego and self-ideal. This new approach to reality is in opposition to the self-ideal of the Diaspora Jew as an introspective intellectual detached from the system of values transmitted from previous generations (Klein, 1978a). It seems that the plasticity of society in Israel allows for the expression of aggression in formalized and acceptable ways. Societal institutions such as political parties or the army and demonstrations and the extreme criticism of past leaders all serve the need for idealization and projective identification of good and bad internal objects.

Considering the intensity of their traumatic experiences, one may say that the survivors of the Holocaust have attained an adequate external adaptation in their new lives. Nevertheless, the Holocaust perseveres in the conscious and unconscious lives, in their dreams and memories, in their speech and associations, as well as in their own identity as survivors. Moreover, it seems that "the Holocaust syndrome" is now a general experience of a large section of the world population. This is evidenced in experiences of loss and mourning of the past and hope for the future. There is also a renewal process of individual and collective identification with the losses caused by the Nazi genocide, but along with this, there is skepticism about the world.

Many of the clinical manifestations of the so-called "KZ syndrome" are now present in altered form. Among some survivors, psycho-physiological symptoms such as gastrointestinal disturbances have acquired chronicity or have achieved a kind of physiological homeostasis. Others have developed true psychosomatic illnesses (hypertension, ulcers, etc.). The development of psychosomatic illnesses among survivors is related to some idiosyncratic somatic and psychological factors connected with oppressive experiences such as repetitive infections, chronic starvation, and the need to suppress aggression in the service of survival.

Psychological factors connected with guilt feelings, memories, and hypermnesis of the traumatic events have also changed over time so that cathexes are now attached to new objects and experiences rather than to those of the past. These cathexes are experienced *de novo*. Such experiences range from a positive involvement connected with building and reshaping Israel as founding fathers or as fathers of their new families to the realization of professional and personal ideals. In Israel, the rebirth of the new-old country came together with the beginnings of the new life for the survivors. This historic event allowed them to fulfill their rebirth fantasies and gave special meaning to their lives. Many survivors report that the nightmares and traumatic memories connected with experiences of the Holocaust are altered, sometimes fading away and sometimes re-experienced with tremendous intensity during the anniversary reactions of their own specific Holocaust experiences or after traumatic experiences connected with the wars in Israel in which their own children are confronted with death.

From a theoretical point of view, the question of the passage of time and its relation to the psychological processes occurring among survivors is extremely complex. From the clinical point of view, we can say that time does not play a role in the unconscious of the survivor and that the suppression and later repression of the traumatic experiences are only partly functioning as a defense against overwhelming anxiety. The use of the unconscious defense mechanism of repression is clearly shown by the fact that traumatic memories are encapsulated and re-experienced when triggered by present-day events. This not only implies the presence of anniversary-type mourning processes but also suggests how the experiencing ego of the survivor contains memories of traumatic events alongside pleasurable ones. Pleasurable memories of the Holocaust include the development of friendships and the maintenance of the self-ideal and specific acts of altruism and love, as many vignettes demonstrate. Memories flooded with unpleasurable affects and content are rejected. Some survivors who appear to be suffering from an inability to express affects and emotions (alexithymia, as described by Sifneos, 1967; Krystal, 1968) are really defending against unpleasurable and chaotic affects that simultaneously threaten their self-concepts and egos. This inability to express affects seems to be functional and can be worked through in psychoanalytic therapy during the most intense transference situation when the patient experiences the therapist as benign, accepting, and containing. Then the analyst is perceived as one who can accept symbiotic longings and who defends the patient and himself via structuring and organizing principles against previously chaotic affects or the repetition of splitting affects toward polarized objects. This is accomplished by accepting ambivalence toward beloved and hated objects.

In psychoanalytic terms, neutralization and the ability to polarize affects and drives in an ego-syntonic way and changes of the self-concept (the longitudinal potential for recathexis of new objects and ideologies) are the means by which survivors have reconstituted themselves. These profound structural alterations can be observed, for example, in the ability to single out particular Nazis as targets of rage as opposed to a collective hatred of all Germans. This makes it possible for survivors to relinquish a paranoid-like loss of basic trust and to reorient themselves in the present. The flooding of the ego with painful memories of the Holocaust (selections and deaths of family members) has diminished both in frequency and intensity. In recounting current dreams, survivors report that they appear as observers rather than as victims. The manifest content of their dreams has also changed so that aggressors appear as current enemies rather than Germans. Dream content is concerned with current life situations and people with whom they are presently involved. Anxiety and guilt feelings connected with past events are experienced with diminished affect and with the potential for neutralization and justification. Resignation to and acceptance of death are themes in these dreams. Death now is experienced in the context of the individual's biological death and life axes.

The life-death axis is the most fundamental dimension in the experience of the survivor; to this must be added the determining element of rebirth fantasies in the creation of new life after the destruction.

Hope and Rebirth
Life
Death

This triangle of themes can be seen deeply imprinted in survivors' individual and family lives since the liberation. Following his encounter with death in the inferno, the survivor had to meet the challenge of rebirth in himself and his reconstituted family in order not to submit to psychological death, even though he managed, against all possible odds, to escape physical extinction.

The knowledge of death awakened in him two antagonistic tendencies: a hunger for life expressed in self-perpetuating activities, autonomy-seeking, achievements, pleasure, and the opposite polarization of a nirvana-like regression, seeking peace, minimal activity, minimal achievements, and dependence on object relations. This polarization corresponds only partly with Lifton's concept of the "death imprint" or "death taint." Lifton, in his formulation of psychological patterns that characterize the survivor, is speaking of "psychic numbing." In studying the life cycles of survivors, we can see styles and modes of adaptation that can be understood as a direct continuation of behavior patterns of survival and coping mechanisms developed during the years of the Holocaust sufferings in the ghettos and the concentration camps. Thus, one whose survival was previously expressed as "Where was I when my friend was killed?" can now say "I had no other choice. I did what I could do in that inferno." Static guilt no longer keeps the survivors locked in the past. This comes about with the acceptance of the present in which reworked reality is separate and distinct from the past. By the increased awareness of the past, with a diminishing of avoidance devoid of repression of the traumatic experience and the acceptance of survival guilt, the symptoms of shame diminish. We also see changes in the synthetic function of the ego, accepting the ambivalence and going beyond the role of society as being responsible for life in the present while not forgetting the past. The potential for a more realistic view of himself and of his role in the traumas of the past make this possible for the survivor. There is now the possibility to experience intensely the deaths of friends and family without guilty self-defense. Thus, he can now see himself as both participant and observer and can free himself for his involvement in the life of the present.

We can say that the observing and judgmental ego emerges when there is a potential for emotionally re-experiencing the past at a distance. Without crippling static guilt, this living and re-experiencing can occur with affects of fear and anguish but without overwhelming anxiety and suicidal self-blame. Among survivors with reconstituted families, the working through of the psychological effects of the traumatization was experienced in the initial phase after liberation through their relationships with their children. These were expressed in feelings of dependency and interdependency and in fears and fantasies of bringing children into a terrifying, dangerous world where they would confront massive death and still survive physically and psychologically. The crux of the survivor's dilemma is that they recognize the human causality of their suffering and feel that they are unable to accept the role of a patient who must relinquish the real anguish over the loss of the family experienced in the Holocaust.

Many of the attitudes and the patterns of behavior seen in the life cycles of survivors concern their attempts to come to terms with having experienced the impossible and the unforgettable. The postwar confrontation with a world which had not gone through these experiences and which was utterly different from their fantasies, hope, and expectations and did not welcome their return from hell was demoralizing in itself.

The survivors developed secondary defenses in the attempt to integrate their Holocaust experiences and the psycho-historical realities in Europe after the liberation and their previous personality structures. They were motivated by a tremendous need to prove to the world and to themselves that they were not destroyed, that they were alive and valuable human beings.

Epilogue

Liberation, May 8, 1945

It seems to me that I denied hearing the Russian tanks in the streets of Theresienstadt. In passing, I registered the shrieking excited voices "The Russians are here!" as if not being able to accept that the long nightmare from which one had wished to awaken was finally coming to an end, as though, with reluctance, to be confronted again with the pain and loss connected with emerging life and with the emptiness of my inner and outer worlds, with so many empty houses and streets in which all that was known and loved no longer existed, some part of me had died with them. So I did not wish to get out of bed and lay stricken with pain, hunger, weakness, and sickness. But the voices grew louder. I could hear Russian songs through the open windows and inmates' excited voices saying that the SS were running away and of people trying to find and kill them. The thought of bread and hot soup seemed like a feast and awakened hunger, and perhaps hunger for life as well.

Hearing and seeing the Russian tanks and Russian faces, I knew that I should be happy; I made the appropriate gestures of greeting. My lips formed the song of the "International" when I heard the melody sung by the soldiers on the main square of Theresienstadt. I remembered a boy with whom I worked who was hanged by the Germans in Plaszow for singing the "International." The picture of his face in my mind awakened waves of pain and hatred.

I could not feel joy. The intense hatred changed into a numbness and amnesia, and there were no feelings at all. Despite the long years of yearning and anticipation, of experiencing freedom in fantasy (the fantasies of "Messianic times," or *Maschiach Zeiten* in Yiddish), and of the joy that would overcome me, there was only sadness and embarrassment. What to do with my freedom? What to do now?

I walked through the streets looking for food until I came to the Elbe. Thousands of soldiers and camp survivors who looked like me in my striped garb wandered in haste, looking but not seeing the late spring, the trees in blossom, the green fields, neighboring Theresienstadt, and the villages near the Elbe. I saw their emaciated bodies with empty feverish eyes. I saw them in my mirror image. I found a box of German preserved meat at the side of the road. I knew I shouldn't eat it but did. Columns of German soldiers in uniform, some missing their SS insignia, came by under Russian guards, by the hundreds, their heads lowered, faces unshaven, with fixed expressions, in some way with the same empty eyes as ours. In only one day, they had become human again in my eyes, changing from omnipotent murderers, masters of life and death, to people in whose eyes I read those emotions so well known to me: grief, shame, and fear.

This meeting of eyes awakened life in me, the teenager who had pity for the defeated, concentration camp inmates of different nationalities who had been slaves of the Germans, among them my own comrades who overran the soldiers, beat them and took shoes and watches. I was surprised to hear my voice call in anger "Don't do to them what they did to us yesterday." But I was not heard. Today it seems to me that this immediate reaction aided to expel the terror and the death from my self-image and began the return to my self-representation of before the Holocaust. Yet I have no full answer to explain the capacity of the human being to save his inner core and recreate. Part of this riddle may have been what formed my motivation to work with children in DP camps and what promoted my own psychoanalytic and psychiatric studies.

I wandered further through the fields and came to the beautiful town of Leitmeritz, now empty of inhabitants. I came to a house, looking for food—or perhaps for something else? I remember the splendid Baroque-style staircase of the house as I entered the gate and walked through the rooms until I reached not the kitchen but the library. It now seems so surrealistic, a mixture of fantasy and reality. Among all the thousands of books, I found a small volume of Heinrich Heine, *Buch der Lieder*. How I found it I don't know. I opened it and read "*Im wunderschönen Monat Mai*"—and I began to cry.

I began my life of freedom weighing twenty-eight kilos. Is it possible? Now, following liberation, I allowed myself the total regression of becoming practically a *muselman*. One day, I fell ill with exantimatic typhoid and dysentery and had to be hospitalized, as were hundreds of comrades, in a hospital in Theresienstadt run by the Russians who took care of the deathly sick patients. I remember one particular woman who cared for me and who told me of her own fate as an actress in Paris and whose "destiny" was to be evacuated to Sudeten. She cried helplessly and fearfully, and again I began to feel a growing interest and emotion in human beings, together with my own awakening life.

I remember my first dream after the liberation. I was on board a beautiful white ship, surrounded by blond Swedish nurses who were caring for me. The wind blew strongly, and the storm and waves endangered the ship. By some miracle, the sea calmed, and the nurse told me that the danger had passed. Years later, I understood the wish-fulfillment dream as a kind of reunion with my sister (the same word as *nurse* in Polish), giving her the role of savior, saving me from the storm and danger in a childlike denial of what had happened. But the dream was also an expression of renewal of life and the hope that I allowed myself to feel again.

In December 1945, in a DP hospital in Munich, after months of hospitalization, I heard of the opening of the theatre by the military government in the nearby residential theatre of Brunnenhof. The old passion and reminiscences for the theatre of my adolescent days returned. Memories of such different performances as Shakespeare's *A Midsummer Night's Dream* in the Slowaki Theatre of Krakow, and of Singer's *Josie Kalb* in the Jewish Theatre of Krakow and of Lessing, whom we had read about in high school and remembered as one of the righteous gentiles in the history of Jewish enlightenment and a friend of Moses Mendelssohn. All of these came to my mind, together with painful feelings of the lost world. The theatre was the expression of another world where joy and compassion existed larger than life. I borrowed clothes, left the hospital without the permission of the station nurse, and walked through the destroyed streets of Munich to the Residence, fearful but also full of excitement and anticipation.

In the theatre, I re-awoke to life. Looking at a scene in Jerusalem, I heard the tale of the three rings. In it, a father gave a ring to each of his three sons, and each one believed that he had received the true birthright, the ring that would bestow strength and work wonders. I felt something moving within me, changing. I felt that each of the sons had in truth received the same message and inheritance; the only difference would be in how they treated it. They were all equal—the Jew, the Moslem, and the Christian. I got my message and accepted the hope for a new beginning. For the second time since liberation, I began to feel and to mourn. The next day, I left the hospital and accepted a job as a youth leader near Dachau for children from the camps. I had begun to feel the courage to hope.

Thirty years later, I met with young German psychoanalysts, some of them children of active perpetrators or of passive onlookers of human destruction, those who did not open their hearts, minds, or mouths when their neighbors were taken away, never to return. There were also German analysts of my generation who as soldiers and young men had neither the courage nor the capacity to fight the evil and who by avoidance, denial, or repression could not be confronted by the question of guilt years after the end of the Thousand-Year Reich. During many hours of supervision, we understood that cognitively and ideologically, they totally rejected the *Weltanschauung* of their fathers; they developed a kind of reaction formation, a total rejection of the state as an instrument of oppression. Emotionally, though, they were unable to be confronted with the Jew who awakened in them complex feelings of uneasiness, anger, and suppressed guilt.

Hearing their pain of having a murderer-father or a mother full of hatred and resentment, their detachment from their parents' generation and their anger and despair awoke in me a complex feeling of responsibility. I felt that for both our sakes, I had to fight the feelings of resentment or pity. I could not forgive them, for I had no right to, but I also had no right to hate. With each individual tale, I understood more and more: that the mythos of the Nazi's total splitting between his world at home, where he was a loving father and husband, and the world of ghettos, camps, and occupied territories, where they were murderers doing the "dirty work" for their beloved homeland, this mythos became more and more implausible. The inability to mourn that Mitscherlich described so vividly seems to be connected with the inability to be in touch with the murderer's world of fathers and mothers or with the lost world of the murdered victims.

In the Universities of Frankfurt, Heidelberg, Tübingen, and Ulm, I experienced the longitudinal process of the courage of these young people, first to hate the evil, to distance themselves intellectually from it, to comfort themselves with the parental representations of perpetrators, and then to encourage in them and in myself the process of forgiving. In this experience of delineation from the evil and the building of boundaries, through ambivalence, splitting, avoidance, or idealization of the Jewish representational world to working through our complex emotions and feelings in the transference and countertransference situations. It allowed both of us the mourning process for the parental representations. It allowed them and me to free ourselves from those toxic introjects of the Nazi era. There is no place for collective guilt and collective hatred; there is no place for formal reconciliation that would amount to a rebuilding of a false self, for them and for me. But there is place for a dialogue for us and for our children to fight against the aggressive tendencies in ourselves, against scapegoating, which is always possible. There is hope for the triumph of the ego, the faint voice in the darkness of silence (*kol d'mama daka*).

During our supervision sessions, I was confronted first with expressions of the uneasiness of the younger generation of Germans toward me as a representative of the world that their parents had tried and succeeded in destroying. They expressed avoidance, denial, and indifference toward the Holocaust and Jews on the surface. There was also an intense ambivalence and manifest distancing from their fathers from whom they were intellectually and rationally removed, although in many preconscious aspects, they identified with the political and psychosocial situation in their country and with their intense fear of an atomic cataclysm in Europe. This obsessive preoccupation with the possibility of an atomic disaster in our teaching sessions awoke the question in me, why here? What is the specific anxiety I felt in Germany? Why did young intellectual Germans become terrorists here, with urges to destroy the social structures? It suddenly occurred to me that this too had an unconscious common denominator. The anxiety was not easily verbalized or enacted, but it seemed to be an expression of a delayed act of vengeance and an expression of justice for the acts of the cataclysmic murders of the fathers and the grandfathers. Years after the Holocaust, there was an avoidance of mourning, not only for the *Führer*, the demonic charismatic parental figure of their parents, but a total avoidance of meeting the Jew who had lived with them for centuries in their streets and towns, their literature and mythology, and more important, their representational world. In many instances, I met their need of over-idealization of me as the messenger of this representative world, as the idealized father, one who could understand them in reference to their real fathers and parental figures. They needed to see in me the one who could accept their ambivalent feelings, their guilt and the verbal and non-verbal pleas for forgiveness.

The theme of forgiveness and the inability to forgive seemed to be the leitmotif in the relations between parents and children in present-day Germany. This was connected with the ability to mourn, not only for their own parental world but also for Jews who left an invisible vacuum in their souls.

In my therapeutic work with survivors and their children and in my teaching activities with young German analysts, it became important for me to fight against re-emerging aggressive and hostile feelings and acts, even when they appeared as expressions of fidelity and justice. I have an obligation toward all victims and toward the children of tormentors who are not guilty of the acts of their murderer-fathers but who cannot deny in their lives the continuity of the burden of responsibility. Here is the tragic meeting point with the children of survivors who in their own continuity take up the burden of their parents' fate.

Participating in the 1983 Amnesty International Conference on Modalities of the Treatment of Victims of Torture, I became aware again of the sickness of those who perpetrate and of those who inject the perpetrators with rationales for their hatred and aggression. From my own experience of loneliness and doubt in times of darkness, I know of those who resist the evil. I know the doubts of people who say, "You are fighting windmills." But I know that the windmills are as old as mankind and feel it is important to fight the ghosts, even when the chances are slim for the victory of reason and the reality principle against hate, self-righteousness, and greed of one nation against another. Our actual life after the Holocaust taught us that those ghosts could return in different images such as self-righteousness or of their own group's national, "legitimate" interests. The Jewish way is not one of vengeance. In any case, the only way to avenge those who perished in the Holocaust is not to forget them, not to make them into holy idealized images but to remember their multiple expressions of life. In spite of the total darkness in the external world, they made life meaningful by cherishing hope.

Afterword

I met Hillel Klein only a few times on his visits to Germany and I was impressed by his serenity and kindness, not to speak of the seriousness of his efforts to make his views and convictions understood and accepted by his German colleagues, and I admired him for what he was trying to achieve and what he did achieve in the end.

I knew, of course, that Hillel Klein's book, originally written in English, had already appeared in a German version in 2003, edited by my colleague and friend Carl Nedelmann and by Gerd Biermann. With Carl Nedelmann I had been working together at the Michael-Balint-Institut in Hamburg for over 20 years. An English version had initially not materialized because it was felt to be impossible to edit Hillel's original in a satisfactory way. As an Israeli colleague once wrote, it needed someone "who is crazy enough to undertake this task". But the pressure continued to produce an English version as well if someone could be found who was crazy enough to undertake the editing of his original manuscript. Since I was in retirement and had the time to undertake this task and because I had always admired Hillel, I offered my services when I was asked and they were gladly accepted.

Now that I have completed my task, I must admit that it was a difficult but in no way impossible undertaking which, however, needed a lot of perseverance, patience and diligence. I think the main editorial problem stemmed from the fact that Hillel Klein's English was that of a Polish citizen which meant that it included many idiosyncracies which are not those of an English-speaking person. One of his relatives once said that Hillel knew many languages but spoke them all rather badly. Moreover, it is evident that Hillel describes the happenings from a Polish point of view. To give you a few examples: Hillel's grammar and punctuation are rather erratic, with many commas where there should not be any – I must have deleted hundreds of commas over the entire manuscript – or missing out on a comma where there should be one; or he speaks of "to not succumb to..."; or a German background is discernible when he asks the question: "What guilt do I have for being born a Jew?" All these examples are taken from chapter 2, and I will add a few more from the remaining chapters. For instance, Hillel writes: "I remember in the ghetto you could see old ladies wandering around with bleached blonde hair" etc. when it should be: "In the ghetto, I remember you could see..." etc.; or he writes: "...through every phase of her life development", where 'development' clashes with 'life'; in chapter 4 we read: "They changed their Jewish identity to a painful secret which could not be shared...", etc. Now I think that from the context it is obvious what Hillel means but the sentence needed editing because it does not make sense as it stands; or we read: "The father developed at the time a paranoid preoccupation..." where the order of the elements suggests an influence from German whereas in English the 'at the time' must come at the end; or we read: "...and feared separating from her." when it should read "and feared to separate from her."; or we read: "He had to deal with not only all that was stirred up inside himself...", when it should be: "He had to deal not only with all that was stirred up inside himself." This shall suffice, and I hope I was able to give you some idea of my problems in editing Hillel's manuscript.

But the editing was also a most rewarding experience, even though the subject matter of the book is rather horrendous and depressing. To be able to share Hillel's feelings before, during and after the holocaust and his amazing recovery and subsequent achievements are quite outstanding, as it is reflected in Yehuda Bauer's Preface to the book and Carl Nedelmann's Introduction. I am therefore extremely glad that his work is now also available in English, a well-deserved monument for this great man.

On 14 December 2010 there was a meeting in Tel Aviv to commemorate Hillel Klein on the 25th anniversary of his death. It was attended by many of his friends and colleagues. In her speech, Dr. Viviane Chetrit-Vatine, then the President of the Israel Psychoanalytic Society, recalled:

> As my personal gesture and with a deep feeling of gratitude I will report briefly the message that I had the luck to receive from him at the very end of his life. Already very weak, he moderated for us students in the third year of the psychoanalytic psychotherapy program a weekly clinical seminar at the Institute. At this time we were all very eager to understand the concept of projective identification, viewed as a communication.
>
> He told us that 'you cannot work as an analyst if you

> do not feel free. Your very task is to realize when your patient keeps you hostage. From this point you have to find the way for you to regain your freedom. Your interventions will be effective on this sole condition. By the process you are going through in regaining your freedom (*Herut*) you will help your patients to regain theirs'.
>
> At this very moment I met a great man who – while being himself the hostage of his terrible illness and close to death – was telling us authentically and very intimately what psychoanalytic psychotherapy is about. He was telling us about freedom, human freedom: a freedom greater than death, when one is able to make room for the other, transforming his being a hostage (*Ben aruba*) of the other man into becoming his very host (*arev lo*) and thus helping him to become a free man. This has been a lesson for me which I will never forget.

In my work as editor I have been greatly helped by Hillel's daughter Esther Ofer who transferred the entire manuscript into her computer and then sent it to me. This saved me a lot of time and I am indeed most grateful to Esther for this wonderful help.

Carl Nedelmann, who wrote the *Introduction* to the English version, was always a great support and help during my editorial work. It was he, in fact, who came back from the commemorative meeting in Tel Aviv with the determined wish to find someone who would edit Hillel's book. And since we have been colleagues and friends for nearly thirty years, he probably hoped that I would take on the job, which I duly did.

We are indebted to Emanuel Berman who was responsible for securing the services of the publishers, the Academic Studies Press. We are most grateful to them for agreeing to publish Hillel Klein's book in its edited entirety.

Last but not least it remains for me to thank Hortense Klein, Esther Ofer and Michal Klein-Honig for their financial support of the project. Financial help also came from the Israeli-Polish Mental Health Association and from the Israel Psychoanalytic Society to which I extend my sincerest thanks.

— Alex Holder

Literature

Publications by Hillel Klein

Klein, H., Zellermayer, J., Shanan, J. (1963): Former concentration camp inmates on a psychiatric ward. In: *Arch. Gen. Psychiat.* 8, 334–342.

———. (1967): Psychiatric disturbances of Holocaust survivors. In: *Isr. Ann. Psychiat.* 5, 95f.

———. (1968a): Problems in the psychotherapeutic treatment of Israeli survivors of the Holocaust. In: H. Krystal (Ed.): *Massive Psychic Trauma*. New York, 233–248.

———. (1968b): Children and social catastrophe. *American Psychoanalytic Association*. Annual Meeting. Boston.

———. (1968c): Symposium on the psychoanalytic treatment of Holocaust survivors. In: *Isr. Ann. Psychiat.* 6.

———. (1971): Families of Holocaust survivors in the kibbutz: Psychological studies. In: H. Krystal, W.G. Niederland (Eds.): *Psychic traumatisation. Aftereffects in individuals and communities*. Boston.

———. Reinharz, S. (1972a): Adaptation in the kibbutz of Holocaust survivors and their families. In: L. Miller (Ed.): *Mental Health and Rapid Social Change*. Jerusalem.

———. (1972b): Holocaust survivors in kibbutzim: readaptation and reintegration. In: *Isr. Ann. Psychiat.* 10, 78–91.

———. (1973): Children of the Holocaust: mourning and bereavement. In: E. J. Anthony, C. Koupernik (Eds.): *The child in his Family. The Impact of Disease and Death*. New York, 393–409.

———. Last, U. (1974a): Cognitive and emotional aspects of the attitudes of American and Israeli Jewish youth towards the victims of the Holocaust. In: *Isr. Ann. Psychiat.* 12, 111–131.

———. (1974b): Delayed affects and aftereffects of severe traumatisation. In: *Isr. Ann. Psychiat.* 12, 293–303.

———. (1974c): Child victims of the Holocaust. In: *J. Clin. Child Psychol.* III, 44–50.

———. Erlich, S. (1974d): Is hospital democracy possible? In: *Mental Health Soc.* 1, 34–48.

———. (1975): Yom-Kippur-War and Holocaust. In: *Proceedings of the Congress of the Israeli Psychiatrical Association*, Tel Aviv.

———. (1978a): Survivors of the Holocaust. *Mental Health Soc.* 5, 1–7.

———. Fleischhauer, I. (1978b): Über *die Jüdische Identität. Eine Psycho-Historische Studie.* Königstein.

———. Erlich, S. (1978c): Some psychoanalytic structural aspects of family function and growth. *Adolescent Psychiatry,* VI, 171–194.

———. (1981): Contribution to the *Yale Symposium on the Holocaust.* Proceedings.

———. (1982): Die Kinder des Holocaust. *Evangelische Akademie Bad Boll. Protokolldienst 23/82,* 260–266.

———. (1983a): The meaning of the Holocaust. In: *Isr. J. Psychiat. Relat. Sci.* 20, 119–128.

———. (1983b): Die Familien der überlebenden Opfer und die Gesellschaft. *Evangelische Akademie Bad Boll. Protokolldienst 31/83,* 36–61.

———. (1984a): Wiedergutmachung—ein Akt der Retraumatisierung. *Evangelische Akademie Bad Boll. Protokolldienst 14/84,* 51–53.

———. (1984b): Nur wer die eigene Verantwortlichkeit akzeptiert hat eine Chance für Selbstfindung. In: Ärztliche *Praxis* XXXVI, 1325–28.

———. Kogan, I. (1985): Some observations on denial and avoidance in Jewish Holocaust and post-Holocaust experience. *The International Symposium on Denial.* New York.

———. (1986): Identification processes and denial in the shadow of Nazism. In: *Int. J. Psychoanal.* 67, 45–52.

———. (1990): Überlebende, ihre Psychologie: Allgemeiner Überblick. In: E. Jäckel, F. Longerich, J. H. Shoeps (Eds.): *Enzyklopädie des Holocaust. Die Verfolgung und Ermordung der Europäischen Juden.* München, 1444–47.

———. (1992): Klein H (1992 [1983]): Von Schuld zu Verantwortung [From guilt to responsibility]. *Psyche* 46, 1177–1186—Transcript of the lecture given largely without notes at the fall conference of the German Psychoanalytical Association (DPV) in Wiesbaden in 1983 (from the taperecording prepared by Christoph Biermann).

Secondary Literature

Anielewicz, M. (1943): The last letter from Mordecai Anielewicz. Warsaw Ghetto Revolt Commander (April 23, 1943).

Anthony, E. J., Koupernik, C. (Eds.) (1973): *The Child in his Family. The Impact of Disease and Death.* New York.

Appelfeld, A. (1979): *Badenheim 1939.* München 2001.

Arendt, H. (1963): *Eichmann in Jerusalem. Ein Bericht von der Banalität des Bösen.* München 1976.

Barocas, H. A., Barocas, C. B. (1979): Wounds of the fathers. The next generation of Holocaust victims. In: *Int. Rev. Pschoanal.* 6, 331–340.

———. (1980): Separation individuation conflicts in children of Holocaust survivors. In: *J. Contemp. Psychother.* 11, 6–14.

Bauer, Y. (1978): *The Holocaust in Historical Perspective.* Seattle.

Bergmann, M. S., Jucovi, M. E., Kestenberg, J. (Eds.) (1995): *Kinder der Opfer, Kinder der Täter. Psychoanalyse und Holocaust.* Frankfurt a. M.

Bettelheim, B. (1943): Individual and mass behavior in extreme situations. In: *J. Abnorm. Soc. Psychol.* 38, 417–452.

———. (1960): *The Informed Heart.* Glencoe.

Blatt, S. (1974): Levels of object representation in anaclitic and introjective depression. In: *Psychoanal. Study Child* 29, 107–157.

Bowlby, J., Parkes, M. C. (1973): Separation and loss within the family. In: Anthony et al. (1973).

Carmel, I. (1969): *An Estate of Memory.* Boston.

Celan, P. (1959): *Sprachgitter.* Frankfurt a. M.

Cohen, E. A. (1954): *Human Behavior in the Concentration Camp.* London.

Czerniakow, A. (1968): *Im Warschauer Getto. Das Tagebuch des Adam Czerniakow 1939–1942.* München 1986.

Danieli, Y. (1980): Families of survivors of the Nazi Holocaust. Some long- and short-term effects. In: N. Milgram (Ed.): *Psychological Stress and Adjustment in Times of War and Peace.* Washington.

———. (1981): Countertransference in the treatment and study of Nazi Holocaust survivors and their children. In: *Victimology. An Intern. J.* 5.

Davidson, S. (1979): Massive psychic traumatization and social support. In: *J. Psychosom. Res.* 23, 84–95.

———. (1980): Transgenerational transmission in the families of Holocaust survivors. In: *Int. J. Family Psychiatry* 1, 95–112.

Des Pres, T. (1976): *The Survivor: an Anatomy of Life in the Death Camps.* New York.

Eitinger, L. (1964): *Concentration Camp Survivors in Norway and Israel.* London.

Erikson, E. H. (1959): *Identity and the Life Cycle,* Monograph, *Psychological Issues,* Vol. 1, No. 1, New York: Int. Univ. Press.

Ettinger, S., Arieli, C. (1969/1970): *Der Zweite Weltkrieg und der Holocaust der Juden Europas.* Recommendation for a curriculum in general and religious state schools. Ministry for Education. Jerusalem (in Hebrew only and unpublished).

Fenichel, O. (1946): *The Psychoanalytic Theory of Neurosis,* London.

Fogelman, E. (1978): Awareness groups for children of survivors. In: *Shoah: A Review of Holocaust Studies and Commemoration 1.*

Freud, A. (1951). Gemeinschaftsleben im frühen Kindesalter, *Schriften,* Vol. 4, 1161–1228.

Freud, S. (1893a): On the Psychical Mechanism of Hysterical Phenomena: Preliminary Communication, *Standard Ed.,* 2, 3.

———. (1917e): Mourning and Melancholia, *Standard Ed.,* 14.

———. (1926d): *Inhibitions, Symptoms and Anxiety, Standard Ed.,* 20.

———. (1930a): *Civilization and Its Discontents, Standard Ed.,* 21.

———. (1939a): *Moses and Monotheism, Standard Ed.,* 23.

———. (1985c [1887–1904]): *Letters to Wilhelm Fliess.*

Friedmann, P. (1948): The road back for the D.P.'s. In: *Commentary* 6, 502–510.

Furst, S. S. (Ed.) (1967): *Psychic Trauma.* New York.

Goldman, N. (1979): *Speech at the Holocaust Conference.* Haifa University.

Greenacre, P. (1952): The puberty trauma in girls. In: *Trauma, Growth and Personality.* New York.

Hartmann, H. (1939): *Ego Psychology and the Problem of Adaptation.* New York.

Hoppe, K. (1968): Psychosomatische Reaktionen und Erkrankungen bei Überlebenden schwerer Verfolgung. In: *Psyche* 22, 464–477.

Kaniuk, Y. (1968): *Adam Hundesohn.* München 1989.

Kaplan, C. (1966): *Warschauer Ghettotagebuch.* Frankfurt a. M. 1967.

Kertész, I. (2000): Die elixierte Sprache. *Frankfurter Allgemeine Zeitung,* November 6th.

Klein, M. (1959): Our adult world and its roots in infancy. *Human Relations*, 12.
Kohut, H. (1971): *The Analysis of the Self. A Systematic Approach to the Psychoanalytic Treatment of Narcissistic Personality Disorders.* International Universities Press, New York.
Kosinski, J. (1965): *The Painted Bird.* Boston.
Krystal, H. (Ed.) (1968): *Massive Psychic Trauma.* New York.
Krystal, H., Niederland, W. G. (1968): Clinical observations on the survivor syndrome. In: H. Krystal (Ed.), 327–348.
———. (Eds.) (1971): *Psychic Traumatisation. Aftereffects in Individuals and Communities.* Boston.
Lemm, M. (1992): *Mordechai Gebirtig—Jiddische Lieder.* Wuppertal.
Lifton, R. J. (1967): *Death in Life. Survivors of Hiroshima.* New York.
———. (1968): Observations on Hiroshima survivors. In: Krystal (Ed.), 168–189.
———. (1979): *Der Verlust des Todes.* München, Wien 1986.
Mahler, M. S., Pine, F., Bergmann, A. (1975): *The Psychological Birth of the Human Infant*, London.
Meerloo, J. A. M. (1962): shock, catalepsy and psychogenic death. In: *Int. Record Med.*, 172, 384–393.
Minkovski, S. (1946): L'anesthesie affective. In: *Annual Medico-Psychol.* 104.
Mitscherlich, A., Mitscherlich, M. (1967): *Die Unfähigkeit zu Trauern.* München.
Modell, A. H. (1971): The origin of certain forms of pre-Oedipal guilt and the implications for a psychoanalytic theory of affects. In: *Int. J. Psychoanal.* 52, 337–346.
Niederland, W. G. (1961): The problem of the survivor. In: *J. Hillside Hosp.* 10, 233–247.
———. (1968a): The problem of the survivor-dynamics of post traumatic symptomatology. In: H. Krystal (Ed.), 1968, 8–28.
———. (1968b): Clinical observations on the "survivor syndrome." In: *Int. J. Psychoanal.* 49, 313–315.
Oz, A. (1979): *Under This Blazing Light.* Tel Aviv.
Rakoff, V. (1969): Children and families of concentration camp survivors. In: *Canada's Mental Health* 14, 24–26.
Rangell, L. (1967): Metapsychology of psychic trauma. In: Furst (Ed.) 1967.
Ringelblum, E. (1967): *Ghetto Warschau. Tagebücher aus dem Chaos.* Stuttgart.

Sandler, J. (1960): The background of safety. In: J. Sandler (Ed.) *From Safety to Superego*. New York.

Schafer, R. (1976): *A New Language for Psychoanalysis*. New Haven.

Schlonski, A. (1971): *Poems*. Tel Aviv.

Scholem, G. (1963): Brief an Hannah Arendt. In: H. Arendt: *Essays und Kommentare* 1, ed. by E. Geisel, K. Bittermann, Berlin 1989, 63–70.

Schur, M. (1955): Comments on the metapsychology of somatization. In: *Psa. Study Child* 10, 119–164.

———. (1972): *Freud: Living and Dying*. London, New York.

Selye, H. (1950): *Stress*. Montreal.

Sifneos, A. (1967): Clinical observations on some patients suffering from a variety of psychosomatic diseases. In: *Acta Medica Psychosomatica*, 452–458.

Spitz, R. A. (1965): *The First Year of Life: a Psychoanalytic Study of Normal and Deviant Development of Object Relations*. New York : International Universities Press.

Steiner, G. (1967): *Language and Silence: Essays on Language, Literature and the Inhuman*. New York.

Stern, M. M. (1959): Trauma, Todesangst und Furcht vor dem Tod in psychoanalytischer Theorie und Praxis. In: *Psyche* 26, 1972, 901–928.

Targowla, R. (1955): Syndrom der Asthenie der Deportierten. In: M. Michel (Ed.) *Gesundheitsschäden durch Verfolgung und Gefangenschaft und ihre Spätfolgen*. Frankfurt a. M.

Tillion, G. (1975): *Ravensbrück*. New York.

Toynbee, A. J. (1975): *Armenian Atrocities. The Murder of a Nation*. New York.

Wangh, M. (1968): A psychogenetic factor in the recurrence of war. In: *Int. J. Psychoanal.* 49, 319–323.

Wiesel, E. (1958): *Nacht*. In: E. Wiesel *Die Nacht zu Begraben, Elischa*. München and Esslingen 1962.

Winnicott, D. W. (1960): Ego distortion in terms of true and false self. In: *The Maturational Processes and the Facilitating Environment*. London 1965, 140–152.

Winnik, H. Z. (1969): Contribution to symposium of psychic traumatization through social catastrophe. In: *Int. J. Psychoanal.* 49, 298–301.

Index of Names

Subject Index